THE OFF-ROAD
4-WHEEL DRIVE BOOK

THE OFF-ROAD
4-WHEEL DRIVE BOOK

CHOOSING, USING AND MAINTAINING GO-ANYWHERE VEHICLES

JACK JACKSON

PSL

Patrick Stephens Limited

First published by Gentry Books
Ltd 1982
Reprinted 1985
2nd edition published by
G.T. Foulis & Co. 1988
This 3rd edition (completely
reformatted, revised and reset)
published 1995.

British Library Cataloguing in
Publication Data

A catalogue record for this book is
available from the British Library.

ISBN 1 85260 544 8

Library of Congress catalog card
number 95-78117

Patrick Stephens Limited is an
imprint of Haynes Publishing,
Sparkford, Nr Yeovil, Somerset,
BA22 7JJ

Designed & typeset by
G&M, Raunds, Northamptonshire
Printed in Great Britain by
Butler & Tanner Ltd,
London and Frome

Dedication

This book is dedicated to all those
who have travelled with me,
sharing not only the joys of remote
areas, but also the trials and tribu-
lations of getting stuck or overturned vehicles mobile again.

Disclaimer

Because vehicles and parts change
and methods of application vary,
the author disclaims any liability
incurred in connection with the
use of any or all of the data and
ideas contained in this book.

Acknowledgements

The author would like to thank
David Bowyer, Keith Hart and the
staff at David Bowyer's Off-Road
Centre, Dave Cadwgan of
Michelin Tyres and Vince Cobley
of Pro-Trax and the Warn
Challenge, for their help during
the preparation of this book.

Contents

Introduction

As a working driver whose life often depends on my vehicle, I am biased towards reliable, tough, workhorse, four-wheel drive vehicles. However, from the manufacturers' perspective, workhorse vehicles are becoming less marketable in comparison with the newer breed of 'designer' vehicles, whose purchasers are more intent on advertising a life-style than venturing seriously off-road.

One remarkable fact of the recent recession in Europe is that, whereas new car sales dropped nearly 20 per cent overall, the sales of four-wheel drive recreational vehicles increased by more than that. Some buyers are changing over from estate cars for transporting larger families or loads, while other purchasers can no longer afford to insure a GTi.

Most vehicle manufacturers now offer four-wheel drive recreational vehicles, including those who used to deride them, even if they have to re-badge another manufacturer's vehicle, or share the cost of development with another manufacturer.

Competition is now fierce, which is good for buyers; but due to ongoing changes it is difficult for manufacturers to keep a good selection of spares available worldwide. Similarly, the constant revamping and updating of vehicles means that any book of this nature soon becomes out of date with reference to the technical details of individual vehicles.

There is a tendency towards independent front suspension. This improves handling on-road, but rigid axles are better off-road, as they keep the ground clearance high and constant. For instance, when one wheel goes over a large rock or hump, the whole axle lifts and the transfer case and differentials are less vulnerable.

Similarly, soft-sprung vehicles, as well as throwing occupants about when off-road, can often get completely out of control if you hit an unexpected bump or dip. Firm springing means better adaptation to off-road conditions, stability and good ground clearance, with consequent driver confidence that he or she is in full control of the vehicle.

Four-wheel drive manufacturers are forced to compromise their designs to cater for the worldwide market, the largest of which is the Middle East, where the terrain is mostly paved or firm gravel road and occasionally sand. This is a vastly different environment from that of expeditions or the off-road enthusiast, where a vehicle may be subjected to extremes from unladen motorway cruising to overloaded off-road use. In consequence, alongside the four-wheel drive market there has developed a considerable industry in four-wheel drive accessories, many of which are purely cosmetic, although some are almost essential, for example to beef up weak or road-type suspensions for serious off-road use.

Some accessories are essential items to particular uses, for example limited slip or locking differentials, which many four-wheel drive manufacturers supplied in the past, but stopped doing so because most of their customers either did not require them, could not handle them, or failed to understand their correct use, and did serious damage to the rest of the drive train by using them in the wrong conditions.

When an experienced four-wheel driver reads a test report on a four-wheel drive vehicle in a normal auto magazine or newspaper, it is painfully obvious that most journalists, no matter how expert they are with two-wheel drive vehicles, have little idea of what a four-wheel drive vehicle should or should not be able to do.

If you want to know about a particular four-wheel drive vehicle, read only test reports in specialist four-wheel drive magazines and talk to owners of such vehicles. Better still, attend four-wheel drive shows or join a four-wheel drive club and see different vehicles in action.

As with most things, you get what you pay for. The extra cost of a stronger item saves money in the end, so think before you buy. If you want to fit oversize tyres and wheels, get the correct axle ratio and engine power in the first place. Heavy duty shock absorbers and road springs are essential for off-road use and towing. If you do not have much ground clearance you can fit underside protection plates, but it would have been better to buy a vehicle with more ground clearance and chassis-protected vital parts.

If your vehicle cannot be used with a high-lift jack without damage, then you cannot afford to get it stuck off-road. If you must have a winch, get one big enough to do the job with power in reserve.

Most people, when they first buy a four-wheel drive, think it can go anywhere and immediately get it stuck. Most four-wheel drive vehicles *will* go anywhere under the right conditions and with the right driving skills. Don't rush into things, learn slowly by trying harder and harder things, a little at a time. Get to know the limitations of your vehicle (for some vehicles the limit will be your own nerve); by staying within these limits you will have a lot of fun.

Why four-wheel drive?

Off-road terrain is more demanding on vehicles than paved roads, though broken-up paved roads such as those in Eastern Europe and Africa can often be worse than gravel roads. Corrugated gravel roads, where the vehicle's wheels hit a ridge, rebound and hit another ridge before the springs can recover, cause vibration to vehicles and their occupants similar to sitting on a pneumatic drill. These conditions cause normal cars to break up and their suspensions to fail; consequently vehicles that are intended for off-road conditions are more strongly built.

Real off-road vehicles are built to truck specifications, and have higher ground clearance and less body overhang at front and rear, in order to lessen body contact with the ground. They have large wheels to iron out bumps and potholes, the wheel wells are larger to give the tyres more room, and the best models have long-travel suspension to keep the vehicle's wheels on the ground in difficult terrain.

Fragile parts, such as fuel tanks, engine sumps, differentials, gearboxes, transfer boxes, drive shafts, steering arms and track rods, are tucked up out of the way of damage and, where necessary, have the extra protection of skid plates.

The best vehicles have engines that produce high torque output at low revolutions and have a sec-

ond, lower, range of gears, for more power and control in difficult or demanding situations. The engines are fitted with filters designed to keep out dust, grit and water, and a cooling system large enough to cope with long periods at low speeds, steep hills and high ambient temperatures.

Axles are fitted with valves or extension tubes that allow them to breathe, but keep out water during wading. Head lights, rear lights and side lights are placed well away from damage by tree branches, flying rocks and ground clearance; there are some exceptions to this, where importers of vehicles from Japan, where fog lights are not required by law, fit them in silly places to comply with local laws.

Most important is four (or more)-wheel drive, which gives better traction on slippery or loose surfaces and shares the load over the components of the transmission. A two-wheel drive vehicle has four wheels, two of which are driven (4x2), while four-wheel drive vehicles have four wheels, all of which are either permanently driven or part-time driven (4x4). There are other vehicles with six wheels, only four of which are driven (6x4), or all of which are driven (6x6), and a few with eight wheels, all of which are usually driven (8x8).

With two-wheel drive vehicles the front tyres drag and skid on turns, as they are pushed against

whatever road resistance they have to overcome. This produces additional load on the rolling capacity of the vehicle, most obvious in mud, sand or snow, where the front wheels plough in, creating a mound in front of the tyres. This makes it more difficult for the rear wheels to obtain traction and force the front tyres over the obstacle.

Adding drive to the front wheels overcomes this problem. More advanced four-wheel drive systems transfer torque to each axle as well as each wheel, when the other is slipping, producing an even smoother, more controlled ride. The net result is rolling smoothly over rocks, through mud, sand and snow, up hills and across ditches, because all four wheels have good traction and, if the suspension is good enough, contact with the ground. Add the extra gear reduction and the vehicle is capable of handling steep gradients, deep mud, sand and snow, and towing heavy loads. Even when travelling on roads in slippery conditions, four-wheel drive gives you better control and consequent safety, a fact well proven by the superiority of four-wheel drive rally cars in competitions.

Four-wheel drive does not double the power to the road, but it does spread the power available to all four wheels instead of two. If a vehicle needs a certain amount of traction to attain a given speed, or cross a difficult surface, driving all four wheels will halve the traction load on the surface and reduce the chance of slipping, skidding or spinning wheels.

In practice, loads are rarely actually halved. Many American four-wheel drive vehicles have large, heavy engines, giving more weight on the front wheels than on the rear wheels, and most long-wheelbase vehicles, when loaded, have much more weight on the rear wheels than on the front wheels. These vehicles, when in soft terrain such as mud, sand and snow, can often break through and bog down on the wheels with the heaviest loads, while the wheels with the lighter load are turning but find little traction.

Only short-wheelbase and specially designed military vehicles have the load equally distributed on both axles; but even with these, steep inclines will put most of the load and traction required on to the wheels on the lowest axle. In fact, equal drive to front and rear axle is not always the best solution, and competitive four-wheel drive rally cars often have more drive given to the rear axle than to the front, for better handling at speed. All-wheel drive is not infallible. Driving skills, or lack of them, can make a difference between getting bogged down or getting through really difficult terrain.

There are occasions when special locking or limited slip differentials can be useful. Some vehicles can be helped by fooling their particular differentials with braking, and others by temporarily locking up one or more of their drum brakes. An example to me was a 1 ton (1,017 kg) Land Rover, factory supplied with 9 inch (229 mm) wide wheels, that was so overloaded in the sand of the Sahara Desert that the engine turned but the wheels did not move against the drag of the sand – the clutch just slipped.

Driver knowledge is all important. By this I mean real knowledge, gained by practise, not fanciful theories that I find in some magazines and books, which I know do not work.

Tread lightly

The Land Access & Rights Association has produced guidelines for off-road drivers. If you haven't owned a four-wheel drive before, you may not be aware of these rules, so they are reproduced below to help you get the most out of your vehicle.

1. Use only vehicular rights of way. Not all green lanes have vehicular rights.

2. Keep to the defined track. Detour only to pass immovable obstacles. Report any obstructions, including low branches, to the highway authority. If the route is not obvious on the ground, ask locally or check on the maps held at the highway authority offices.

3. Travel at a quiet and unobtrusive speed and, when travelling in groups, keep to a small number.

4. Ensure that your vehicle and yourself are fully road-legal. Green lanes are subject to the same laws as surfaced roads.

It is a criminal offence to drive on beaches, dunes, open moorland commons, parks and farmland without permission.

5. Pay attention to the Four Ws:

WEATHER – do not travel on green roads when they risk being damaged beyond a point of natural recovery when the weather improves.

WEIGHT – do not use lanes that may be seriously damaged by the wheel pressures applied by your vehicle.

WIDTH – do not use lanes that are too narrow for your vehicle. Avoid damage to trees, hedgerows and boundaries.

WINCHES – use only when unavoidable – your priority should be to avoid damage to trees, walls or the surface while recovering the vehicle.

6. Respect the life of the countryside. Be courteous to other road users, including walkers. Take great care when passing horses. Be prepared to stop your engine if necessary. Always fasten gates and take care near livestock.

7. Remember that wildlife faces many threats and green lanes can be valuable.

For further information contact:

Land Access & Recreation
    Association (LARA)
PO Box 9
Cannock
Staffs
WS11 2FE

CHAPTER 1

Available options

When you set out to buy a four-wheel drive vehicle, there are various options from the factory that enable you to select a basic vehicle according to your requirements. Obviously there will be a necessary compromise between what a buyer requires and how broadly a manufacturer covers the market. The buyer then has to make up the difference by selecting from accessories and components available as 'aftermarket sales'.

For example, the Mercedes Unimog, some specialist low-volume manufacturers' vehicles and earlier Land Rover vehicles have various options and power take-off points of special interest to agricultural and industrial users for pumps, compressors, saws, generators and winches that would be in long-term use. The buyers of this type of vehicle formed most of the original four-wheel drive civilian market, but nowadays vehicles for these uses have developed apart from and alongside the recreational four-wheel drive market.

European and Japanese manufacturers offer their vehicles in one or two wheelbases, with body options of truck, soft top, hard top or estate, petrol or diesel engines, manual or automatic gearboxes and various specifications of trim, power steering, lockable or limited slip differentials and part-time or permanent four-wheel drive. American manufacturers tend to offer more options, covering different weights of suspension, engine sizes, power steering, cosmetic trim, etc. The situation is

Options – a Land Rover Series 1 chassis with a capstan winch driven by power take-off (PTO) from the engine.

complicated by the various anti-pollution laws in different states.

Further complications arise from the fact that European and Japanese manufacturers make more vehicles for export; these have to be more standardised and this, together with local regulations in the country of manufacture, results in less options. Obvious difficulties include lights having to be near to the edge of the vehicle, which are then vulnerable on narrow off-road tracks. British Land Rover 12-seat estates are built with uncomfortably cramped seats to avoid the VAT levied on ten- and seven-seat versions, while European and Japanese manufacturers are mindful of EU laws on the tachographs, special licences and paperwork required with vehicles of more than nine seats.

Manufacturers do not always get their products absolutely right and often ignore feedback regarding customer requirements – until some other manufacturer gets it right and their sales start falling.

PART-TIME (SELECTABLE) FOUR-WHEEL DRIVE

Part-time four-wheel drive is the simplest four-wheel drive system and is usually available on cheaper vehicles. With this system you mostly drive in two-wheel drive with the front axle, half-shafts and propeller shaft idly spinning, unless disconnected by freewheeling hubs. On reaching difficult terrain you lock up the freewheeling hubs, if fitted (see below), and change the transfer box into four-wheel drive, high or low range according to conditions.

Both axles are now locked together. If one wheel loses traction there should still be traction on the other axle, but if the second axle also has a wheel that slips and you have open differentials on

both axles, then you are stuck.

Part-time four-wheel drive works best if you also have axle differential locks, or a limited slip differential, on the rear axle. Limited slip differentials are not wise on the front axle, as they cause handling problems; however, I have also had rear limited slip differentials cause handling problems on wet asphalt roads, by 'fish-tailing'. (Limited slip differentials are dealt with in detail later in this chapter.)

With part-time four-wheel drive you are either in two-wheel drive, or have both axles locked in – there is no central differential that can adjust the differential travel between front and rear axles. If you have freewheeling hubs you can also save a little on fuel and reduced wear, though real savings are debatable.

When a vehicle makes a turn, the various wheels go through different arcs – those on the outside of the turn travel further than those on the inside of the turn. If the vehicle has both axles locked together, as in part-time four-wheel drive, then there is a 'wind-up' of stress between the front and rear axles, which puts considerable strain on the transmission. On loose surfaces the wheels will spin and release this strain, but on a firm surface this is more difficult. If the vehicle is lightly loaded, the wheels will spin and the tyres scrub, but this cannot happen if the vehicle is heavily loaded. So the strain causes excess wear to the gearbox, transfer box, half-shafts, hub drive members, differentials and universal joints.

Many books tell you to engage four-wheel drive as soon as you leave the paved road. If you have part-time four-wheel drive this is the wrong thing to do. On firm gravel tracks you will soon get transmission 'wind-up', tight steering, difficult gear changing and either nasty bangs as the wheels spin to release the stress, or complete failure of the weakest components. You are doing unnecessary and costly damage to your vehicle.

Many part-time four-wheel drive

vehicles do not have constant velocity joints (see below) on the front wheels, so when in four-wheel drive the speed at which you can travel without damage to the universal joints on the front wheels is limited. On firm tracks, therefore, you are much better off in two-wheel drive. Even on firm sand you are better off in two-wheel drive. The driving is easier, you have better control and, if the terrain is safe, you can travel faster without damage to the universal joints on the front wheels.

With part-time four-wheel drive, only use four-wheel drive when you require it. If in doubt engage four-wheel drive and drive slowly. Except for very steep inclines, boulders, or starting off when towing a heavy load, do not use it on firm ground; but do learn how to engage it quickly, or on the move where possible.

If you do not spend much time in four-wheel drive, there are drivers who prefer the part-time system for 'sporty' driving in two-wheel drive. You do have a slightly more positive feeling to the steering and it is easier to drift the rear wheels on bends.

Constant velocity joints

The more expensive vehicles (though not all of them) have constant velocity joints to the front wheels. These enable vehicles to travel at high speed without vibration and damage in four-wheel drive. Vehicles that do not have constant velocity joints on the front wheels should not be driven faster than 30 mph (48 kph) in four-wheel drive, or you will get vibration and possibly damage. Some quite expensive vehicles even have open joints.

Freewheeling hubs

If you have a part-time four-wheel drive vehicle and only use it off-road, and then not too heavily and for little of its working life, you can save a little on fuel by fitting freewheeling hubs to the front wheels. These hubs disconnect the drive from the hub to the axle half-shafts, saving on the rolling resistance of the front differential, half-shafts and propeller shaft. However, the wear on the relevant transmission parts is so small as to be unmeasurable, and the saving in fuel consumption is also small, though you may notice easier steering and less front tyre wear if you do not have constant velocity joints to the front wheels.

There are freewheel adaptations to permanent four-wheel drive vehicles, but it would be nonsense to fit them and it would require an awful lot of driven miles to make up for their cost.

If you have manual freewheeling hubs you must always remember to put the hubs into lock before engaging four-wheel drive; you should not engage four-wheel drive on the move, because you might damage them. Freewheeling hubs do not stand up to hard four-wheel drive use in hot countries, particularly with heavy going in soft sand. If this is your main use of four-wheel drive, forget them!

For expedition use, if you need fuel savings on the road, take your vehicle's original hub driving members and hub caps with you and refit these for difficult areas.

Never lock a hub on one side and not the other – this will damage the differential. If you have the type that can be turned by hand, check regularly that children or hooligans have not moved them! On some vehicles you must also lock them in for a few miles each month, to get lubricating oil around the moving parts.

Some automatic freewheeling hubs engage when you engage four-wheel drive; some only engage when forward traction is required, and release again in an overrun situation such as when braking downhill. This can cause problems, particularly on loose ground or when towing. To correct this, some automatic hubs can also be locked manually; being realistic, you should lock them up manually before going off-road.

Manual freewheeling hubs.

Automatic freewheeling hubs or 'stuck-in' manual freewheeling hubs are usually disengaged by driving backwards for a few yards while swinging the steering wheel from side to side with two-wheel drive selected; but you may have to jack up one wheel if there is heavy transmission 'wind-up'.

New gaskets and 'O' rings will be required for the hubs when you service the hub wheel bearings.

Front half-shaft disconnect

Some vehicles have a system to disconnect the front half-shaft, which enables changing into and out of four-wheel drive on the move at reasonable speeds ('shift-on-the-fly'). All of the front drive components continue to revolve, so there is no gain in fuel consumption or component wear. There will be a small reduction in tyre wear and you can enjoy sporty driving if you like to drift the wheels when cornering.

PERMANENT (FULL-TIME) FOUR-WHEEL DRIVE

The advantages of a permanent

four-wheel drive system are now apparent to manufacturers and are standard on more expensive vehicles. Several manufacturers who derided them when they first became available on the Range Rover now fit them to their vehicles.

In 1919 William Walter worked out a truly optimum four-wheel drive system. In the typical bevel gear spider of a differential, the device can run forward or backward at equal ratio. This balances the drive load between wheels, but if one wheel slips it takes all the traction and spins, and nothing goes anywhere. Walter replaced the bevel gears by a worm gear, which is essentially irreversible, or can be cut to the degree of reversibility required. So then he had a differential on which a tractionless wheel could not spin; it would let an outside wheel go faster than an inside wheel, but if one wheel tried to go a lot faster than the other, it could not. This was a true all-wheel system without any limited slip clutches, dogs or locking mechanism, usually fitted to large commercial equipment.

Apart from this system, the answer to the transmission 'wind-up' problem on hard surfaces is to put a third (centre) differential between the front and rear axle to let wheels travel their different distances. The original Range Rover system and Borg Warner's early Quadra-Trac system has this third differential fitted with a limited slip system of clutch cones, pre-loaded by springs. The spring pressure is designed such that the cones will not slip under normal torque loads, so that if one wheel slips, traction is transferred to the other axle. In situations of excessive 'wind-up' on hard surfaces, when the torque goes beyond the pre-determined spring pressure, the cones will slip and release the 'wind-up'. This provides the optimum performance for most on- and off-road use, but for extreme conditions there is a lock-in device, to give total four-wheel drive without limited slip.

Other systems use an open third differential between the front and rear axles, so that if a wheel on one axle slips, no traction is applied to the other axle, which means no drive at all. There is of course a lock-in system, to give conventional four-wheel drive. In both systems, if you use the lock-in device you must remember to unlock it again before returning to a firm surface, or you will get transmission 'wind-up'.

Limited slip centre differentials do have their problems, but these only occur in high-speed cornering, as achieved in rallies and off-road racing. At these cornering speeds, with wheels momentarily changing between traction and no traction as all four wheels struggle for a grip on a loose surface, the vehicle can suddenly change from understeer to oversteer to neutral steer and back again, without warning.

The Range Rover's limited slip system was dropped soon after the first models, Land Rover claiming that it made very little difference. Other systems have since been added to Range Rovers that are more effective and less troublesome, to inexperienced drivers.

The most advanced four-wheel drive system, the Ferguson FF, was used in many racing cars in the 1960s, winning one Grand Prix, many hill climbs and twice nearly winning the Indianapolis 500. It showed definite superiority on a wet track, and was a combined mechanical and hydrostatic system, using pumps and electrical sensors to provide limited slip at each wheel. This also gave improved anti-lock braking. The system was only used in one production car in the 1960s, the Jenson FF coupé, and, due mainly to its cost and complexity, was not taken up elsewhere until much later, except for specialist competition cars.

The Ferguson FF system used a centre differential with a viscous fluid coupling, which cut out snatch in the transmission and was arranged to give 63 per cent power to the rear wheels and 37 per cent power to the front wheels. Having the dominant drive at the rear wheels ensured that a near neutral steering attitude could be maintained while accelerating round a corner, instead of the understeer normally caused by permanent four-wheel drive.

The viscous coupling centre differential system continues to be developed and is fitted to many modern vehicles, including Range Rovers, Mitsubishi Pajero/Shoguns, Jeep Grand Cherokees, Toyota Landcruiser VXs and Volkswagen Synchros. For most off-road vehicles the system gives 50 per cent drive to front or rear axles. The advantages of this system are that there is no transmission 'wind-up', less noise and smoother operation. Driver knowledge or input is neither required nor desired – all the driver has to do is to move the transfer box into low range for difficult terrain.

One drawback on some systems is that just as torque is driven to previously non-driven wheels, so braking torque can be delivered the other way. This is undesirable, especially with ABS. There are complicated ways around this by pumping the viscous fluid back and forth as conditions vary, but it is simpler to have the ABS disengaged automatically, either altogether or to the axle concerned.

When a permanent four-wheel drive system has the centre differential locked, you have the same problems as with a part-time four-wheel drive system put into four-wheel drive, except for the speed limitation. Most permanent four-wheel drive vehicles have constant velocity joints to the front wheels. Except for very steep inclines, boulders or starting off when towing a heavy load, do not lock-in the centre differential on firm ground.

On most vehicles you can reduce transmission 'wind-up' problems with permanent four-wheel drive systems by only locking the central differential in when you require it. On a muddy track you can lock the system in for bad sections and out again as soon as you are through. This is fine so long as you are sure of the terrain, but if in doubt it is best to leave the system locked in.

Full-time four-wheel drive produces some 'torque-steering' due to the driving torque applied to the wheels, and you have to fight this. Most drivers would only notice some understeer, and for most this system is safer, but out and out sporting drivers would consider the steering less positive.

Some vehicles have a choice of methods of four-wheel drive, but very few owners of these vehicles would have enough knowledge to make realistic use of this.

WHEELBASE

Short-wheelbase vehicles have less distance between the wheels, which gives them more ground clearance as far as ramp break-over angle is concerned. This gives them a better overall performance in terrain where vehicles have to cross any kind of hump, including large boulders, tree stumps, ramps, ruts, sharp hilltops and sharp dune crests. Most short-wheelbase vehicles also have good angles of attack and departure, which improves their performance further.

They are also smaller, with a shorter turning circle, which makes them more manoeuvrable and less likely to get damaged in confined spaces. The weight is more evenly distributed between all four wheels when loaded, which gives them better all over traction. Powered by smaller engines, they are more economical on fuel; however, they are most useful in sand, where a bigger engine is preferable. With the rear of the vehicle close to the rear axle, they have considerably better control and tow hitch ground clearance when towing, so long as the towed trailer does not exceed the recommended weight limit.

On the debit side they have little room or load-carrying capacity, and can become unstable at speed,

especially on corrugated tracks and slippery roads, where they are prone to skidding, sometimes turning over if they clip a rock or kerb. Sensible driving is essential with these vehicles.

If outright off-road performance is not all-important, long-wheelbase vehicles have more room, better load-carrying capacity and give a smoother ride. Despite larger-diameter wheels, the longer wheelbase usually gives less ground clearance between them as far as ramp break-over angle is concerned, and most such vehicles have poor angles of departure. They can get by on small engines with careful use of the gearbox, but have a larger turning circle, making them less manoeuvrable in cramped situations.

There is a modern tendency with up-market vehicles to have the length of their wheelbase designed more towards paved road, ride and rear passenger legroom comfort than off-road ability. The Range Rover's variable height suspension goes some way towards improving this.

ENGINES

When fuel was cheap it made sense to have the biggest engine you could, but things have changed and now it is best to use the smallest reliable engine you can obtain. Here I must stress *reliability*, for although bigger engines use more fuel they usually last longer and are relatively more trouble-free than smaller, faster-revolving, engines. Most four-wheel drive vehicles have a hard life, so the larger engine will work out cheaper.

Obviously if most of your driving is in civilised surroundings and your off-road work never far from civilisation, small engined Suzukis can give you a lot of fun. However, if your vehicle is to be working hard with lots of slogging, operating power machinery from take-offs, or working away from civilisation, you will require a large engine.

Small engines with appropriate gearing will do all that is necessary in most off-road conditions, so long as you do not have power-sapping ancillaries such as power steering, automatic transmission or air-conditioning and are not over-loaded in deep mud, deep snow or soft sand. If you must have automatic transmission, power steering and air-conditioning, you will require the largest engine available, and in soft sand the larger engine's ability to power through will work out cheaper on fuel and your own energy and nerves. In countries where air-conditioning is necessary and fuel is cheap, as in the Middle East, you can afford to use the biggest engine available; but most people must compromise on engine size.

There is a tendency for some manufacturers to fit their existing engines to four-wheel drive vehicles without regard to the requirements for good torque at low engine speeds, and using components that are fine for normal vehicle use but not sensible for vehicles that may be working in extremes of temperature away from civilised help.

Two major problems are glass-reinforced fibre camshaft drive belts and electronic engine management systems. The former can cause serious damage on failure, and the latter cannot be repaired in the field. The failure of either means a dead engine.

Turbochargers

Turbochargers are now common. Those sold as standard by four-wheel drive manufacturers will be reliable for Third World use, so long as you use top-quality engine oil and change it and the oil filter at the correct intervals. If you cannot get the recommended engine oil, change it and the oil filter at half the recommended interval. An oil cooler is essential, and inter-coolers are worth having, if available.

Turbochargers get very hot in use and can get sprayed by cold water when wading. Allow the engine to tick over long enough to allow the turbocharger to cool down before wading, and also for at least 30 seconds before switching the engine off.

On vehicles where the manufacturer has taken one of its normal range of engines for four-wheel drive use, the turbocharger may cut in too late for the low-down torque that is preferable.

Various turbochargers are available as add-on fitments, but you must make sure that your engine can handle the extra power produced. I would not advise these for Third World use.

Choice of fuel

Most four-wheel drive vehicles have petrol (gasoline) engines. Usually the same engine is used in other vehicles on the manufacturer's production line, so it is cheaper to make, produces more power and is lighter in weight than an equivalent diesel engine. Petrol engines are also more easily repaired by the owner or a competent mechanic. Under normal conditions, therefore, the petrol engine is the preferred choice, apart from the high cost of petrol.

In countries where liquid petroleum gas (LPG) is cheap, several companies make conversions for petrol engines so that they can be run on either LPG or petrol at the flick of a switch. A slower-burning fuel, LPG produces more low-down torque and a saving on fuel costs.

Petrol engines have disadvantages in hot, dusty or wading conditions. In hot countries, beside the fire risk, even the best-designed petrol engines suffer from vapour lock in the fuel system, and this problem is worse on steep or long climbs at altitude. Dust, which often contains iron, gets into the distributor, shorting it out, and, when wading, water gives trouble to the electrics. In these situations there is an advantage in using diesel engines.

In most less developed coun-

tries, diesel is considerably cheaper than petrol and more commonly available, as it is used by trucks and tractors. Another advantage of diesel to long-range expeditions is that, with the extra low-down torque, the vehicle is often in a higher gear in the rough and thus has improved fuel consumption, which in turn means carrying less weight in fuel for a long section without fuel supplies. This in turn improves the fuel consumption further.

Having done away with most of the electrics, diesels have very few problems other than sluggish performance, and require less maintenance than petrol engines. With many diesel engines you have to push the clutch pedal fully down to the floor to attain a clean gear change. The only real problem with a diesel engine is that, if the injector pump goes wrong in the outback, there is very little you can do about it, but modern-day injector pumps are very reliable. For Third World or dusty country use, add a second fuel filter in the fuel line – this will prolong the life of your injector pump. A sedimenter is useful, near to the fuel tank, to remove water and rust without the need to bleed the engine, but the glass must be protected from thrown-up stones.

There is a modern tendency to use faster-revolving diesels, to get more power from the weight and better on-road performance. These are the opposite of that required for off-road use, where the older type of engine, revolving more slowly, is preferable for its extra reliability and low-speed torque. For these reasons the six-cylinder diesel in the Toyota Landcruiser is very popular in North Africa, and several companies specialise in fitting larger diesel engines into Land Rovers and Range Rovers.

Diesel engines have a reputation for being hard to start in cold weather, but the answer is a large battery in good condition. Japanese diesel engines often have a 24-volt electrical system for better starting. In really cold weather

mix one part petrol to 15 parts of diesel to stop the fuel from waxing – in extreme conditions use one to ten. Technically this is illegal and could possibly cause some damage to modern engines, but it is customary in countries where severe cold is normal. The petrol should preferably be unleaded, and *must* be unleaded if your diesel engine is fitted with a catalytic converter. Anti-waxing additives are also available for this purpose, but they are not easily obtainable.

In theory diesel engines should give better engine braking downhill, but this is not always true.

Oil coolers

Oil coolers are necessary for vehicles being used stationary for power take-off use, and in hot countries where high-speed highway driving is expected. They are also useful in hot countries with long steep inclines, especially at altitude, as in the mountainous areas of South America, Afghanistan, Pakistan and the Sahara Desert. As already mentioned, they are essential with turbocharged engines. If you have automatic transmission, a separate oil cooler is necessary under these conditions.

Catalytic converters

Catalytic converters are a legal requirement in many countries, though some manufacturers argue that the same reduction in dangerous emission gases can be achieved by better engine design, for more efficient burning of the fuel. In the UK new regulations enforce the fitting of catalytic converters to most new petrol and diesel engines. Petrol engines with carburettors will be replaced with fuel-injected versions, and more powerful engines will have to be fitted to allow for power losses due to the catalytic converters.

For serious off-road use, catalytic converters are easily damaged, both by physical contact with the ground or rocks and by vibration.

Even driving heavily over speed restriction humps ('sleeping policemen') can damage them. The catalysts are expensive, rare metals, usually platinum and rhodium, made up in a very fine and fragile honeycomb, and can be irreparably damaged by water if you stall the engine with the exhaust outlet under water. Catalytic converters are also damaged if an engine goes out of tune, misfires or burns oil; some fuel additives, leaded petrol and bump starting the vehicle – when raw fuel is pumped into the unit then ignited when the engine fires – are also harmful. Even one faulty sparking plug can cause damage. A damaged catalytic converter will easily show up in yearly Ministry of Transport testing, and they are costly to replace. If you are off-roading in countries where one is not required by law, bearing in mind the low-quality fuel and corrugated tracks in some countries, you should seriously think about removing it.

The catalysts operate at very high temperatures. In hot dry areas, beware of parking over long grass or dry leaves, as they could start a fire that will engulf your vehicle.

TRANSMISSION

Automatic or manual?

The American market and, increasingly, the more luxurious vehicle market prefers automatic transmission. There is also an increasing awareness amongst fleet operators and the US Forces that automatic transmission lowers the incidence of transmission shock loads from driver misuse and gives smoother gear changes and thus less chance of loss of traction by inexperienced drivers.

If you fail on a hill and have to reverse back down again with an automatic, you are in a dangerous situation. On big boulders and the up-and-down of heavy, slow going, manual transmission is best;

Manual transmission gives more positive engine breaking down steep inclines.

it will give instant engine compression and gear hold-back, which the automatic cannot. When descending steep hills, engine hold-back using the gears is more secure with manual transmission than with automatic transmissions, which have been known to change up a gear, increasing the speed, despite being locked into first gear.

In continuous heavy slow going, the automatic transmission's oil may overheat, unless an extra oil cooler is fitted. Fuel consumption is increased and the special fluids used can be difficult to obtain in the Third World. A further problem for serious off-road use is that you cannot push-start or tow-start the vehicle if your battery fails – you will have to use another battery or jump-leads from another vehicle. If your starter motor has failed, even another vehicle will not be able to get your engine started.

Automatic transmission produced for four-wheel drive vehicles should have a manual lock-in drive on the lowest gears to allow engine braking, but you may not be able to engage this if the speed is too high. When going up a steep hill, over a crest then steeply downhill, you may not be able to stop on the crest, and will have to think ahead and lock low gear in early.

Transfer box

Some four-wheel drive vehicles do not have a low-range transfer box. They may have an extra crawler gear instead, but for serious off-road use this is not enough. Some predominantly sporting four-wheel drive vehicles have a low-range transfer box that is not low enough to give good engine braking downhill. With these vehicles you will have to use first gear in low range in most situations where I recommend second gear for 'working' vehicles.

Cross-axle differentials

As has already been mentioned, when a vehicle makes a turn the outside wheels travel a greater distance than the inside wheels. Within the axle the differential is the device that differentiates between the speeds of the two wheels on the axle, allowing one

Land Rover manual main gearbox and transfer box levers.

wheel to turn at a different speed from the other, while still transmitting the power to each axle half-shaft and hence each wheel on that axle.

Conventional 'open' differentials work fine on paved roads and give predictable handling. Most four-wheel drive vehicles are fitted with 'open' axles front and rear and, although front and rear axles can be locked together through a four-wheel drive lever or centre differential lock, it is still possible for one wheel on either axle to lose traction and spin, leaving the second wheel on that same axle without traction.

There are four answers to this problem: limited slip differentials, locking differentials, electronic traction control and torque-biasing 'Torsen Gleason' differentials.

Limited slip cross-axle differentials

Limited slip differentials use friction plates, cones and/or gears to reduce slippage between each of the wheels on the same axle. A certain amount of clutch pre-load is built into the unit; when one wheel loses traction, the amount of power that can be transmitted to the other is dependent on this pre-load (friction) on the clutch plates.

The friction may not be enough to power the vehicle if one wheel totally loses traction, but in general off-road performance is improved without excessive

handling problems, so long as these units are only fitted to the rear axle.

Limited slip differentials restrict the true differential action, and tyre wear is increased, as is the wear on the differential itself. Special lubricants are required and there can be handling idiosyncrasies, particularly on short-wheelbase vehicles. These do not only occur off-road – I have also had problems on wet motorways.

At highway speeds on slippery surfaces, on corrugations, or when traversing slopes laterally, one wheel can slip slightly, causing the differential to grab and swing the rear end out, often to reverse again as the clutches slip and grip. This action is sometimes referred to as 'fish-tailing'. Limited slip differentials are also sensitive to differences in tyre diameter; a difference in air pressure between two tyres on the same axle, a mis-matched spare wheel, or a punc-

A Vauxhall Monterey shows lack of axle articulation as the limited slip differential refuses to work on this occasion.

ture, can cause this fish-tailing. Therefore if you fit snow chains, they must be on all four wheels.

Because of fish-tailing problems, some modern limited slip differentials have the friction set so that they do not always seem to work when you want them to off-road. If you have a handbrake on rear drums, a short application of this may tweak them into action, otherwise try a quick jab on the foot brakes.

Some specialist vehicles also have limited slip differentials on the front axle, but I cannot recommend this. On narrow tracks one front wheel might grab traction and pull you off the track before you can stop it, and on a slippery road the limited slip could pull you from side to side and at worst induce a spin, as the torque goes from wheel to wheel.

Limited slip differentials have been fitted to many production four-wheel drive vehicles and some two-wheel drive road vehicles in the past. They are currently fitted to a few four-wheel drive vehicles, but many manufacturers have now dropped them.

Automatic lockable cross-axle differentials

Automatic locking differentials transmit power to each wheel through a pair of dog clutches. When one wheel rotates faster than the other, the appropriate clutch is disengaged, and this results in the differential action occurring in ratcheting stages, rather than being smooth and progressive. If one wheel loses traction, the other wheel on the same axle will receive the total power applied to the differential, to maintain vehicle mobility. Off-road this system is superior to limited slip differentials, but handling on paved roads suffers.

During turns on paved roads and on loose, slippery or corrugated surfaces, or when traversing slopes laterally, unlocking can be sudden, resulting in rapid changes in direction, particularly on short-wheelbase vehicles. On sharp turns, loud bangs and ratcheting noises occur as the unit locks and unlocks, and tyre wear and internal differential wear is increased. This system is for rear axles only; on the front axle there can be extreme problems with steering. Again, if you fit snow chains, they must be on all four wheels.

Manually lockable cross-axle differentials

Manually lockable differentials use a conventional differential with a mechanical locking device that can be used at the driver's discretion. When unlocked there is no increase in tyre wear and no difference in the vehicle's steering. They can be installed on the front axle as well as the rear, without compromising on-road handling, and are not sensitive to differences in tyre diameter.

These differentials have been fitted to tractors and military vehicles for many years, and more recently to four-wheel drive recreational vehicles; but the market leapt forward when Tony Brown's ARB Company brought out their 'Air Locker', where, by using a small 12-volt air compressor, these units could be fitted to either or both axles and controlled pneumatically and separately by push-button switches on the vehicle dashboard. No special maintenance is required and paved road handling is not affected with the differential unlocked. The air compressor can also be used to pump up tyres.

ARB have led the market for many years, but by the time this book is published Kam Differentials of Godalming will have a British-built unit on sale, with a manual override to allow for damage to the air lines.

Jack McNamara has a differential lock operated by the vacuum supply from the engine manifold or brake booster, and a simpler system that can be engaged under the vehicle by removing a bolt on the differential.

Locking differentials give you the confidence to tackle difficult off-road situations at a slower, safer speed. The half-shaft driving the one wheel that has traction can be under considerable torque. Consequently, individual half-shafts must be strong enough to take whatever torque the engine can deliver, particularly if the vehicle is to be used fully loaded. It is best to have uprated components fitted.

Fully locking differentials should only be used when really necessary, over short distances, and should never be engaged while the wheels are spinning, or mechanical damage can occur. It is these problems, with lack of driver education, that have stopped many manufacturers from fitting them as standard, and caused others to abandon them after short production runs.

With a locked front differential you will not have proper steering. Both wheels must travel at the same speed, so you will go straight ahead, unless slipping sideways on a slope. They should therefore be used even more selectively, only on very short sections where no change of direction is required. If the vehicle is leaning sideways on a slope, with the lower wheels on soft ground, the use of cross-axle differential locks tends to cause the lower wheels to dig in faster and deeper, making the vehicle lean more and possibly turn over.

Torque-biasing cross-axle differentials

'Torsen Gleason' differentials, invented by American Vernon Gleason, can be fitted front and rear. They allow normal differential action while the tyres grip, but proportion the torque in accordance with the available traction when they do not.

They consist of two or more pairs of planetary gears meshing with two central helical gears, the planetary gears being mounted across the axis of the differential. The inherent inefficiency of the helical gearing crossing at right angles acts as a limited slip.

The system has instant reaction to unequal traction between wheels, and the 'bias ratio', the ratio of axle torques that the differential can support, remains constant over a wide range of operating conditions.

Some feedback torque is required, so once a wheel spins freely there will be no torque on the driving shafts, so the vehicle stops. Stabbing repeatedly at the brake pedal ('cadence' or 'modulation' braking), causes some torque on that wheel's half-shaft, allowing some to be transferred across the axle. This does not always work, but when it does the vehicle is jerked along until normal traction is resumed.

Electronic traction control

The Range Rover's electronic traction control system is a technically more sophisticated answer to the problem, with the advantage that it does not load up either half-shaft; the torque is maintained evenly across the whole axle, even if only one wheel is actually finding traction.

With additional circuits in the ABS braking system, the electronic control unit senses when one wheel is travelling so much faster than the other that it must be slipping, and applies the brake on that wheel only, to slow it down and maintain drive to the wheel that still has traction. There is no requirement of driver knowledge as to when it is necessary to use it, and no handling idiosyncrasies. The system is fast and smooth – a brief lighting of the advisory lamp on the central warning display is often the only indication to the driver that the system has come into use.

Using cross-axle differential locks or electronic traction control

Cross-axle differential locks or electronic traction control are most useful when crossing ditches, humps or boulders, where one or more wheels may end up in the air without traction. The better your axle articulation, the less this is likely to happen, but all vehicles have their limits.

Other situations where these aids are useful are in mud or snow and when you have the two wheels on one side of the vehicle on mud or wet grass and those wheels on the other side on a paved road or firm track, particularly if you are towing a heavy trailer. Remember that you will not have any steering when a front cross-axle lock is locked-in.

If you do not have cross-axle differential locks or electronic traction control and are stuck in this way and have an adjustable drum brake on the spinning wheel, locking the brake shoe on, with its adjusting cam, can help over short distances.

Axle ratios

A few manufacturers offer a range of axle ratios, allowing prospective buyers to match up their requirements according to their preferred wheels, tyres and engine. More often, however, axle ratios are changed as an aftermarket accessory, when wheels, gearing or engines are changed, or the differential is given stronger components.

SUSPENSION AND STEERING

It is not practicable to attach the road wheels directly to the chassis frame or body construction – every shock caused by variations in the road surface would be transmitted to the vehicle and its occupants. The function of the wheel suspension and springs is to absorb these shocks and allow the vehicle to proceed on a level course, regardless of road conditions.

Ideally, when a wheel strikes a bump it should be thrown upwards and its energy entirely absorbed by the suspension system, while the vehicle remains level. In practice, the extent to which this occurs depends largely on the weight of the wheel and its appendages relative to the weight of the vehicle. For this reason on-road cars have these components made as lightweight as possible, including the use of small wheels. However, off-road, larger wheels are preferable, as they iron out pot holes and give more ground clearance.

Long-travel suspension, which gives good axle articulation, is

With cross-axle locks front and rear you will be able to traverse very difficult terrain, although with the front cross-axle lock engaged you will have no control over the steering.

A modern Land Rover shows particularly good axle articulation, while the Nissan Patrol demonstrates poorer articulation.

has disadvantages, including high unsprung weight and a tendency for gyroscopic interaction between the wheels; also the beam axle acts as a lever, tilting the whole vehicle if one wheel is lifted by a bump. This last action is advantageous off-road, as it keeps the whole axle at the same height above the ground, therefore less liable to hit any obstruction.

Independent suspension

Most on-road light vehicles have independent suspension on the front, if not on all four wheels, and many four-wheel drives now have independent suspension on the front for improved ride and handling on paved roads. Each front wheel is separately hinged, such that the up or down movement of one wheel does not affect the other. There are several ways of achieving this, but for off-road use when one wheel lifts over an obstacle the rest of the axle loses ground clearance, making it more likely to hit any obstacle or, in some situations, the ground itself.

Springs and shock absorbers

Springs support the vehicle's weight and, in conjunction with the wheel and tyre size, set the vehicle's ride height. They determine the limits of the suspension travel and, in conjunction with shock absorbers and anti-roll bars, determine the vehicle's ride quality and handling characteristics.

When a spring is compressed or released, it will continue to bounce up and down several times unless some form of damping device is fitted.

Older-type high-friction 'leaf' springs are to a certain extent self-damping, but modern anti-friction leaf springs, torsion-bar springs and coil springs could go on bouncing for some time unless shock absorbers are fitted (of which more later). The name is misleading, for the spring actually absorbs the initial shock of the

advantageous off-road, as it gives more chance of keeping all wheels in contact with the ground, thus maintaining traction without the requirement of limited slip differentials or cross-axle differential locks. However, such a suspension allows the vehicle to roll more when cornering.

If you have a choice, and if you work in rough country, it is always worth going for the heaviest suspension offered. Most of the time you will get a hard ride, but this is better than having regularly to replace broken springs and shock

absorbers. If you to spend 95 per cent of your time on the road, a softer suspension will give you a more comfortable ride.

Non-independent suspension

On older vehicles the rear suspension of most four-wheel drive vehicles and the front suspension of most serious four-wheel drive off-road vehicles is non-independent: the wheels are mounted at the ends of a beam axle, which couples them rigidly together. This system

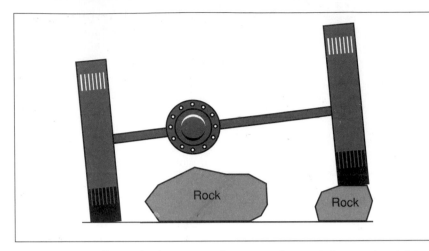

With a beam axle, if one wheel goes over a hump or rock ground clearance is maintained along the whole axle.

bump. The shock absorber prevents any further oscillations and is better described as a spring-damper. In simple terms, the springs provide flexibility in the vehicle's suspension so that it can

With independent suspension, if one wheel goes over a hump or rock the opposite end of the axle and the differential are not raised, and in extreme situations are actually lowered, making the differential liable to grounding.

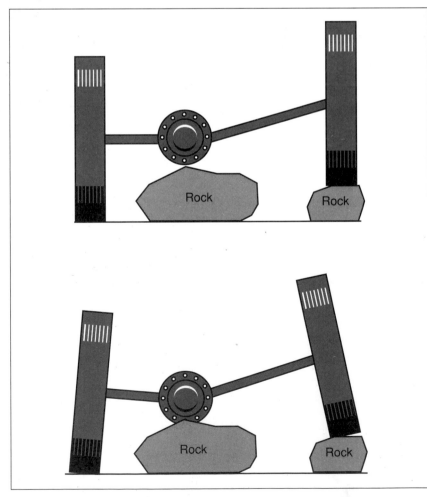

ride over uneven surfaces, while the shock absorber damps down the recoil so that the vehicle does not bounce out of control.

Leaf springs

Laminated semi-elliptic leaf springs – good old-fashioned 'cart' springs – are relatively cheap, strong, easily repaired (or extra leaves can be added for extra load-carrying capacity), and have the advantage of positively locating the axle. However, they can be improved upon: they can be inter-leaved, graphite-coated or given additional anti-friction pads to decrease friction, given a flat shape if necessary (where the 'U' bolts seat them to the axle) to reduce stress, fully scragged to ensure that they take a permanent 'set' shape, reinforced with extra, flat helper leaves, to progressively absorb heavier loads, and have more than one leaf wrapped around the bushes for extra safety. There can also be improvements in the materials used for the spring bushes, and spring shackles can be made with grease nipples.

Torsion bars

Torsion bar springs consist of a straight steel rod or tube, or are built up from several leaves into a bar, which is square in cross section. The springing effect is obtained by holding one end of the rod and twisting the other.

Coil springs

Coil springs are best described as torsion bars wound up into a helical shape. They have the advantage of allowing longer wheel travel and hence axle articulation. There is not much that can be improved with torsion bars, other than using a heavier fitment, but coil springs can be improved, or those for a heavier-weight vehicle fitted.

Spring packers can allow the vehicle's trim to be adjusted for weight and the spring wire diameter itself can be tapered for part

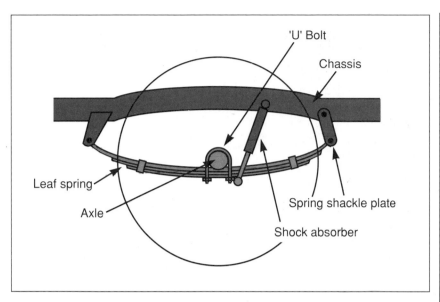

Leaf spring suspension, with the spring holding the axle in place.

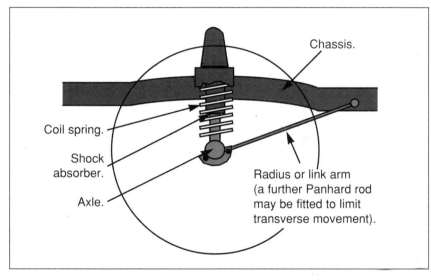

Coil spring suspension, with a radius arm to hold the axle in place fore and aft.

of the spring length, to produce a variable spring rate. Constant spring rate is fine on the front axle, but variable spring rates are useful on the rear axle, to provide better ride comfort when unladen.

Another way to achieve a variable spring rate is to vary the pitch (distance) between the individual spring coils. Pneumatic 'helper' springs (air bags) are also available to fit within rear coil springs, to handle progressively greater loads, or you can fit stronger springs, designed for a heavier vehicle.

Neither torsion bars nor coil springs positively locate the axle, so various extra locating rods, link arms and bushes have to be employed to locate the axle and limit its horizontal movement.

Other suspension systems

Various rubber 'springs' have been used in the past, and now that the Range Rover has an air system, other such systems are likely to follow. Both types provide soft suspension under low deflection, but stiffen up rapidly under increasing loads. It cannot be too long into the future before active suspension

systems are fitted to four-wheel drive vehicles.

Anti-roll bars

The adoption of independent front suspension, particularly long-travel suspension, and the use of softer springs has caused a tendency for vehicles to roll sideways when cornering. This can be reduced by fitting an anti-roll bar (or stabiliser). This is a torsion bar fitted across the car and connected to the suspension links in such a way that it resists any tendency for the wheels to move up and down in opposite directions to each other. The bar is not anchored rigidly to the chassis, so it does not stiffen the springing if both wheels move up or down together.

Shock absorbers

On production vehicles shock absorbers are a necessary compromise between the conditions of on-road and off-road use. The basic design is of a piston moving within an oil-filled cylinder, with a 'designed-in' rate of leakage, so that the amount of dampening for a heavy bump is very much larger than that for small bumps. Some can be adjusted for firmness, either manually or from within the vehicle.

Cheaper designs of shock absorbers suffer heat build-up and lose efficiency as the oil becomes aerated in use. More expensive designs have larger bores, use pressurised nitrogen instead of air and more sophisticated valve systems.

Shock absorbers have a hard time on-road and a much harder time off-road – they do not, in fact, last very long at all. Worn shock absorbers can seriously affect your safety at highway speeds, so they should be checked regularly and, if worn, all four units should be replaced at the same time.

Steering dampers (stabilizers)

Steering dampers are a simple form

of shock absorber. Mounted laterally between a tie rod and the chassis, they dampen and bring under control the movement of the tie rod, which connects the steering wheel to the front road wheels. The result is smoother steering off-road, with less twisting of the steering wheel over bumps and more lateral control on paved roads.

A steering damper is essential if you have oversize tyres, because their greater unsprung weight compounds wheel shimmy and wear on front-end components.

Power steering

Power steering is not essential, except on the largest four-wheel drive vehicles, and is another component that does go wrong, especially in heavy off-road use; but it can be useful for those who find steering heavy, especially when parking. On some vehicles there is no 'feeling' built in, so it is difficult to know which way the wheels are pointing. On some systems the built-in 'feeling' increases with speed.

BRAKES

Servo brakes

Servo brakes are not necessary on short-wheelbase vehicles, but make a big difference to all other models. Presently available systems are very reliable.

Anti-lock braking systems (ABS)

If available, ABS braking can make a big difference on slippery, paved roads, as well as on loose surfaces and mud off-road, especially with larger vehicles whose heavier weight makes them more prone to skidding if the wheels lock up.

The brakes are applied until wheel speed sensors identify that a skidding wheel is likely, then the brake pressure is released. The cycle of brakes on/brakes off is repeated many times per second, a more efficient version of 'cadence' ('modulation') braking. If you have ABS, do not perform cadence braking yourself – maintain pressure on the brake pedal to allow the system to work effectively.

Some ABS systems work individually on the front wheels, but treat the rear wheels together as a pair. Some are fooled by loose gravel or corrugations, so it helps if they can be disengaged.

ABS can not work efficiently on individual wheels if cross-axle differential locks are engaged, and some systems may be fooled when centre differential locks are engaged, so where these locks are used ABS is automatically disabled where necessary.

Transmission brake

True off-road vehicles should have a handbrake or foot parking brake connected to the rear propeller shaft, rather than directly to the rear wheels. The advantage of this system is that if the vehicle is in four-wheel drive, this brake is acting efficiently on all four wheels, particularly important in off-road situations and more so when the vehicle is parked on a steep incline and/or has wet brakes at the wheels.

The only disadvantage of this system is that you must engage four-wheel drive and lock the centre differential if you have one before jacking up the vehicle to change a wheel. It is also wise to chock up the other wheels and put the vehicle into gear.

Transmission brakes should never be used when the vehicle is moving – they will put severe stress on the transmission and the heat build-up can cause the adjacent transfer box oil seal to fail. The only exception to this rule is a very gentle application, with the ratchet disengaged, to dry the brake out if its use for parking on a steep incline is likely to be required soon after deep wading. In this instance, put the vehicle into gear for extra safety.

Do not use the transmission brake to slow down the vehicle on a steep incline. If this is necessary, use cadence braking.

WHEELS AND TYRES

Vehicle manufacturers go to great lengths to design transmission, suspension, steering and braking systems for performance, handling and safety within strict regulations. The wheel and tyre combination is an important factor in this.

Many four-wheel drive owners fit larger wheels and tyres without thought for the legality of the final vehicle, or their own safety, as well as whether the vehicle's components can handle the extra stress. If the EU bureaucrats get their way, any such alterations will become illegal on the public highway within the European Union. It is therefore essential to check with the vehicle manufacturer, as well as the wheel and tyre salesman, before making such changes.

When you fit oversize wheels and tyres you increase the unsprung weight, causing increased impact on and bounce of the wheels. Springs and shock absorbers may require up-rating and axle ratios may require changing.

All tyres are designed to fit specific widths of rim and, of course, the appropriate diameter of wheel. The profile of the wheel rim varies according to the preferred type of tyre to be fitted and whether it is tubed or tubeless. Wheel sizes and profiles often change between older and newer versions of the same vehicle, and the number of wheel studs may also vary.

Wheel offset is another variable. The original wheel rim may be set 'in' or 'out', so that the path of the load through the hub lies between the inner and outer wheel bearings. Changing this, as well as placing additional strain on the wheel hub bearings and steering components, may adversely affect

Oversize tyres on a Jeep Wrangler.

the handling and braking characteristics of the vehicle. Brake discs and associated guards may also be exposed to possible damage in deep ruts.

Wider rims and larger tyres can also reduce the clearance between the tyre and the chassis, body, suspension and brake components, particularly on full lock and/or maximum suspension travel.

Alloy wheels generally weigh less than steel wheels, but if damaged they are difficult to repair. They are designed with 'poser' appeal and are an eminent target for thieves. Steel wheels are cheaper to replace and in a Third World situation can be knocked back into reasonable shape in an emergency.

Divided wheels (split-rim wheels) make tyre changes and repairs easier, but only use those supplied by the vehicle manufacturer for that vehicle (for example Toyota Landcruisers in the Middle East). I have seen several split-rim wheels break up.

Another problem is that many American and Japanese tyres are only available for 15-inch (381 mm) diameter wheels. These tyres may actually be of a larger overall diameter than those fitted to 16-inch (406 mm) wheels. However, fitting a 15-inch wheel where a 16-inch wheel was originally fitted can reduce the cooling airflow around

the brakes, leading to brake fading. Larger (heavier) tyres will also require the brakes to work harder, as the moment of rotation is greater. At slow speeds off-road you may not have any problems, but at higher speeds on paved roads, especially under heavy braking, things could be different.

Excessive increases in overall tyre diameter can alter the caster and camber angles, reduce the self-centring ability of the steering and alter the vehicle handling characteristics. The toe-in should be set as close to 0° as possible, especially with wider tyres and wheels, while caster should be within the manufacturer's specification. Wide tyres suffer reduced traction on wet grass and on loose or slippery ground, due to reduced ground pressure.

Tyres

Whatever the abilities of your vehicle, its ultimate performance in any terrain will depend on having the correct design of tyres for that terrain. Tyres are air containers, and it is the air that carries the load. The larger the quantity or pressure of air contained in the tyre, the higher the load the tyre can support.

Each tyre has a specified load capacity. To carry an increased

load it may be possible to change to a higher load capacity tyre in the same size, which would take a higher pressure, or change to a larger-size tyre, providing the components are compatible.

The load index, or ply rating, gives the load the tyre can support at a given speed when correctly inflated. For reasons of cost manufacturers supply their vehicles with the minimum cross-country tyres they consider necessary; with so many different tyres on the market for different uses, it is impracticable for them to do otherwise. You have to select the tyre for your own needs.

Some self-cleaning tyres are directional and must be fitted the correct way round to be effective; such tyres will not be self cleaning in reverse. For this reason some commercial off-road vehicles are fitted with the front tyres self-cleaning on forward movement and the rear tyres self-cleaning on reverse movement. Tyres are not self-cleaning if they are spinning.

Nowadays there are four basic types of off-road vehicle requirements in tyres, plus various specialist uses. The luxury Range Rover/Mitsubishi Shogun-type vehicle owner requires a high-speed, low-noise, good-road-holding, attractive-looking tyre, that is a highway saloon car tyre that can handle a wet grass car park, snow or a wet slipway when launching a boat. Tyres of this type use advanced compounds, a high ratio of tread to groove, and a high-technology firmly braced tread design to give precise steering; wide circumferential channels and numerous cross slits to ensure good water dispersion to avoid aquaplaning; a staggered tread block of different sizes to reduce high-speed road noise; and a wide flat crown to give maximum road holding with even wear and square shoulders to give positive cornering.

The all-round Discovery/Suzuki Vitara-type user, who uses the vehicle predominantly on-road, but also for weekend off-

An Olympic Super Mud Plugger – the direction of rotation is marked on the side of the tyre.

The Michelin XM+S244.

The Michelin 4x4 A/T.

road fun, is looking for long life, good grip on wet roads and adequate performance on muddy tracks, snow and ice. Tyres of this type try to be all-rounders, with a multi-block tread pattern with sharp-edged 'sipes' (knife cuts) to give good performance in wet and snowy conditions; firm tread blocks on the tyre shoulders to give directional stability and extra grip in mud; variable tread block size to give a quieter ride on paved roads; and progressively widening channels across the tread to eject surface water and wet mud.

The farmer, vet, doctor and relatively serious off-roader, who could be driving any type of off-road vehicle, require all-terrain capability and rural road comfort. This user looks for damage resistance, traction on grass, mud, snow and ice, and reasonable performance on paved roads. Such tyres have a taller but reinforced side wall, supple enough to absorb bumps, rocks and potholes; deep tread with a high percentage of tread pattern (grooves and sipes); channels across the tread surface that open out towards the shoulders, for self-cleaning in mud; and angled shoulder blocks and large rigid tread blocks to give good traction and control in most conditions.

The serious Land Rover Defender-type off-roader requires a tyre to go anywhere, regardless of the weather and ground conditions. Unfortunately, tyres with the aggressive open-tread patterns suitable for mud are the opposite of what is best for sand. So these have to be different tyres.

Off-road tyres for uses other than sand require a deep aggressive tread pattern on a tyre that is relatively narrow, so that it cuts through mud and snow to reach the firmer ground below; large, widely spaced tread blocks in a self-cleaning pattern, for mud or loose surfaces; large, sharply angled tread blocks on the shoulders, to give extra grip in longitudinal ruts or on steep slopes; and a supple casing to allow use at pressures as low as 15 psi (1.0 bar), but also reinforced side walls against damage. These tyres will not have particularly good performance on the highway, where they may also be noisy and wear down quickly.

For use predominantly in soft sand a tyre must be large and supple (balloon-like), so that it can be run at pressures down to 15 psi (1.0 bar). Sand tyres should have almost no tread pattern so that they float over the sand, only compressing it and causing little disturbance to the surface, because the surface crust is usually firmer than the sand underneath.

Sand tyres should not be used over stony or mixed ground – the side walls cut up easily and sharp stones will penetrate the shallow tread. These tyres are excellent for their specialist use, but are not designed to be used on paved roads, where they have poor directional stability. New, ultra-tough sand tyres are appearing in the USA, with Kevlar in their construction. Pure sand tyres have only circumferential grooves for directional stability, but Michelin supply one tyre, the XS, that is more usable on the road, as it does have a tread pattern, though it can be dodgy on ice.

Overlanders and expeditions, who have to cover mixed terrain, will find broad buttress tread, truck-type tyres are best; they have a good road performance, do not cut up easily on sharp stones and can be run soft in sand. For deep mud and snow, this type of tyre fitted with snow chains will be better than most specialist mud tyres. One tyre, the Michelin XZY, stands out for this use, because it has a greater load-carrying capacity

4X4

Superb wet road grip, excellent braking and precision steering make this the perfect fit on and off the road. Specially developed multi-siped tread gives extra grip on snow, ice and wet grass, while the advanced radial construction gives a smooth ride on the road. The ideal all-round 4x4 tyre with a very long life.

4X4 A/T

An excellent all-round tyre that is tough enough for arduous off-road use, but still performs well on the road. Deep, self-cleaning tread gives excellent mobility on mud. Very smooth on rough ground with special undertread protection rubber for extra damage resistance.

4X4 H/W

Designed mainly for road use, it ensures precision handling and excellent grip at all speeds. Comfortable and quiet it will improve safety while returning a very long life. Striking white sidewall lettering makes it a stylish choice to match any 4x4 vehicle.

4X4 O/R

The ultimate off-road tyre ensuring maximum traction on the muddiest, roughest ground. Self cleaning and comfortable, with tough tread rubber and heavy sidewall protection for high damage resistance and a long working life. Ideal for professional, military and enthusiast use.

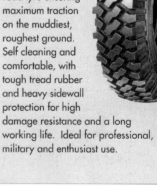

A selection of Michelin 4x4 tyres.

Balloon sand tyres on a Toyota Landcruiser, essential for crossing the Arabian empty quarter, Yemen.

The Michelin XS.

The Michelin XZY.

than those of the same type by other manufacturers. Overlanders and expeditions are always overloaded! Michelin XZY tyres almost fall off the rim when flat, making it very easy to break the bead to repair punctures.

Further specialist tyres used off-road are tractor or dumper tyres, which have exaggerated self-cleaning treads that are particularly good in mud and clay, but very poor on paved roads, and very

large balloon 'terra' tyres, which spread the load lightly over a large 'footprint'. These are used on boggy ground or where the vehicle has to go over a farmer's field without damaging the crop.

There are hundreds of different tyres for four-wheel drive vehicles, with all manufacturers competing for what has become a large market. All the top manufacturers are constantly developing new tread designs, but with prices being so

high, many enthusiasts favour the good old-fashioned Firestone SAT for off-road use.

The manufacture of tyres is not an exact science, which is why wheels fitted with tyres should be balanced for paved road use. Larger-sized wheels and tyres are more difficult to balance, and the balance weights rarely stay on in off-road conditions.

Tyre construction

In cross-ply tyres the ply cords extend to the bead, so as to be laid at alternate angles of substantially less than 90° to the peripheral line of the tread. Cross-ply tyres have more rigid side walls that flex less and therefore give a harder ride. At correct pressure they are less prone to damage from striking the side of rocks or the kerb and less prone to damage from snow chains. They are also better for cutting through mud, to grip the firmer ground below. They are relatively cheap and, when fitted with aggressive treads, are good in mud, so they are popular for trialing, and with farmers and operators working on mixed terrain of mud, snow and rocks. However, they wear out relatively quickly.

In bias-belted tyres the ply cords extend to the bead so as to be laid at alternate angles of substantially less than 90° to the peripheral line of the tread, and are constrained by a circumferential belt comprising two or more layers of inextensible cord material, laid at alternate angles smaller than those of the ply cord structure. Bias-belted tyres are more common on the American market, but are old technology that is dying out. They exhibit properties mid-way between those of cross-ply and radial-ply construction.

Radial-ply tyres pioneered by Michelin have the ply cords extending to the bead, so as to be laid at 90° to the peripheral line of the tread, the ply cord structure being stabilised by an inextensible circumferential belt. Radial-ply

Extreme exaggerated self-cleaning tractor tyres on a Land Rover for forestry work.

Enthusiasts like the Firestone SATs for trialling because they give good traction at a low price.

Remoulded tyres

With the high cost of tyres, remoulds have reappeared. They are a cheap alternative for vehicles used predominantly off-road and at low speed on-road. You should beware of physical size differences from different manufacturers' original casings.

Speed rating

For public highway use, the speed rating should be matched to the top speed possible in the vehicle to which they are fitted, regardless of the speed at which the vehicle is driven or its off-road use.

Cross-ply tyres have slightly less grip than radial tyres on paved roads, so they are not recommended for high-powered vehicles on the highway. They have correspondingly lower speed ratings.

New tyres should be bedded in at low speed and correct tyre pressures for the first 300 miles (500 km).

Mixing tyres

Legally, except for temporary use of the spare tyre at low speeds, you must not use:

1. Cross-ply tyres or bias-belted tyres on the rear axle, if radial-ply tyres are fitted to the front axle.

2. Cross-ply tyres on the rear axle if bias-belted tyres are fitted to the front axle.

3. Any two tyres of different construction on the same axle.

In situations 1 and 2 the tyres on the rear would have a greater slip angle, causing excessive oversteer. In situation 3 they would give inconsistent handling.

Tyres and transmission 'wind-up' in four-wheel drive

As explained elsewhere, when vehicles are in four-wheel drive

tyres are more expensive, but their extra flexibility gives a softer ride, which is better for the vehicle and its occupants. This flexibility gives the tyres an under-inflated appearance and lowers the ground clearance slightly. They also have a lower rolling resistance, which improves fuel economy and gives longer life. They run cooler and are better suited to running at lower pressure for extra flotation

on soft ground. For really heavy work, steel-braced radials are preferable, and some tyres have stronger side walls to reduce damage from side impact.

Radial-ply tyres 'set' in use, so when changed around to even out tyre wear, they should be kept on the same side of the vehicle; for example, the nearside front wheel should be moved to the nearside rear wheel, or vice versa.

Rotation of four radial tyres.

Rotation of five radial tyres.

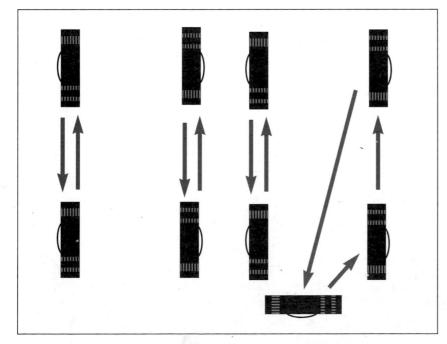

with any centre differential locked in, the different distances travelled by each wheel can cause transmission 'wind-up'. To minimise this, all four tyres and the spare tyre should be of the same size and tread pattern and have roughly the same degree of tread wear. This is essential across any axle that is fitted with a limited slip differential, where the tyres must also be at the same pressure.

Tubed or tubeless?

Most modern vehicles are fitted with tubeless tyres, because they hold their pressure better, especially around small penetrating objects. For hard off-road use at ultra-low pressures, tubeless tyres can give problems and therefore they should be fitted with tubes. This prevents problems with the bead when driving over rocks, the kerb, when wheels are damaged or when sand gets between the bead and the seat. Most punctures are tears and resealing a tubeless tyre requires a high-pressure compressor and possibly a bead expander, ie, a circumferential strap or tourniquet, which are rarely available. For these reasons most true off-road vehicles are supplied with tubed tyres.

Competition vehicles using tubeless tyres would have back-up trucks and crews, but in general, if you have trouble with tubeless tyres off-road, you should fit an inner tube; but there are some wheel rims to which you should not. Wheels that are designed with an asymmetric hump rim profile, to retain the tyre bead on the rim at very low pressures, should not be fitted with tubes, because the tubes can chafe on the internal wheel rim humps. Check with your vehicle manufacturer and the tyre manufacturer. Most manufacturers are not going to recommend that inner tubes be fitted to their tubeless tyres, but it is widely recognised as common practice in the real world.

Only use inner tubes with short valves. Long truck-type valves can rip off on sudden deflation, and in off-road conditions a flat rear tyre may not be noticed until irreparable damage has occurred.

Valve caps

Always fit valve caps that have a seal. These help to keep the air in and dirt and mud out.

Tyre pressures

For paved road use, tyres at the recommended pressure for the load on the axle will have their tread flat on the road, giving optimum contact area ('footprint') and lateral stability. If the pressure is too high, the tread expands in a balloon shape, and the effective 'footprint' is reduced. Most of the load and hence, wear is on the centre of the tread, with the outer tread and shoulder little used. Lateral stability is reduced and the ride becomes hard.

If the pressure is too low, the tyre flexes more than it is meant to, generating extra heat and tending to roll about when cornering. The tread in contact with the ground arches upward in the centre, reducing the 'footprint' and increasing the wear on the outer tread and shoulder. The sidewalls immediately above the 'footprint' bulge out under the load, making them vulnerable to impact damage.

The amount of tread in contact with the ground and the amount of deflection of the tyre side walls depends on the load on the axle and, hence, each tyre. Tyre and vehicle manufacturers issue tables of recommended tyre pressures for given axle loads. With loaded long-wheelbase vehicles, there will be more weight on the rear axle than on the front axle, so the rear tyre pressures should be higher. These recommended tyre pressures are important for tyre life and vehicle handling characteristics.

On-road, correct tyre pressures are important, but off-road there are times when you gain improvements by breaking the rules, so long as you travel at reduced speeds. In areas of sharp stones, for example, increased tyre pressures will help to keep sharp stone contact away from the vulnerable side walls and on to the thicker tread at the centre. With radial-ply tyres increased tyre pressures will help the tyre to cut through mud or snow, into firmer ground below. With a lightly loaded vehicle on radial-ply tyres, increasing the pressure to the maximum allowed will fractionally increase the ground clearance and ramp break-over angle.

On soft ground there are considerable advantages to lowering tyre pressures, particularly with radial-ply tyres. Normally the lower limit would be 15 psi (1.0 bar), below which there is a chance that the tyre bead could move on the rim, or tubeless tyres deflate and the wheel rim be damaged. An accurate pressure gauge is essential. For some military uses, pressures down to 10 psi (0.7 bar) are used.

Vehicle manufacturers stipulate minimum tyre pressures for handling reasons and the possibility of a tyre being dislodged. Some Michelin tyres are cleared by Michelin, structurally and operationally, for pressures down to 9 psi (0.6 bar) where the absolute limit of flotation is essential. You must fit inner tubes for use on sand, obey Michelin's published tables on axle load and speed limit, be extra vigilant for possible side wall, damage and avoid sharp steering movements or side slopes that could cause a tyre to roll off a wheel rim. As a general rule the maximum permitted speed would be 12 mph (19 kph).

As the tyre balloons out, the curling up of the centre of the tread makes little difference on soft ground (true sand tyres are shaped to allow for this) and the 'footprint' is lengthened, so overall the weight of the vehicle is spread over a larger area, giving less ground pressure. This enables the vehicle to float over soft ground into which it might otherwise have sunk.

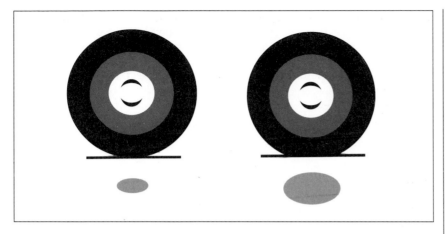

Hard tyre – small 'footprint'. Soft tyre (lowered tyre pressure) – larger 'footprint'. This spreads the load over a larger area, giving less chance of slipping and more traction.

There are situations, such as deep, relatively firm snow or mud, where it can be difficult to decide on the best tactics – hard tyres to cut through or soft tyres to float. You may have to try both. Remember that if you fit chains, you must use the correct tyre pressures.

Whenever tyre pressures are altered, you must return them to normal as soon as the terrain permits – hard work if you do not have some form of engine or electrically driven compressor. When returning tyre pressures to normal while continuing a journey, the warm tyres will not register correct 'cold' pressures, so the pressure should be re-adjusted at the next 'cold tyre' opportunity, or wait until the tyre is cold before checking and proceeding.

General tyre care

- Check tyres regularly and, where possible, remove stones, thorns or nails from the tread before they can work into the casing. Thorns are a major problem for tyres in many countries. They break off, but the pointed ends continue to work through the tyre, causing punctures long after you left the area where you picked them up. If you can carry the weight, it is worth carrying an old set of tyres for off-road use in thorny conditions, and a good, legal set of tyres for on-road use.

- Oil, fuel and paint damage the tyre compound. Remove these with detergent and water.

- Tyres are also damaged by ultraviolet light in direct sunlight, excess heat and ozone concentrations near to welding and electrical machinery.

- For public highway use all tyres must have more than the legal minimum depth of tread and be free of cuts and blisters. Cut or blistered tyres should normally be scrapped, but they may be of use off-road at low speed. Tyres wear out faster off-road, mostly due to impact damage and sharp stones or thorns. They also wear out faster on-road if subjected to high-speed cornering, rapid acceleration and heavy braking.

- Tyre pressures should be checked when cold. When running, tyres get hot, more so at high speed and over corrugations. The air inside is not able to expand, so the pressure increases. Tyres are designed to accommodate this, and should not be bled to lower this pressure.

Tyre nomenclature

Nowadays all relevant information is moulded on the side walls of tyres. If this is not so, do not buy the tyre.

The tyre sizing nomenclature is confusing, being different in different countries and for different manufacturers, and it is constantly changing. Even more confusing is that some nomenclature mixes both metric and imperial measurements. The old ply ratings no longer apply, each ply nowadays being much stronger than the old plies. Now you get a load rating and a maximum speed rating.

Cross-ply tyres are usually straightforward, for example '7.50

Some of the tyre nomenclature on a Michelin XZY.

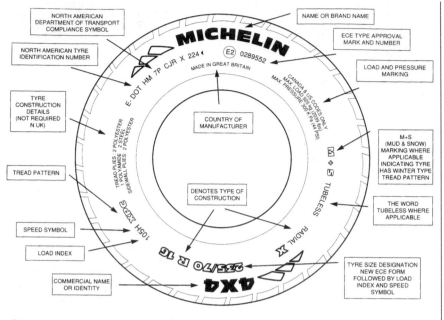

Tyre nomenclature.

x 16'. This has a section width, that is the width across the tyre walls, when inflated but unladen, of 7.5 inches (191 mm), and it fits on a 16-inch (406 mm) diameter wheel. Some American and Japanese figures include the total size, for example '31 x 10.5 R 15' means that the overall diameter of the inflated tyre on a wheel is 31 inches (787 mm), the section width is 10.5 inches (267 mm), the 'R' refers to radial, and the tyre is designed to fit on a 15-inch (381 mm) rim wheel.

In the accompanying diagram showing the tyre nomenclature of a Michelin tyre, '4x4 235/70 R 16 105H XPC' means:

4x4	all-purpose tyre
235	nominal section width of the tyre in millimetres, on standard radial tyres (aspect ratio approximately 82 per cent). The aspect ratio is not shown, for example 205 R 16.
70	nominal aspect ratio of the tyre, that is the height of the tyre's cross-section expressed as a nominal percentage of its width.
R	radial construction.

Although international standards specify the use of the letters 'B' and 'D' to indicate bias-belted or cross-ply construction respectively, they are rarely used and a hyphen replaces the letter R on tyres not of radial construction.

16	nominal diameter of the wheel rim to which the tyre should be fitted – almost always shown in inches.
105H	service description, comprising Load Capacity Index (numerical code) and Speed Category Symbol (alphabetical code).
XPC	tyre type and tread pattern
4x4	AT – All Terrain Tyre
4x4	O/R – Off-road Tyre
4x4	H/W – Highway Tyre
ORWL	Outline Raised White Letters

Load Index Markings

The 'Load Index Capacity' (as '105' in the example above) is one or two numbers that indicate the load(s) that the tyre can carry in single or in single and dual formation at the speed corresponding to the associated Speed Category Symbol.

Load Index	Kg
095	690
096	710
097	730
098	750
099	775
100	800
101	825
102	850
103	875
104	900
105	925
106	950
107	975
108	1000
109	1030
110	1060
111	1090
112	1120
113	1150
114	1180
115	1215
116	1250
117	1285
118	1320
119	1360
120	1400
121	1450
122	1500
123	1550
124	1600

Note: On some tyres a second Service Description is marked. This is a Unique Point and provides an additional rating at the specific conditions of load and speed indicated. Unlike the basic Service Description, it must not be used as the basis for calculating bonus loads at reduced speeds, or higher speeds at reduced loads.

Speed symbols

The 'Speed Category Symbol' is a letter or letter and number that indicates the speed at which the tyre can carry the load, corresponding to the associated Load Capacity Index.

Symbol	mph	kph
J	62	100
K	68	110
L	75	120
M	81	130
N	87	140
P	93	150
Q	100	160
R	105	170
S	113	180
T	118	190
U	124	200
H	130	210

BODY AND INTERIOR

Ergonomics

We all have different body sizes and shapes, so one has to test drive a vehicle to be sure that one can comfortably reach all the necessary controls and that the seats are comfortable. One can get accustomed to a heavy clutch or steering, but look out for poor headroom, legroom or elbow room, windscreens too low, body pillars obscuring forward vision and accelerators that are so sensitive that every bump translates into a blip on the pedal. Also, vehicles with small and/or closely spaced foot pedals will not allow you to drive easily, when wearing

The Land Rover Defender's foot pedals are suitable for boots.

boots or wellington boots.

Rear doors

Rear doors come in a variety of configurations, from various forms of split tailgate, split rear doors of different widths and one single large rear door. Some vehicles have rear doors that open the 'wrong' way for loading from the kerb in the UK.

Air-conditioning

Many four-wheel drive vehicles are used in areas where air-conditioning can be an aid to comfort, especially where the climate is hot and humid, rather than just hot. Air-conditioning with its filters can also be useful to those who suffer from hay fever or other problems induced by pollen, dust and vehicle emissions.

Air-conditioning uses a lot of engine power, so you will require an engine with enough power to drive it without affecting the performance of the vehicle. Another disadvantage is that it spoils your acclimatisation to the outside air temperature, and you can feel 'knocked out' if you have to leave the vehicle to do some work. You will also have condensation prob-

lems on spectacles, cameras, camera lenses and any other instrument when you exit the vehicle.

Adhesive polarising sheet is available for windows, which both keeps the internal vehicle temperature down and makes it difficult for people outside to see in.

Front air ventilators

Adjustable air ventilators at the front of the vehicle are very useful in dusty areas, as they greatly reduce the amount of dust sucked into the vehicle from the rear by increasing the pressure within it.

Electrical supply

Larger alternators can usually be ordered for new vehicles and are essential if you are to fit ancillaries that cause increased battery drain.

Seats

If seats are made for hard work they are not comfortable and vinyl covers make you sweat in hot countries. If they are made for comfort they break up and, if cotton covered, they fade and soon tear in direct sunlight.

Due to British tax laws, Land Rover 12-seater estates have

terrible passenger seats with no legroom. This can be improved by fitting fewer seats after purchase, so long as the VAT has not been reclaimed.

Most seats seem to be designed so that a tall driver has to bend down to see out of the windscreen. Various specialised sprung seats are available, which are good for dirt roads and for crossing fields, but for really bad surfaces, such as the huge corrugations of the Sahara, as opposed to the unsealed roads of Australia and South Africa, the going is so rough that these seats make little difference.

The best answer for long expeditions or bad roads seems to be to use the seats supplied with the vehicle and use a folded blanket between you and the seat back to cut down perspiration, and a foam cushion to sit on. Whatever you use, it should be easily washable – a high-pressure water hose is the only way to really clean all the sand, dust or mud out of a fully used four-wheel drive vehicle.

Seat belts

Most developed countries now insist on seat belts being fitted to vehicle front and rear seats, and some insist on them being worn on the public highway. For off-road driving there are extra problems. If the seat belt is correctly tight, most drivers will find it difficult, or impossible, to reach extra gear levers, such as the four-wheel drive and transfer box levers. If you have full-time four-wheel drive, this is less of a problem.

Some inertia-type seat belts tend to tighten up with each bounce when used off-road in rough terrain. In really rough terrain or over corrugations you will find a full competition harness more comfortable.

Safety air bags

Modern safety air bags can be used without problems on four-wheel drive vehicles off-road. So if your vehicle comes fitted with them, there is no need to worry about them inflating by mistake – they are a useful addition to safety.

Where air bags are fitted, the front of the vehicle will have been engineered for the correct crush-rate, compatible with the air bag triggering devices. Therefore any extra fittings at the front of the vehicle, for example winches or nudge bars, should have the vehicle manufacturer's approval so that these triggering devices will operate satisfactorily.

Seating and European law

Under British tax laws vehicles with 12 seats are VAT refundable, hence the minimal leg room in the Land Rover 12-seater estate. If you have claimed back the VAT, you cannot remove any of the seats, not even the extra centre seat in the front, or you will have to pay back the VAT. Customs & Excise generally apply this rule for six years from new, though this has never been tried out in court, so it could be enforced for longer if they wished.

Within the EU, but outside of the UK, vehicles with more than nine seats are required to be fitted with a tachograph. This is not really a problem in itself, apart from the cost and the room it takes up; but there are accompanying laws on driving hours and enforced rest periods, etc, with which you also have to comply as though you are driving a bus.

If you wish to take a 12-seater Land Rover across the Channel, the Department of Transport suggests that you take the rear seats out, but again they stress that this has never been tried out in court. If you have already claimed back the VAT, you should really remove these seats on the ferry or train, to remain within British law!

Windows

You rarely have a choice in this area. Up-market vehicles almost invariably have electric windows, in response to customers' choice. However, off-road they can be a disaster, especially if you have an accident or turn the vehicle over and cannot get the doors or windows open. Make sure that you have a pointed hammer, designed to break such windows, easily to hand at all times.

In dusty or sandy areas, electric windows regularly fail to operate – invariably sticking closed in a hot climate and open in a cold climate!

Tinted windows reduce vision.

Lights at the rear

For off-road use all lights should be as far as possible out of harm's way. However, manufacturers and importers have to comply with 'Construction and Use' Regulations. These include the maximum distance that lights can be situated from the extremity of the vehicle and the road surface, and state that rear lights must not be obscured by the back door or rear-mounted spare wheel when the back door or spare wheel carrier is open. This is why you will find vehicles with rear and/or fog lights housed within the bumper, which on some vehicles is a safer place to put them than below the bumper fittings.

You can buy additional lights and fit them in more sensible places, including the blanked-off apertures where they were originally meant to be on some vehicles, but they must be in addition to the legally situated units, and the latter must all be working when you return to the public highway.

Windscreen wipers

For use in sunny countries, windscreen wipers should not be chrome-plated, but matt black, to avoid dangerous reflections. Some vehicles that have been converted from left-hand to right-hand drive have not had the windscreen wipers converted, so the driver has poor vision.

Wing mirrors

Wing mirrors should also be matt black for the same reasons; they should also be capable of being folded back to avoid damage by trees and branches on narrow tracks.

Bumpers

Metal square-section bumpers or chassis are more suitable for the use of a high-lift jack off-road.

Several modern vehicles now have plastic bumpers, often part of a designed-in crumple zone to deal with a head-on collision. You cannot use a high-lift jack with these designs unless there are jacking points that such a jack can be adapted to fit.

Gimmicks

Many Japanese vehicles have unnecessary instruments such as altimeters and inclinometers – but they give you something to occupy your mind in traffic jams!

SUMMARY

- Part-time four-wheel drive is effective and cheaper, but requires more thought beforehand so as to engage it in time.

- Do not use locked-in four-wheel drive on firm surfaces.

- Freewheeling hubs save a little on fuel and front tyre wear and give smoother steering, on part-time four-wheel drive vehicles.

- Permanent four-wheel drive is more easily available when you require it, and, if the vehicle is fitted with constant velocity joints to the front wheels, allows higher speeds.

- Short-wheelbase vehicles have better off-road performance, but less load-carrying capacity and easily become unstable at speed.

- Long-wheelbase vehicles have less off-road performance, but more load-carrying capacity, comfort and stability.

- Petrol engines are cheaper, have better performance for their weight and are more easily repairable by Third World mechanics. However, they give electrical problems in water and dust and the fuel is a fire risk.

- Diesel engines are better in water and dust, have less fire risk and good low-down torque. They use less fuel and the fuel is usually cheaper than petrol.

- Catalytic converters are easily damaged off-road, but are often required by law.

- Manual transmission is superior to automatic transmission for off-road use, but where driver knowledge is minimal or the vehicle may be driven by several different drivers, automatic transmission may be preferable.

- Cross-axle differential locks have advantages in really difficult conditions, but driver knowledge is essential. Limited slip and automatic locking cross-axle differentials cause handling problems and are unwise on front differentials.

- Limited slip or viscous coupled centre differentials reduce the requirement for driver knowledge, and viscous coupling reduces snatch loads.

- Electronic Traction Control gives the same result as cross-axle locks, without any requirement of driver knowledge, no extra stress on components and no problems with 'fish-tailing'.

- Independent suspension gives better handling on-road, but reduces ground clearance in many situations off-road, where non-independent suspension is preferable.

- Shock absorbers must be in good condition.

- Long-travel coil springs give better axle articulation.

- Power steering is useful on larger vehicles, but many systems lack 'feel'.

- Servo brakes are essential on long-wheelbase vehicles.

- Anti-lock braking is a considerable advantage. If you do not have it, learn to 'cadence' brake.

- Transmission handbrakes are better off-road than those connected to rear drum brakes.

- Fitting large wheels and tyres causes increased stress to other vehicle components, which may require upgrading. If you fit large wheels and tyres, drive slowly.

- Steel wheels are cheaper to replace and can be temporarily knocked back into shape in an emergency or in the Third World, where spares may not be available.

- There are hundreds of tyres available and most of them are good. Where possible use the correct type for the terrain to be crossed. All-terrain tyres are fine until you encounter the extremes of sand and mud.

- Only use low pressures when absolutely necessary, and where possible use tyres with inner tubes for serious off-road use. Never use aggressive tread tyres on sand.

- Radial tyres have proved their superiority in most situations, and their 'Achilles heel' of side wall damage is fast being improved.

- Prices are high, so many enthusiasts favour the good old-fashioned Firestone SAT tyres for off-road use.

- Remoulded tyres can be physically different in size.

- High-performance vehicles require tyres with the correct speed rating.

- Check the ergonomics of the vehicle for your own body by a test drive.
- Air-conditioning has advantages in dusty, hot, humid or polluted conditions, but is a disadvantage if you have to get out of the vehicle often. It also uses a lot of fuel and saps engine power.
- Air ventilators at the front of the vehicle reduce the amount of dust sucked into it at the rear.
- Choose the windows, rear doors and seating arrangements that suit you best.

Aftermarket accessories

TRAILERS AND TOWING

Tow rings and hooks

Properly fitted, strong towing rings or hooks, front and rear, will make it easier for you to help, or be helped by, another vehicle or winch and avoid vehicle damage caused by attaching tow ropes, etc, to parts not designed for such stress. These rings or hooks must be strongly attached, preferably to the chassis.

Some vehicles have fittings under the chassis that are designed for lashing the vehicles down on transporters or ferries. These are not strong enough for towing out

Do not use lashing down eyes for towing – replace them with 'JATE' rings, as shown here.

a stuck vehicle, but they can be replaced with stronger 'JATE' rings and then used as a pair linked by a bridle.

A correct tow ring properly fitted on a Land Rover 90/110 Defender – part of the plastic radiator grill has to be cut.

Tow bars, tow balls and tow hitches

If your vehicle does not have a separate chassis, make sure that any tow bar system you fit is strong enough. If you have a towing system fitted to a chassis, unless the trailer is specifically designed for off-road use you will have to fit a towing plate to lower the ball or hitch to the correct ground clearance for the trailer or caravan concerned. Some are adjustable for height.

A second towing ball, hitch or pin on the front bumper can greatly facilitate the positioning of your trailer or caravan into an awkward

A towing ball lowered to the correct trailer height. This lowers ground clearance considerably off-road, where the towing hitch can dig in like an anchor.

A combined tow ball/pin jaw mounted on the passenger side of the front bumper for easier trailer manoeuvring.

A military NATO-type pintle.

Do not use towing balls that are an extension of the pin – they can pull out.

parking spot. It should be placed off-centre, to the passenger side, so that the driver can see clearly past the trailer. In some countries this will be illegal on the public highway.

The standard 2-inch (50 mm) ball hitch has a 7,700 lbs (3,500 kg) limit. The combined ball hitch/pin jaw has the same limit on the ball and 11,000 lbs (5,000 kg) on the pin. For serious off-road towing a towing ball is not secure enough, and you should use a heavy duty NATO pintle or a pin.

Do not use tow balls off-road that are an extension of the removable pin – the securing coil can break and the pin pull out when the trailer pitches.

There are some designs of tow ball/hitch that can be removed easily when not required, thus retaining the vehicle's original departure angle. Not all of these are particularly strong, so choose with care and check with the vehicle manufacturer.

Tow ropes, straps and strops

Tow ropes should have a quoted breaking strain approximately

To protect a tree wind the webbing strap a full turn around the trunk.

Ropes are easier to feed through pulleys, eyes, hooks or shackles, easier to knot, can be spliced or knotted if broken, are more pliable to handle and have more stretch and therefore absorb more shock than straps.

Strops are straps with stitched loops at each end, for connecting with shackles. Ropes are best used with spliced ends on .75-inch (190 mm) shackles. Knots are usually impossible to undo after towing.

Special nylon Kinetic Energy Recovery Ropes (KERR) are available for 'snatch' recovery. Instead of having the usual three strands of rope laid in the same direction, hawser laid to the right, cable laid to the left, KERR ropes have eight strands, four laid to the left and four laid to the right. With a breaking strain of 11.8 tons (12 tonnes), they are suitable for most recreational vehicles. They can stretch by 40 per cent, storing up a considerable mount of kinetic energy, which is then applied to the stuck vehicle, in addition to the pull of the towing vehicle. They are normally around 7 yards (8 m) long.

However, being nylon, KERR ropes have a finite life, shortened by the strain to which they are subjected, abrasion, sand and grit amongst the fibres, and ultraviolet light in direct sunlight. Therefore wash out any grit or sand, thoroughly dry the rope and store it in a close-weave breathable bag.

Ropes with some stretch are

equal to the laden weight of your vehicle. They are best made of nylon, polypropylene or terylene, as these materials do not rot when damp. However, they will lose strength if exposed to direct sunlight (ultraviolet light). Manila ropes absorb water, swelling up and shrinking when wet and stretching again as they dry.

Webbing straps do not damage live trees, roll up neatly for storage, are easier to clean and dry more quickly when wet. They have little stretch so can be safely joined with shackles. When used on trees they should be wrapped at least one full turn around the trunk close to the ground, unless they have to be higher so that the rope or cable clears a hump. Webbing straps

should have sewn loops, but you can convert straps using overhand knots to make end loops, and the tape knot to join ends together.

Tying a webbing knot.

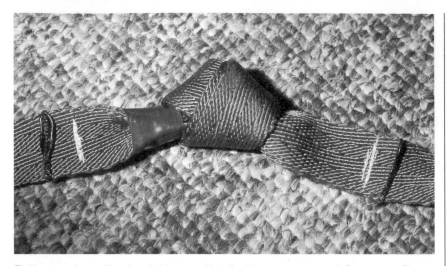

Finish a tape knot either by stitching or with adhesive tape to prevent it from coming loose.

How to tie a double sheet bend knot.

The double sheet bend knot pulled tight.

preferable for towing to absorb shock loads. For on-road use 15 feet (4.5 m) should be the maximum distance between vehicles, so this is the optimum length; but off-road, where angles can be difficult and you may have to right an overturned vehicle, four times this length is useful.

Off-road in difficult terrain, have a suitable tow rope already attached to your vehicle and either wrapped around the front bumper or nudge bar if on the front, or tucked through a window into the vehicle, or coiled and stowed up on the roof rack if on the rear.

However, do not leave ropes permanently like this, as they will pick up mud and grit and be damaged by direct sunlight. Long lengths of rope are best stored coiled, ready for instant use, in an open-top plastic barrel of appropriate diameter, cut down to the height taken up by the coiled rope. Keep ropes away from petrol, diesel and battery acid, and remember that tolypropylene ropes float on water. Wash and dry all ropes before storage.

Where tow ropes are to be joined together, never use a shackle or a rope with metal-lined eyes. If either rope breaks, the shackle or eye will become a lethal high-speed projectile, aimed directly at either vehicle and its occupants. Shackles and metal-lined eyes are fine where they can be securely fixed to either vehicle. Link ropes together through their eyes or knot with a double sheet bend.

For heavy recovery, do not use the lifting shackle fitted to air portable vehicles.

Shackles

Shackles for towing or recovery, except for connecting to high-lift jacks, should be .75 inch (19 mm), and bow shackles are more versatile than 'D' shackles. For short sections, shackle pins should be screwed fully home, then unscrewed half a turn to prevent them seizing in use. For longer

A tow strap already fitted and wrapped around the bumper for quick availability.

towing and on-road, shackle pins should be screwed fully home to stop them vibrating undone.

Snatch blocks

'Snatch block' is a nautical term for a pulley block that can be opened so that a rope or cable can be inserted from the side instead of threading it through the end.

As shown in Chapter 4, using a snatch block doubles the mechanical advantage and halves the line speed when towing or winching. Also more than one snatch block can be used at the same time to improve things proportionally. They are also invaluable to alter the line of pull where the towing vehicle or winch cannot obtain a clear one.

Choker chains

Chains are inextensible and are not cut through by sharp attachments so they have many uses. Choker chains have a semi-closed hook that can be clipped over the chain's own links for easy attachment and shortening. They are ideal for use as bridles, or when using a high-lift jack for winching.

'A' frames

For towing a vehicle over long distances a rigid 'A' frame, which has two anchorage points for the front of the towed vehicle and an eye for the towing vehicle, gives the towing vehicle more control, safer braking and can do the braking for the towed vehicle.

EXTRA TANKS

Extra fuel tanks

If there is room for extra fuel tanks to be fitted under the vehicle chassis and you can afford their high cost, this is the best way to carry extra fuel, but most people have to resort to using jerry cans, either on the sides or roof rack, or in the vehicle. Fuel should not be carried

Snatch blocks.

in jerry cans on the front of the vehicle – it is a fire risk in an accident.

Side- and front-mounted jerry cans are fine for Third World use, but are illegal in much of the first world. As with bull bars they have been happily ignored until recently, but the bureaucrats in Brussels have gleefully spotted another idiosyncrasy that they can jump on; so EU directives are being dis-

cussed and insurance companies can use these as yet another let-out for non-payment after an accident. If therefore you are travelling out through Europe to your overland or expedition destination, do not fit any of these to the vehicle until you clear any restrictions; you should also clear their fitting with your insurance company.

Jerry cans are the cheapest way to carry extra fuel and have the

Only carry water on the front, never fuel. Spare main leaves can also be carried here.

added advantage that they can be unloaded from the vehicle, as an aid to recovery, if it is stuck.

German-style jerry cans have a good narrow-neck pouring-spout, whereas the American style has a wide, circular spout that is difficult to use. Spare rubber seals for the spouts should be carried.

If you carry petrol in jerry cans in a hot country, always earth the can and the vehicle before touching the open jerry can to the fuel tank filler, otherwise static electricity can cause a fire.

Extra fuel tanks are sometimes built into the rear of vehicles, or under the rear seats; these are fine for diesel fuel, but not for petrol. Additional fuel tanks should have internal baffles to minimise fuel movement and avoid fuel pouring out of the vents on steep inclines.

If you have jerry cans on a roof rack, put a thin sheet of marine plywood between the roof rack and the cans; their welded seams can stand proud, and if they come into direct contact with the metal roof rack they will split with the vibration. Also allow room for the cans to expand in the heat of the day.

It is surprising how many people still carry jerry cans upright on the roof, untie them, then lift the heavy cans down to fill the tank. I always put the fuel cans on their backs at the rear of the roof rack and tie them down permanently with the filling spout pointing towards the rear of the vehicle. I can then fill the cans in situ from fuel station pumps. When I need to fill the vehicle's tank, I park the vehicle facing slightly downhill so that the fuel does not pour out of the can when opened, then fill the tank by plastic siphon tube. Each can is not completely full, but you save a lot of work, strained muscles and bent jerry cans.

If you use a clean, transparent siphon tube, you will not get any fuel in your mouth, and if you put your finger over the bottom of the tube as each can empties, you can move the top of the tube into the next can and allow the siphon to continue.

Never fill fuel tanks completely. If the vehicle warms up in the sun the fuel will expand and escape through the breather pipe, possibly causing a fire. The same thing can happen if the vehicle is parked on a camber, with the fuel tank filler spout facing downhill. Overfull fuel cans can spray out fuel when opened.

Keep vehicles and fuel cans well away from camp fires. Remember that empty fuel cans contain explosive mixtures and are therefore more dangerous than full ones.

Water cans

Military surplus polypropylene jerry cans are available for carrying drinking water. These are impervious to sunlight, so they avoid the growth of algae that takes place in water in normal plastic cans that sunlight can penetrate. If you do not have a winch fitted, a couple of water cans can be carried on the front bumper without overloading the front springs.

I like to keep a second plastic filling hose, of a different colour and the correct size to fit most water taps, and use this to fill my water cans. This hose must be kept clean and never be used for fuel.

Nalgene bottles

If you require small plastic bottles to carry liquids, detergents, medicines, etc, without leaking, the American-made Nalgene series, available from quality camping and trekking suppliers, are the best.

ELECTRICAL EQUIPMENT

Increased electrical power

Off-road vehicles, particularly those going well off into the wild, invariably have ancillaries that increase the drain on the battery, from extra lighting, refrigerators and tyre compressors to the massive drain of an electric winch. Despite their intended use, most modern vehicles leave the factory with smaller batteries than are sensible.

German-style jerry cans in a lockable frame – illegal in Europe.

When travelling slowly over difficult terrain, the alternator output may not be able to keep up with the battery drain, unless you switch off ancillaries. For off-road, especially recreational and expedition use, a larger alternator and larger battery are almost essential, together with a split charge system and a second, separate battery for the ancillaries that is not damaged if regularly run flat.

Where space is at a premium, there are special batteries that are in fact two batteries in one unit. One of these is a deep cycle unit, which can be allowed to run flat powering ancillaries without being connected to the side of the battery used for starting the engine. Deep cycle batteries, manufactured for marine use, are ideal units for separate second batteries. Some of them have additional fittings that allow extra cables, such as winch cables, to be attached without overloading the conventional clamps. There are also batteries where the acid is contained in microporous glass beads, that almost completely eliminate acid spillage.

Any main battery that starts giving trouble should be replaced before you venture off-road. Sealed batteries are useful in hot countries, as water loss by evaporation shortens battery life.

Jump leads

Always carry a pair of heavy-duty jump leads, at least 3 yards (3 metres) long. If you use them to start another vehicle, make sure that the vehicles are not touching each other. Jump leads are essential for starting vehicles fitted with automatic transmission and/or catalytic converters, in the case of a flat battery.

Refrigerators

Battery-operated refrigerators work for short trips of no more than two days. Beyond that length of time I have never known one work well enough for food in a really hot climate, but it will help keep film and beer cool. Battery drain is high, so a second, separate battery is essential. The less efficient heat transfer-type units can also be run on gas when the vehicle is at a standstill.

Solid-state units are useful in four-wheel drives, for there are no moving parts (other than a fan) to be affected by awkward vehicle angles and bumpy roads. The Koolatron series work well, and their efficiency is greatly improved by using freezer packs; they may also be reversed to keep things hot. Engel refrigerators are more efficient, but considerably more expensive with more to go wrong. Both types have mains voltage adaptors so that you can take them into a hotel, or use a generator, at night.

Battery-operated refrigerators never work well enough to keep frozen food frozen – remember that frozen food that has thawed must not be re-frozen.

Internal fans

Internal fans can be fitted for cooling if you do not have air-conditioning, but if they are used without the engine running they should not be run from the main battery.

Air horns

Air horns are essential in third world countries, but remember that older pedestrians may be completely deaf anyway.

LIGHTS

Front lighting

Most vehicles are supplied with sealed beam headlights. On paved roads the failure of one of these is at worst illegal, and spares are readily available. Off-road your life may depend on them and spares are large, fragile and difficult to carry.

Quartz halogen headlights are a legal requirement in some countries, so bulb replacement units are usually available, though rather more expensive. They give greater light output and the small bulbs are easier to carry as spares. The main disadvantage is the high cost of the reflectors (three times the price of a complete sealed unit, without the bulb). Mine tend to rust, presumably due to wading and the fact that they are not fully sealed.

Extra spotlights are useful at night off-road, but you will require protective covers against thrown-up stones when they are not in use.

Rear lighting and fluorescent lighting

Reversing off-road at night can be tricky, and is the quickest way to get stuck. A good rear-mounted spotlight, mounted safely out of the way near to or on top of the roof, can make life a lot easier, and

A rear spotlight mounted safely out of harm's way.

Lights strung on ropes between vehicles illuminate the mess area of this comfortable camp near Bilma, Niger.

is useful for pitching camp after dark. The switch should have a light-up indicator – it is illegal to have this light illuminated while moving forward on a public highway.

In addition, it is always worth carrying a couple of 12-volt fluorescent striplights on extension cables. These lights make little demand on the battery and are useful as camp lights, reading lights or for working on the vehicle. Gas and storm lanterns save on batteries, but break easily and are not safe inside the vehicle.

A rope stretched between the roof racks of two vehicles, or one vehicle and a tree, is useful for setting up these striplights over a working, eating or cooking area. They can also be hung on the side of a roof rack.

VEHICLE BODY AND PROTECTION

Fly screens

In hot countries, on forward-facing vents, fly screens are essential, not so much against flies as against the swarms of bees, wasps and hornets through which one often has to drive. They can also be useful against mosquitos if you sleep in the vehicle.

Bug deflectors

Horizontal strips of plastic or sheet metal fitted transversely across the front of the bonnet can deflect the airflow enough to stop your windscreen being splattered with dead flying insects, but will not divert heavier items such as mud and gravel.

Radiator screens

In many countries there are times of year when insects swarm and plant seeds fly around in the wind. At these times, and any time that you travel across grassland and scrub, your engine is likely to overheat due to a clogged radiator matrix, which is difficult to clean out. A fine mesh screen across the front of the radiator, which is easy to remove for thorough cleaning, is useful in these situations.

Window guards

In hot Third World countries a heavy wire mesh, securely fitted to windows that open, will allow the vehicle to be parked or slept in

safely with the windows open, so that it does not get too hot inside.

Laminated windscreens

Laminated glass windscreens crack when stones hit them, instead of completely shattering as toughened glass windscreens do. So for off-road use, where stones hit windscreens regularly, a laminated windscreen is an advantage. Cracked windscreens are now illegal on public highways in many countries.

Sun visors

Sun visors are useful for vertically challenged drivers, but taller persons such as myself already have to stoop to obtain clear vision through most windscreens, and sun visors make the problem worse.

Rear windscreen wipers and washers

Four-wheel drive vehicles tend to spend much of their time on muddy roads, and their body shape tends to plaster the rear windows with mud very quickly. A rear windscreen wiper and washer kit is therefore very useful.

Light guards

Light guards are almost essential off-road. Most designs on the market are either made of weak wire or more strongly with bars, but then fitted with silly self-tapping screws. You will require a design that is strong, securely fitted and has easy access to the glass to clean off the mud. Some designs hinge forward to allow the glass to be cleaned, but the hinges are usually weak and the holding screws rust in. I prefer a design with enough room between the guard and the lamp glass for my large hands to get into with a rag.

Having had my headlights smashed by attacking bandits in Iran, I consider strong headlight guards essential in the Third

A strong light guard with a sensible gap between it and the lamp glass.

Roll cages

An overturned vehicle is always a possibility in difficult off-road conditions, so a roll cage is very useful on a soft-top as well as on a hard-top vehicle, if you can afford it. Beware of designs that are purely cosmetic, with little real strength – get one that is manufactured to competition standards.

Wing protection steps

Wing protection steps are useful for climbing over the wings to the roof rack, but the use of those on sale made of polished aluminium would be madness in a sunny country, where they can reflect the sun into your eyes and blind you while driving – paint them matt black.

Bull bars, nudge or brush bars

These originated where bush contact with kangaroos or bulls was common, and the vehicles to which they were fitted were built more substantially than those of today. Nowadays they are mostly sold for 'posers', though there are more substantially built items

World, and there must be a large enough space between the guard and the glass to allow for their being struck with a club or large stone without the guard deforming enough to break the glass.

Front headlight wipers

Front headlight wipers tend to drop off in off-road use, especially when wading. They are best removed when off-road and replaced when on-road.

Tree branch deflector cables

Thin cables stretched between the front of the roof or roof rack and the front of the wing or nudge bar on each side of the vehicle will help to deflect branches clear of the windscreen.

Deflector cables to ward off tree branches.

A Land Rover fitted with a roll cage.

Polished aluminium wing protection steps should be painted matt black to avoid blinding reflections from the sun.

A vehicle fitted with an integral winch bumper and nudge bar.

available, well designed to absorb impact and to include fittings for winches and light protectors. They are certainly useful as nudge bars in bush or forest country, but in a more severe impact they are another item to straighten out.

On vehicles that have a separate chassis, these bars should have a strong mounting to that chassis. Unfortunately, in a medium impact this may cause unnecessary and expensive damage to that chassis, which would normally have only occurred in a severe impact. On vehicles without a separate chassis, there would be little difference.

Some of the most up-to-date four-wheel drive vehicles have designed-in crumple zones and safety air bag triggers to minimise passenger injury in head-on collisions. Nudge bars can negate their effectiveness, so check with the vehicle manufacturer.

EU bureaucrats have their eyes firmly set on adding nudge bars to their never-ending list of directives and regulations. Like most such regulations they are unlikely to be retrospective, but some insurance companies are already becoming difficult over payments after an accident. If you have a bull bar fitted, make sure that you clear it with your insurance company or, if necessary, change your insurance company to allow for it. Even the UK Department of Transport is against nudge bars. It seems that the Transport Research Laboratory has shown that pedestrian injuries are likely to be more severe if struck by a vehicle fitted with a nudge bar. One wonders how much difference this would really make – the front end of any vehicle is a hard object to be struck by! However, with possible new regulations in mind, manufacturers are now offering nudge bars constructed from deformable materials.

Number plates

Make sure that these do not project below the bumper where

The wrong place for a number plate.

Wheel steps are too close to the vehicle for sensible work.

rough terrain or a high-lift jack will damage them. It is also best if they do not project above the bumper, or you will break them if you stand on it. If you fit nudge bars or any other extras, the number plates must remain clearly visible and you must wash the mud off before you return to the Public Highway.

Wheel steps

Steps that fit over the wheels have recently appeared on the market. They could be useful if you are one of the few that washes the roof manually, but they are not that clever an idea for working on the engine because they are too close to the vehicle to be comfortable. I put the spare wheel on the ground to stand on and adjust its position for comfort and convenience. You can also move the spare wheel to the front of the vehicle, but cannot do this with a wheel step.

Protection plates

These are heavy metal shields attached to the underside of the vehicle to protect those parts that are vulnerable to impact damage, usually the engine sump and fuel tank. In general you will only need these plates if you spend your time bouncing over tree stumps and rocks. Universal joint guards are not very effective and tend to clog up with grass in scrub country. Some vehicles require protection for their steering rods and links, or the fitting of stronger units.

Side steps, side runners and running boards

Side steps, runners and running boards are useful to help the vertically challenged and ladies in fashion dresses gain entry and access to high-ground-clearance vehicles, and some designs protect the body sills against being chipped by thrown-up stones. However, most of them lower the vehicle's ground clearance and make it difficult to dig out sand or mud when the

Protection plates on a Range Rover.

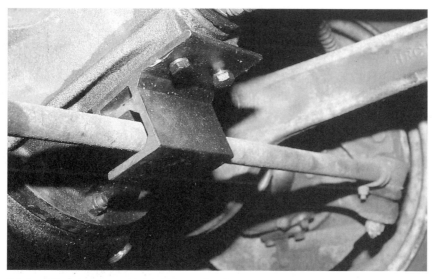

This Land Rover accessory track rod protection does not cover enough.

Land Rover accessory front steering protection.

vehicle is bogged down, or to get sand ladders into position under the rear wheels.

One manufacturer has argued with me (correctly) that the lowest point under a four-wheel drive vehicle is usually the differentials. My answer is that if the differentials are grounded, the side steps/running boards make it more difficult to get a shovel under the vehicle to clear them and that off-road the terrain is rarely level. So when the vehicle is lower on one side, it is the side steps/running boards on that side that are the first to ground.

Some manufacturers have produced side bars intentionally strong enough for high-lift jack use, for vehicles where this would not normally be possible; they are normally set high enough to make no difference to the ground clearance. Warn produce running boards secured by spring clips that can be removed without tools for off-roading. Folding side and rear steps should be folded up any time that the vehicle is moving.

JACKS AND THEIR USES

The pillar or scissor jacks supplied as standard with most modern vehicles are not normally up to tough use, and are often not strong enough to lift a fully loaded four-wheel drive vehicle at the rear. You will almost certainly require a good bottle or hydraulic jack with enough lifting power to lift your vehicle fully loaded.

Scissor jacks tend to seize up in sandy conditions, and many hydraulic jacks will not operate on their sides, so also have a screw jack or high-lift jack. Off-road you often need two jacks in a difficult situation, and to repair a spring a jack on its side is often required to locate the axle. Transmission brakes can cause trouble when jacking because wheels at opposite ends of the vehicle can contra-rotate through

This side bar fitted for use with a high-lift jack will also protect the sill.

and potentially damaging.

For really soft ground it helps if your jack support plate can be fitted inside the rim of your spare wheel, spreading the load over a wide area. For long expeditions, where it is often necessary to work under the vehicle on soft ground, I use axle stands that fit into spare wheel rims.

In short, if your vehicle has a sensible chassis and bumpers, you will save yourself a lot of grovelling, time and energy with a high-lift jack. This plus your hydraulic jack will get you out of most awkward situations. For off-road travel, never leave home without one!

the differential if the wheels are not chocked.

Hydraulic jacks may be too tall, even at their lowest point of travel, to site under the vehicle axle if you have a completely flat tyre. There are two ways round this. You can either use low-range first gear to drive the wheel with the flat up on to a rock so that you can get your hydraulic jack in position, or start with the original manufacturer's jack to get the vehicle high enough to use the hydraulic jack. If the vehicle is heavily loaded, you may have to unload it first. A high-lift jack solves this problem.

On soft ground you either need a 1 foot square (305 mm sq) thick piece of plywood or hardwood, or a similar piece of thick metal, as a support pad for each jack to give it a sensible base area. With a light vehicle you can use the blade of your shovel, but it will slide around in mud. I have met drivers who have drilled a hole in a shovel and put a long bolt through it, under the jack, for positional stability, but this is not very successful in soft mud or sand.

At least one book on how to cross the Sahara, recommended by a leading motoring organisation, shows pictures of jacking the wheel rim and hub driving member directly, to get sand ladders under the wheel; this is both dangerous

A high-lift jack on a jack pad.

High-lift jacks

The high-lift jack was originally made for farm use in the 1930s, where it got its original name of sheepherder's jack. It is used at many times the extension of a normal jack, so it and its load are unstable and more likely to slip. This can sometimes be used to advantage, but in general you should be extra careful.

As with any jack on soft ground, you need a strong jack pad to increase the ground area and give a firm base, but as a high-lift jack is more likely to slip, locating dowels or strips should be added to the jack pad to stop any slipping at the base. In mud the area of your jack pad can be increased as already described, by placing it on the spare wheel, perforated plate or sand ladders.

A couple of shackles, the largest possible to fit the holes in the jack's rack, can be used to attach ropes or chains from the jack to trees or ground anchors to enable the jack to be used for winching or lifting. One can also be placed temporarily below the jack mechanism to avoid it slipping if someone tampers with it. The reversing latch should never be dropped with the handle in the down position – the leverage can work back to front, so the handle can fly up and continue ratcheting, injuring the operator.

For vehicles without flat, strong bumpers, and late-model Land Rover vehicles, an adaptor can be made or bought to fit into the jack locating sockets. For Japanese 'U'-shape bumpers, for example Toyota Landcruisers, you can buy a hook accessory to fit. In wet or muddy conditions a piece of wood or thick cloth between the toe of

Warning: When using high-lift jacks, always walk the lifting mechanism up the rack taking the handle fully past the audible 'clicks' at each end of the arc of travel.

Shackles that fit the holes in the rack of a high-lift jack.

A bumper suitable for use with a high-lift jack – the number plate has been cropped so that it will not be damaged from below (but this may soon become illegal).

An adaptor that enables a high-lift jack to be used on late-model Land Rover jacking sockets.

A high-lift jack being used as a winch.

the jack and the bumper or chassis can help to stop it slipping.

Soft mud has a suction effect that may be so bad that the rack of one high-lift jack alone can bend. If there are two available, use them in unison.

There are innumerable other uses for high-lift jacks, including spreading and clamping for bodywork repair, building construction and fencing work (though you will have to make a stronger top clamp than most jacks are supplied with), winching, and lifting trailers to fit to the vehicle's tow hitch.

When used as a winch, the jack can only manage a few feet at a time. Ropes stretch, so chains are best used to connect the jack to the vehicle and its anchor (use a webbing strap to protect a tree being used as an anchor). A second chain or rope from the anchorage to the vehicle may be necessary to hold the load while resetting the jack between runs. In the same way you can pull aside fallen trees if the vehicle is suitably chocked.

For a vehicle immobilised by spinning wheels, or 'high centred', the vehicle can be lifted until 'packing', for example sand ladders, brushwood, logs or stones, can be placed under the spinning wheels.

You can break the bead on a tyre by placing the base of the jack on the tyre adjacent to the wheel rim and jacking it down using the weight of the vehicle. Use the front of the vehicle if it is not loaded at the rear.

Shunting a vehicle to one side

Vehicles trapped in ruts or with one wheel over an edge can be shunted sideways with a high-lift jack. This is a common procedure, and you can minimise the chance of the toe of the jack slipping by fitting a metal plate with vertical 'U'-shaped grooves in it behind the rear tow hitch, and a similar plate or two pieces of angle iron to locate the jack positively below the centre of the front bumper. Put the vehicle into gear in low range with the handbrake on, and if available have two people, one at either side, to steady the vehicle as you jack it up.

Place the jack vertically to the centre of the front bumper and jack it up as high as is sensible off the ground, then hold the top of the jack's rack with one hand and the outstretched handle with the other and push the vehicle over in the desired direction, ensuring that the helper on that side stands well clear. As the vehicle falls, release the hand on the rack and use the handle to pull the jack clear of the vehicle. Repeat the procedure at the rear of the vehicle. You may have to repeat the whole procedure several times, to reach safe ground.

High-lift jacks come in two sizes, 4 feet (1.2 m) and 5 feet (1.5 m). The latter is necessary

A bumper designed for an integral winch that also contains sockets and fittings to stop a high-lift jack from slipping.

Jack the vehicle as high as possible while helpers steady it at either side.

As the vehicle falls release the hand on the rack and pull the jack clear using the handle.

A 4-foot high-lift jack easily stored mounted on the rear of a Land Rover.

for high vehicles such as Unimogs, is useful for winching, recovery from deep ditches and will shunt a vehicle over further. The 4-foot model is, however, sufficient for most uses, and is a more convenient length to mount

The 'Stabilizer Jack'.

on, or carry in, a vehicle.

A recent addition to the high-lift jack range is the 'Stabilizer Jack' by Jackall, an adjustable accessory that will remain in position holding the load with the main high-lift jack removed. Off-road its use is limited, unless you can place it on a perforated plate. The design of its base is such that it is meant to be used on solid ground for working under the vehicle, but you would be safer with axle stands under the axle.

New high-lift jacks will be more efficient if you scrape off the paint and file down any burrs on the rack. After use in mud or sand the jack should be thoroughly washed down and lightly oiled.

There will come a time when the holes in the rack become burred. The burrs can usually be filed down, but the rack can also be reversed.

To summarise, off-road you will need a good jack, preferably two, and a strong jack pad to give a firm base over a larger area. A high-lift jack is the off-roader's best friend, but it can be dangerous if not used carefully.

Air jacks/bull bags

Various companies produce air bags for use as jacks. They are blown up by the vehicle's exhaust gases (if you have a twin exhaust, one side of it must be blocked off), and some are good enough to pass military specifications. Be careful where you place the bag, not just because of hot exhaust pipes and sharp projections, but because exhaust pipes and many other components under the vehicle are not designed to carry its weight. A heavy blanket can be put between the air bag and the vehicle to protect the bag. Vehicles wobble about on air bags and may slip off, but you can change a wheel with care.

Air bags are particularly useful for caravans and trailers, and in mud, sand or on high-centred vehicles. Each side of the vehicle can be lifted in turn and sand

An air jack in use.

ladders, stones, brushwood, etc, placed under the wheels to increase the ground clearance. When used in mud, deflating and replacing the unit afterwards can be messy! Always have a high-lift jack as a back-up. Air jacks puncture easily on thorns or sharp stones and the valves can leak due to ingress of sand, grit and mud.

RACKS AND INTERNAL CARGO

Roof racks

For expeditions you may require a roof rack; even for normal camping a roof rack is useful for carrying light, bulky items. Roof racks must be strongly built and strongly fitted otherwise, off-road, especially on corrugations, everything will break up. Weight for weight, tubular section is stronger than box section, and it should be heavily galvanised.

Several companies advertise Safari preparation including roof racks extending beyond the front of the roof over the windscreen. The designer and manufacturer of such an item can never have driven a loaded four-wheel vehicle on a corrugated track, let alone off the track! Even an ordinary roof rack, properly loaded with most of the weight to the rear, will, in such conditions, cause breaks to the bulkhead or a non-reinforced windscreen frame. To put jerry cans of water or petrol over, or even beyond, the windscreen, as some designs do, is absolute lunacy!

Even worse are designs that extend the roof rack to the front bumper. In the Sahara and the Middle East I have seen vehicles fitted with such roof racks, causing broken front springs and bent front axles on corrugated roads. Such extended roof racks also mean that when you are going downhill you cannot see forward properly, as the roof rack obstructs your vision. Roof racks of this type should only be for very lightweight awkward loads, or used as a filming platform.

Full-length roof racks can be safely fitted, but remember that the weight of such a roof rack is usually on the manufacturer's limit for roof weight. Good roof rack designs will have supports positioned in line with the main body supports of the vehicle, for example the posts between the doors. There should be fittings along the back of the vehicle to stop the roof rack juddering forward on corrugated roads and making holes in the roof.

Land Rover 90/110s and Defenders have aluminium roof channels. Roof racks fitted to these vehicles should have additional supports to the top of the bulkhead at the front and to the top of the lower rear body at the back.

A roof rack can be fitted to soft-top vehicles, or heavier loads be supported by using a roll cage to support it. You must remember that any extra weight on the roof will raise the vehicle's centre of gravity, so it will turn over more easily.

If you intend to sleep on the roof rack, and many do to avoid snakes and scorpions, it is worth putting wooden slats or thin marine plywood along it to lie on. Do not fix it with self-tapping screws – they lead to rust and fall out. Instead drill holes in the wood and tie it down. Leave a gap on either side and cut holes at strategic points in the centre so that you can get to the rack to lash things down. Some manufacturers make fold-up tents for fitting to roof racks.

If a roof rack is fixed to the roof of a Land Rover, Landcruiser or Unimog, it should not be further fixed to the chassis, for the bodies are designed to flex on the chassis. A strong waterproof cover is required in wet areas and is useful

Additional roof rack supports to the top of a Land Rover bulkhead . . .

. . . and to the top of the rear lower body. Note also the roof rack access ladder.

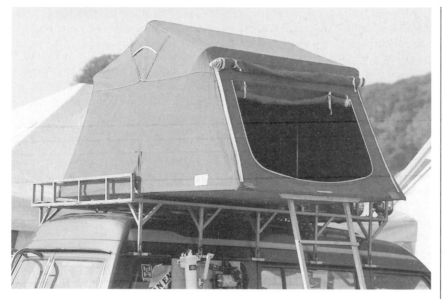

A folding tent fitted to a roof rack.

Other racks

Various 'racks' are available for specialised uses: spare wheel shuttles, for carrying bicycles or canoes, even nudge bars that hinge down and on which farmers can carry bales of straw, etc, off-road.

Ratchet tie-downs

Ratchet tie-downs of nylon or terylene webbing are ideal for securing items firmly on to trailers, roof racks or within vehicles. Be careful not to over-tighten them or you may break the item you are securing, or the base to which you are securing it.

Barriers, nets, boxes and bags for internal cargo

Off-road, cargo stored in the rear

to keep out dust in dusty areas. If you have a full-length covered roof rack you will not need a double-skinned safari roof for hot countries. Modern Land Rovers do not have double-skin roofs, so a loaded roof rack, or one with a plywood cover, is useful to keep the vehicle cooler inside.

Nylon or terylene rope is best for tying down baggage. Hemp rots quickly and also holds dust and grit, which tears your hands in use. Rubber tie-downs, as sold in Europe, soon break down in strong sunlight; a more practical method is to cut old inner tubes longitudinally into 2-inch wide strips and make your own hooks from wire tent pegs for the ends. These straps will stand up to constant harsh sunlight, without breaking.

Sand ladders can be hooked along the side of the roof rack out of the way, yet become quickly available when you get stuck.

A fixed ladder to the roof rack from beside the back door will minimise body damage when climbing on to the roof rack.

To summarise, roof racks should be sensibly designed and fitted. Ideally they should not be used for heavy loads, but we are all guilty of this. Wood on the rack makes a good sleeping platform and helps

to keep the vehicle cool in hot countries.

A specialist rack for carrying a spare tyre.

of hard top vehicles, but not tied down, can move dangerously into the passenger area, as can dogs or farm animals if carried. Even items as small as drink cans or audio cassettes could cause a disaster if they get under foot pedals.

Metal cargo barriers or heavy cord nets can be fitted to keep larger items separate. However, metal boxes are noisy and produce messy metal dust or filings, so loose items are best stored in plastic crates or soft bags.

Tie-down rings, hooks and cleats

Very few non-military vehicles are supplied with tie-down rings for lashing baggage down to stop it moving about dangerously in the back of your vehicle. Those that are sold as aftermarket accessories often have weak fittings, so you may have to make up your own backing plates. If you fit any to the floor, the recessed type that lay down flush with the floor when not in use are preferable. For side or bulkhead fitting you can save money by using exhaust pipe 'U' bolts with home-made backing plates.

Centre console cubby boxes

Useful centre console cubby boxes between the front driver and passenger seats can double up as armrests for those of the right body height. If these are fitted to a 12-seat vehicle in the UK you could have to pay back the VAT if it has been reclaimed.

WHEELS AND TYRES

Spare wheel

Where the spare wheel should be carried is a perennial problem for four-wheel drive vehicles. Inside the vehicle they take up a lot of room and, when flat and covered in mud, can be objectionable.

Many vehicles carry them on the back door, but they reduce rear vision and off-road they damage the door hinges. I am tall enough to prefer them on the front bonnet, but shorter drivers find this restricts their forward vision.

A remarkable number of vehicles have the spare wheel slung underneath the vehicle where not only is it difficult to remove and will often be covered in mud, but also when you have a flat tyre off-road it can be difficult and in some situations dangerous to get out. Therefore it is strongly recommended that you do not have the spare wheel under the vehicle when off-road.

If you are not strong enough to be able to lift a spare wheel on to a roof rack, there are swing-away rear wheel carriers that can be fitted to the rear of the vehicle.

Spare wheel covers

Fast becoming *de rigueur* in the posers' market, wheel covers now come in all types from cheap cloth to lockable polished stainless steel, with attendant blinding reflections in sunlight! In hot sunny countries the cover is more useful for keeping strong ultraviolet light off tyres, which causes cheaper makes to split. In damp climates such as the UK, waterproof or water-resistant versions trap moisture, leading to premature rusting of steel wheels.

Tyre pliers

Tyre pliers are effective for breaking the tyre bead from the wheel rim on smaller tyres, but are not very effective on 16-inch (406 mm) rims.

Tyre pumps

If you spend much time off the road you will get punctures from thorns and sharp stones. On a

A shiny spare wheel cover could cause dangerous reflections from the sun.

long off-road journey there comes a time (often many times!) where you run out of spares and just have to repair one. Pumping up a large tyre with a foot pump is hard work, and if you are doing it on sand the pump, being on the ground, picks up sand and soon fails. Just as much a problem is putting enough air back into four tyres that you may have let down for that soft stretch.

Several types of tyre pump are available. There are various models of battery-operated compressors – most are Japanese, but are usually made for car tyres and will not quite manage a 7.50 x 16 in (191 x 406 mm) tyre to 45 psi (3.11 bar). However, there is the American-made Schrader model 202 12-volt compressor which just manages it. In a hot climate it will get from zero to 36 psi (2.5 bar) in 15 minutes. You should then let the pump cool down again before topping up to final pressure. The pump uses quite a high current, so the engine should be kept running. If you have a diesel engine, which does not have its own compressor, then this is the only type of pump you can use. I have worked one of these pumps very hard for several years in the Sahara,

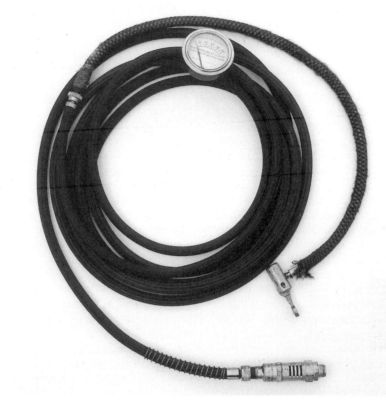

Some sparking plug tyre pumps are fitted with a manometer, but do not trust the accuracy of such a gauge.

without any problems.

Even more useful are the compressors supplied to operate the ARB and Kam differential locks, which operate to 135 psi (9.32 bar) and 120 psi (8.28 bar) respectively. None of these compressors require any special maintenance. They can all be used to inflate air beds and inflatable boats, while the ARB and Kam compressors will also drive low-pressure air tools.

All compressors should be used on or inside the vehicle, not on the ground, where they can pick up dust and sand.

If you have a petrol engine, you can carry a pump that fits in place of a sparking plug. In the UK you can only get the Schrader version, but other makes are available in America. Some of these are fitted with pressure gauges, but these are not very accurate and tend to break in transport. Use accurate displacement pressure gauges and always carry a spare. Keep a valve core tool and spare valve cores with the pump.

Puncture repair kits

I am always surprised to see punctures repaired in the UK with

The Schrader 12-volt tyre compressor and Schrader tyre pump that fits in a sparking plug socket. The former should be used in or on the vehicle, never on the ground.

patches and rubber cement, while throughout most of the world hot vulcanising machines are used, which are superior for hard-worked off-road and truck tyres. All over the Sahara and Middle East punctures are repaired in this way, and even in the far outback you can find home-made versions with a clamp on a domestic clothes iron and even, in Southern India, using a primus stove.

The sensible thing to do on a long expedition is to carry several spare inner tubes and, each time you get a puncture, replace the tube and get all the punctured tubes vulcanised properly when you reach the next place where it is possible to do so. Even in the UK I always carry a spare inner tube, as few tyre repair centres stock larger sizes.

Even so, there will come the odd time when you just have to mend one yourself out in the bush (most punctures seem to be caused by thorns, so you tend to get many at once). The best puncture repair kit is the German Rema 'Tip Top' brand, but you have to be very careful with cleanliness and, once opened, it is difficult to stop the cleaning solvent from evaporating. Use a course file to rough up the inner tube before patching it.

Match-ignited hot patches never work with heavier four-wheel drive-type inner tubes.

ENGINE, EXHAUST AND TRANSMISSION

Timing gear replacements for camshaft drive belts

Many modern engines have belt-driven camshafts. From the manufacturer's viewpoint they are cheap, quiet and do not require lubrication. From the owner's viewpoint, however, they stretch, which affects the timing of injection pumps, and often fail, with disastrous results. Nowadays it is recommended that they be replaced around 40,000 miles (64,500 km) in normal use, but for off-road use, particularly in hot, dusty countries, you would be wise to halve that figure.

In the UK Zeus Design Patents of Exeter produce a conversion to good old-fashioned timing gears for several engines, which costs little more than that of replacing the belt. There are many satisfied taxi and Land Rover owners with this conversion, but I have not found anyone who has put one to the test of hard work in hot, dusty countries.

Raised air intakes

Most production four-wheel drive vehicles have their engine air intake low enough to pick up dust and water in extreme conditions, so there are aftermarket systems to raise this, some of which tend to break off under high vibration such as on corrugated tracks.

Polyethylene stabilised against ultraviolet radiation lasts better than metal in this respect, but whatever system you fit, it will have a flexible rubber connection somewhere, which, like the rubber connection between the air filter and the engine itself, should be regularly checked for holes.

Auxiliary vehicle and engine pre-heaters

If you use a vehicle in low temperatures, systems that burn fuel independently of the engine are useful. They can be fitted either to heat the interior air of the vehicle, particularly useful to rear seat occupants in larger vehicles and those sleeping in the vehicle, or to heat the engine water cooling system, additionally heating the vehicle interior via its own existing heater system.

Pre-heating both the engine and the vehicle makes a big difference in cold and, in particular, snowy conditions, both cutting down on engine wear, by starting a warm engine, and providing the extra comfort and safety of a warm vehicle with defrosted windows for clear vision.

For those who regularly operate in snowy conditions, these heaters are cheaper to operate than leaving the engine running in traffic jams, and if you are trapped in a snow storm, they are safer than leaving

A raised air intake fixed to a roll cage for extra strength.

the engine running, which, in extreme situations, has killed vehicle occupants by carbon monoxide poisoning.

Simpler mains electrical pre-heating systems are available, but of course can only be used where you have access to mains electricity, usually at your home or garage, though in most Arctic countries many buildings have the required electrical sockets available.

Extra engine cooling

Conversely, a fan with an extra blade or two will help cooling in a hot climate. There will be an increase in noise and more problems in water crossings, but it is worth it. Electric radiator cooling fans reduce fuel consumption, and on short journeys in cold weather they decrease engine warm-up times. However, they do not produce enough cooling in hot countries.

Oil coolers may be necessary for some engines in hot countries and those with automatic gearboxes, and are essential if a turbocharger is fitted.

Stainless steel exhausts

Stainless steel exhaust pipes last longer than normal exhaust pipes for on-road conditions, especially where salt is used on roads in winter. In off-road use, however, exhaust pipes usually require replacement after physical damage rather than due to corrosion, so the extra cost of stainless steel is not warranted.

Swivel pin housing gaiters and propeller shaft gaiters

Where swivel pin housings are fitted, they are vulnerable to dust and grit getting under the seals. Leather gaiters are available for Land Rovers and are easily made to fit other vehicles.

It is possible to fit a similar system over the sliding joint on the propeller shaft, but at high speed you could get damage due to them putting the propeller shaft out of balance.

Overdrives

Many modern vehicles have a fifth gear, which is really an overdrive, this system being stronger than bolt-on units. Bolt on units are available for other vehicles, but for those who spend 90 per cent of their time on paved roads, the reduction in noise and vibration at cruising speed is worth more than the amount of fuel they save.

Overdrives have a tendency to wear quickly if used for heavy off-road work or towing. Do not believe manufacturers' claims that they double the number of usable gears – if used in low gear the stress is too high, they are best used only on the top two gears in the high range.

ANTI-THEFT DEVICES

Vehicle theft is a major problem in the UK, and is not limited to luxury off-road vehicles – well-restored older four-wheel drive vehicles also get stolen for their parts and accessories. If you have fitted valuable extras, do not have window stickers advertising the fact!

Vehicle theft is not so much a problem in other countries, and is almost unknown in Japan, so vehicles manufactured there tend to be easier to break into. Older Land Rovers and the Defender series vehicles, with their intentional flexible body, are particularly easy to break into by those who know how.

There are many high-technology car alarms available, and your insurance may insist on one of these for an expensive luxury vehicle, but those with a tendency to go off when a vehicle is buffeted by wind can be a nuisance when you are parked in open fields – and who is likely to hear them, when parked in a remote glen?

Systems that cut the fuel flow to the injection pump are good for diesel engines, as well as fuel-injected petrol engines. In off-road and Third World conditions, cheaper solutions such as a battery isolator or ignition cut-out hidden from sight and simple devices that lock the gear lever or over the steering wheel, with an arm attached that stops the steering wheel from being turned, are effective.

Professional car thieves in cities often cut the handbrake cables and tow vehicles away with the front wheels raised. This is more difficult (but not impossible) on vehicles fitted with transmission brakes.

CB radios and GPS units should be removed or locked in a safe box when a vehicle is left unattended.

Battery isolators

Battery isolators are a useful theft deterrent on any vehicle, and are particularly useful on off-road vehicles, where fires may be caused by short circuits when wading, by turning a vehicle over, or, more commonly, when the insulation on cables is worn through by constant vibration against metal parts on bumpy or corrugated roads.

You can buy battery isolators fitted with a fuse across the terminals that will allow side lights, clocks and radio memories to remain active, but which will blow if the starter motor is used; alternatively you can easily fit your own fuse across the terminals.

Steering, bonnet and fuel cap locks

Many four-wheel drive vehicles are manufactured in countries where steering locks have to be fitted by law, in an effort to deter car thieves. They are usually fitted using bolts with snap-off heads to make their removal difficult.

In dusty areas the tumblers within the lock itself tend to seize up, causing difficulty with inserting or removing the key. Locks of this type, including those on the doors that require a key to operate them, should only be lubricated with dry graphite – oil will make things worse.

If you are having trouble with a steering lock in dusty conditions, leave the key permanently in the lock, rather than break it by force, until you reach an area where you can remove and replace it. The key itself will help to stop any more dust getting in, and the whole unit can be permanently covered with a plastic bag or rubber glove to help keep the dust out.

Steering locks are difficult to remove – an operation requiring a hacksaw. In a dusty climate it is best to either remove the steering lock completely, or to replace it using normal bolts and carry a spare lock. Would-be car thieves would not expect the lock to have normal, headed bolts. A battery isolator is often a better theft deterrent and has an additional safety factor.

It is also wise to have the bonnet, fuel cap and any jerry can holders locked – this is essential in less developed countries. Keep it simple and use padlocks; you can replace these easily if they go wrong. Jerry cans and boxes on the roof can be locked down with a strong chain sheathed in plastic tubing, threaded through their handles.

Land Rover 90/110 and Defender vehicles do not have a strong enough spring on the in-cab release for the bonnet to release it if it has the weight of the spare wheel on it. You must therefore either have a second person to pull the release while you raise the bonnet, or else use a piece of wood with a channel cut into it to hold the release open while you go round and lift the bonnet.

Safe and waterproof boxes

As has already been mentioned, four-wheel drive vehicles are not difficult to break into and are often used in terrain or Third World countries where theft is common. One or more strong metal boxes, securely fitted to the vehicle and fitted with tamper-proof locks, are therefore useful for carrying money, documents, cameras and other valuables. A small safe for money and passports can be fixed to the chassis, but for larger items such as camera and filming equipment, there are folding safe boxes that can be folded up flat when not in use, to give more room in the vehicle.

Another useful item for off-road use is a Pelican or Underwater Kinetics case. These plastic cases come in many sizes, are extremely tough and have a replaceable neoprene seal to make them waterproof, so they are also dust proof. The sealing system is so efficient that after descending 984 feet (300 m) downhill, or landing in an aircraft, you will have to release the purge valve before you can open the case.

First aid kit

A first aid kit must be carried by law in some countries, and should always be carried in any vehicle. You should also know how to use one and preferably take a First Aid course. Remember that medicines, antiseptics and sticking plasters will be affected by heat.

Radio

A radio receiver in your vehicle is useful on paved roads for news of road hazards and traffic jams. Unfortunately, in Britain such warnings are usually two hours late, but the system works better in the rest of Europe and the USA. Off-road, a radio is essential if you wish to know what is going on in the rest of the world. Overlanders and expeditions can get the world news on a short wave radio.

Two-way radio is illegal in many Third World countries, usually the ones where you would most like to have it! Usually the country is scared of spying. Short-distance Citizen's Band radio is popular with off-road vehicle users in

A channelled piece of wood used to keep the bonnet release pulled while the bonnet is lifted by hand.

developed countries and is a boon when 'green-laning'.

Radio telephones only work over relatively short distances, but satellite telephones using folding dishes have been regularly used in some of the world's most in-hospitable places, including the summit of Everest, often with sponsorship from the supplier. Remote desert expeditions could find such a system a useful safety factor.

Cassette player

I have often had to drive a four-wheel drive vehicle alone, from London to Tehran, Kabul, Rawalpindi, Algiers or Casablanca, and in such situations have found a cassette player and several tapes almost a necessity. Such things are very much a matter of taste, but any fast music is useful if you are a little tired. Do not use tapes in dusty, humid or seaside areas, where the tapes tend to slip, while in hot countries long-play tapes tend to stick. Likewise CD players are best avoided in dusty, damp and salty areas.

Speakers do not last long with the dust and damp, so they have to be replaced frequently. In Third World countries radios and cassettes are best hidden – they are highly prized by thieves.

GETTING OUT OF TROUBLE

Shovels, pickaxes and axes

Shovels are useful when camping, for digging latrines, digging a safe hole for a fire, or burying rubbish. For recovery in soft sand or mud, two shovels are essential – two people can be digging the vehicle out at the same time. Avoid shovels with too big a blade, as they can be very tiring to work with, while military folding or trenching tools are too small.

A long handle is necessary to clear away sand from right under

Short-handled shovels are useful when you are on your knees digging out sand.

the axle, while additional short-handled shovels are useful on sand, where you may be digging on your knees. A pointed blade is better than a flat one and a steel shaft less likely to break when most needed. Narrow-blade spades are useful in mud and clay.

When travelling on mountain tracks carry a pickaxe and, for camping where firewood is available, a sharp hand axe. Most travellers in Africa, including the Sahara, pick up wood as they find it during the day's travelling, for cooking in the evening.

Saws

Where you may find brushwood as a traction aid, a bow-type tree saw is useful and, where it is permitted and fallen trees may block the route, you could carry a chain saw.

Perforated steel or aluminium plate

Interlocking steel or aluminium plate dates back to bush airfield use in the Second World War. It can be interlocked over an area, but most vehicles would only

carry two sheets. Each sheet is quite heavy and is only really nec-essary for trucks, so it is senseless for Land Rover/Toyota Landcruiser-size vehicles to carry them, as one often finds in Africa. They can bend upwards and snag the underside of the vehicle, and they are not really strong enough on their own for bridging use, though they work well over logs and stones.

Perforated plate is designed to be used with the projecting side on the ground, that is the side with the projections that are meant to fit into the holes on another sheet of plate, facing down. This is cor-rect for placing on sand, grass, ice, thin snow or wood.

In mud, deep snow or on stones, I prefer to place them the other way up. In mud or snow they will sink under the weight of the vehicle, the holes will produce enough grip on the mud or snow and the vehicle's tyres will get a grip on the projections instead of slipping, as they often do on the smoother side of the plates. If you put the projecting side down on stones the projections are likely to be damaged and then will no

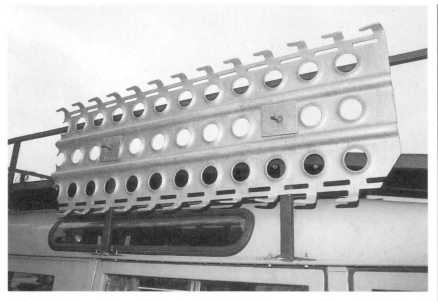

Perforated plate, seen here with the projecting side to the camera. The method of fixing is too slow for fast use.

longer interlock with other sheets of plate.

Sand ladders

Vehicles of the Land Rover/ Toyota Landcruiser type should carry sand ladders, which are lighter in weight and easier to handle and recover than perforated plate.

Sand ladders are short lengths of strong steel ladder, just long enough to fit comfortably between the vehicle wheelbase. One vehicle alone would carry four of these, while two or more vehicles travelling in convoy would only carry two per vehicle, as they can be shared in a difficult situation.

Sand ladders are less useful in mud, as the vehicle tyres tend to slip on them, but they are usually stronger than perforated plate for unsupported bridging use over ditches.

Square-section rungs are more efficient for traction, so much so that the ladder may have to be dug out afterwards. They are also more efficient in mud, if the vehicle tyres have large lugs. With ladders

under the rear wheels, the front end of the ladders often kick up when the wheels begin to grip, sometimes damaging the chassis or exhaust pipe. This can be avoided if the ladders are made in two pieces with hinges half way, which allow them to articulate vertically, but you then lose the bridging ability.

'Waffles', a new design of sand ladder by Frank Luxton, are based on the floor grids of oil rigs. Manufactured of glass-reinforced fibre, they are lightweight, do not rust and are strong enough for bridging. They will be marketed by David Bowyer's Off-road Centre.

Sand channels

Sand channels are lightweight aluminium channels with a mesh centre. Each unit comes in three pieces 19.7 inches (500 mm) long, with ropes to link the three together longitudinally. Individual sections are not long enough to damage the chassis if they kick up. Sand channels are lightweight to carry and convenient for package and storage, but being in three pieces you cannot pick them up and drop them again efficiently in line with a moving vehicle.

They also have no bridging ability, the mesh would tear up if placed on stones and they are of little use in mud, where they may fly out backwards from under a driving or spinning wheel, with possible injury to anyone pushing the vehicle from behind.

Perforated plate, metal sand ladders and sand channels, all become bent in use. When you reach hard ground place them with the ends on the ground and the bend in the air and drive over them to straighten them out again.

In any terrain where you might require the use of these items, they should be hooked on the outside of the vehicle, where they can be quickly and easily taken off for use. In real deserts you may require them 20 or more times per day!

Sand ladders on the sides of vehicles ready for instant use, here in the Hoggar Mountains in the Sahara Desert.

'Waffles' in use.

Stones, logs and brushwood are also all usable, if available.

Snow chains

Snow chains are just as useful in mud and clay as they are in snow. Normal closed-tread on-road tyres fitted with chains are more efficient in mud and clay than most open-tread off-road tyres, so much so that if you are off-roading on someone's land check with the owner before using them, as they will really cut up the ground.

Snow chains come in many varieties: on-road types designed to do minimum damage to road and tyres and produce minimum noise; off-road types with more chain per tyre area and designed to give maximum grip, particularly uphill; and many types in between, with various systems for tensioning and easy fitting.

If you have long-travel suspension, check with the vehicle manu-facturer as well as the chain distributor. The wrong type of chain on the front wheels may cut through brake hoses or cause other damage at extremes of axle articulation and full steering lock.

Ideally you should fit chains on all four wheels. There are several books that tell you to fit chains on the front wheels, if you only have one pair. I can only assume that the authors of these books have never tried this in practice.

With American four-wheel drive trucks that have large, heavy engines over the front wheels, fitting chains to the front wheels only works fine on level ground. However, when going uphill the vehicle weight is thrown on to the rear wheels, and going downhill the front wheels with the chains are gripping, but the rear wheels have less weight on them so they slide from side to side ('fish-tailing'). Eventually, and especially if the brakes are touched, this will cause the rear end of the vehicle to overtake the front in a spin.

If you fit chains only on the front of most European and Japanese four-wheel drive vehicles, you will find that even on a level road traction is poor and touching the brakes can cause the rear end to spin round. On any hill they will be useless. Therefore if you only have one pair of snow chains, fit them to the rear wheels! However, if you have a limited slip or automatic locking rear differential, you must have chains on all four wheels to minimise loss of control when fish-tailing.

NAVIGATION

Compass

For off-road navigation you need to be well acquainted with the use of a magnetic compass. Those fitted to the vehicle will be affected by the metal and electrical fields within the vehicle, but you can use them if you allow for the vehicle's magnetic deflection.

Suppliers of good vehicle compasses will supply you with literature on how to 'swing' your vehicle and adjust the compass as accurately as possible. Even so you should not rely on it entirely, but stop often and double-check with a good hand compass, well away from the vehicle and any cameras, exposure meters, keys or Swiss army knife that you may be carrying.

For long-distance desert work a sun compass is useful if you can find one and learn how to use it, but for serious work you should learn how to navigate by sextant or theodolite. Never rely on desert markers left by departed Colonial Powers. Local guides may have moved them so that travellers have to pay them for guiding.

At sea you can follow a compass bearing for ever, just allowing for wind and currents, but over land you will have to adjust your direction around mountains, gullies or soft sand. Therefore write down the distance that you travel on each compass bearing, so that you can work out your true position accurately and be able to backtrack if things go wrong.

Trip meter

Off-road navigation is greatly simplified if you have a trip meter on your odometer and you have accurate knowledge of how correct it is in relation to the tyres and gearing that you have fitted. A cheap way to calculate the accuracy is to check your odometer reading against the survey markers that are numbered every 109.36 yards (100 m) along the side of motorways. You can of course go to the cost of a full Rallying system.

Global Positioning Systems (GPS)

Satellite navigation has been around for many years, particularly in marine use, but it had problems with high cost or rental charges, low number of satellites, equipment or battery malfunction and the poor accuracy of charts in less developed areas.

Enter the US Military which, after some setbacks since the first two Navstar satellites were launched in 1978, has completed its current programme with a total of 21 satellites plus three active, spare satellites in orbit. These orbit 12,400 miles (20,000 km) above the earth twice a day, inclined at 63° to the equator, each transmitting its precise position and correct time accurate to Nanoseconds. Earth stations monitor the satellites, correcting any conditions that may affect their accuracy. The result is continuous 24-hour global coverage.

Having tracked three of these satellites, triangulation can give three fixes, converging on a single point, but if you add a fourth line of fix, any error will be realised because the four fixes will enclose a volume of space, rather than converging on a single point. This is mainly due to less accurate quartz clocks in the receiver, so it recalculates the fixes until they converge on a single point, then corrects its own clock setting. Correcting for internal clock errors and the time it has taken to receive each signal, a GPS can compute its own latitude and longtitude with accuracy down to ±16 feet (5 m).

With four satellites the fix is in three dimensions, complete with altitude. Where possible some models compute from up to 12 satellites. GPS works best when the satellites are well spaced out, to minimise Geometric Dilution of Precision (GDOP). It finally came of age in the Gulf War.

The world is not a perfect sphere, so GPS requires datum corrections so that charts and maps match its calculated position. Make sure that any model you buy has datums for the regions in which you wish to travel, or has a manual adjustment option.

In theory GPS is not affected by weather or terrain, but the signals can be affected by electrical phenomena in the atmosphere. During the Gulf War GPS receivers often came up with the message 'cannot get good reception' half an hour before sunset and half an hour after sunrise. With so many vehicles drafted in quickly, many had civilian GPS receivers, so the standard positioning service was switched off and extra satellites moved into the area for more accurate fixes. They also fail to work through metal, solid objects or heavy tree cover; they must have a clear line of sight to the sky.

The Navstar satellite transmits two signals, Precise Positioning Service (PPS), which is encoded for military use, and Standard Positioning Service (SPS), which is degraded for civilian use to an accuracy of around ±110 yards (100 m), ±164 yards (150 m) for altitude – good enough for visual sighting.

Enter Differential GPS (DGPS). If a GPS receiver is sited at a fixed, accurately known position, software can be programmed to calculate the difference between the real position and the GPS-calculated position from the downgraded signal. So with accurate maps and fixed sites GPS can put back the accuracy the US military have taken out, giving accuracy good enough for hiking, mountaineering and green-laning. A six-figure grid reference only gives a position to ±110 yards (100 m).

A network of differential beacons is being set up throughout the world, though mostly around coasts, so you are unlikely to be near one in a large remote desert. If there are differential beacons in the area that you are operating, you can connect an extra 'black box' costing around £450 for more accurate fixes.

In the long term, just as the US Military has given up plans to charge for the system because it would be too difficult to administer, they may drop the downgraded system. Being realistic, any government wishing to use the system militarily would have computer experts to break the code and use the accurate version.

GPS units can be fixed or portable, and some portable units can also be fitted into a fixed docking bay. They come in varying levels of weatherproofing. Some 'hand-held' units are in fact too large to be comfortable in the hand.

As with their predecessors, they are not infallible and the hand-held units eat batteries! In cold weather alkaline batteries soon fade, so lithium or nicad batteries are more useful. As with many electronic items, total, unexpected battery failure can leave you hunting for the handbook, and, with some models, repeating an initial set-up programme.

For off-road use there are advantages to having the unit powered by the vehicle battery, but current antennae systems available for vehicles are not that good and you might prefer to be able to remove the unit, both for theft reasons and to continue a journey on foot.

The Magellan Trailblazer hand-held GPS unit.

Displays can be either alphanumeric or pixel; the latter can also display full graphics to feature route plots. More advanced systems can store up to 100 'way-points' (a series of positions linking a route) in their memory by entering the coordinates, so you can plot a course and back up along it if necessary. Some will calculate direction and speed on the move and estimate journey time.

Some systems on sale in the UK are customised with the Ordnance Survey Grid System, as well as standard latitude and longitude and Universal Transverse Mercator Grid System (UTM). Depending on your area of use, you can also find systems offering Australian, European, Swedish, North American and Japanese grid

systems. Prices are falling so fast that remote expeditions could carry two or even three units.

> **Warning:** You must remember that anything that relies on batteries or electronics can go wrong and is subject to operator error. Before relying on GPS for real navigation in remote areas, you must be able to navigate accurately by traditional methods first. You should write all route changes down, so that you can continue manually if the unit fails and back up with or without the unit if you get lost.

GPS units are developing fast, being leading edge technology, slightly outdated models are reg-

ularly sold off cheaply. It is worth shopping around and especially checking out marine suppliers, who handle larger ranges and greater quantities.

THOSE FINAL ITEMS

If a four-wheel drive vehicle goes wrong off-road, then inevitably you will have to lie under it, either in mud, thorns or blowing sand. Therefore have a boiler suit handy, and if you do not already have a cover on a roof rack, then you will be glad of some form of ground sheet to lie on. In an area of wind-blown sand, build a shelter around the part of the vehicle on which you are working. To keep the sun off and sand out and for working underneath, a pair of goggles can save you a lot of eye problems.

A small hand brush is also useful for brushing out your vehicle and for brushing engine, wheels or bodywork clean, before you work on them.

Vice

For serious off-road work, over-landers and expeditions, a strong metal-worker's vice, which can be bolted to a bumper or tailgate, is useful.

Starting handle

Few vehicles still have starting handles, but they are equally useful for setting-up tappets, etc, when working on the engine.

Fire extinguishers

Off-road vehicles tend to be used in fire risk situations and may be your only way of getting back to civilisation. Therefore one or more good-sized fire extinguishers should always be carried and regularly checked.

CHAPTER 3

Off-road driving

Safety warning: Vehicles designed to go off-road have a higher centre of gravity than normal cars. Their higher ground clearance and often shorter wheelbase makes them suitable for off-road terrain, but they are not designed for cornering at the same speeds as conventional passenger vehicles. Sharp turns or abrupt manoeuvres can result in loss of control, spinning, or the vehicle turning over. Therefore always travel at sensible speeds – corner, accelerate, change gear and brake smoothly, and always wear a seat belt.

DRIVING FOUR-WHEEL DRIVE VEHICLES – GEARING, STEERING AND BRAKING

Four-wheel drive vehicles driven competently and fitted with the appropriate tyres can traverse seemingly impossible terrain. Conversely, with an inexperienced driver and inappropriate tyres they can get stuck in a flat field on wet grass.

The controls

Before you go off-road, read the vehicle driver's handbook and thoroughly acquaint yourself with the extra controls available for four-wheel drive. Ten years ago most of these were standardised for all vehicles, but nowadays there is a bewildering and often unnecessary variety. There will also be limitations to the speed at which some controls on some vehicles can be operated without transmission damage.

If the vehicle has manual freewheeling hubs, these should be locked in before the vehicle leaves the paved road, or for conditions of snow and ice on paved roads. With the freewheeling hubs locked in, you can easily engage four-wheel drive if you require it.

If the vehicle has part-time four-wheel drive, there will be either a lever or a push-button control to convert the transmission from part-time to full-time, and vice versa in high range. There may also be a maximum speed at which this control may be operated. This speed will vary from vehicle to vehicle – on some it may be accomplished at any speed, providing that the road wheels are not spinning at different revolutions. Some variation in the operation of this control, or a separate control, will change the transfer gear ranges from high to low and vice versa. There will be a maximum speed at which this may be done without damage (sometimes only with the vehicle stationary), and on some vehicles the use of the double declutching technique may be required to accomplish this on the move.

If the vehicle has permanent four-wheel drive, there will be either a lever or push-button control to lock the centre differential. On most such vehicles this can be accomplished at any speed, providing that the road wheels are not spinning at different revolutions. If you are on loose ground where there may be differences in wheel or inter-axle speeds, ease the accelerator and disengage the clutch before engaging the centre differential lock. The neutral position on this centre differential lock and the transfer box should be used if the vehicle is to be towed, the vehicle is winching other than in self recovery, or a power take-off is being used. (The new Range Rover does not have a selectable neutral position for dead engine towing, and this can only be obtained by fitting a 5 amp fuse in position 11 in the under-seat fuse box.)

An advantage of permanent four-wheel drive systems is that you can easily engage and disengage the centre differential lock, locking in before any difficult section, and locking out to free transmission 'wind-up' on easy sections. On some vehicles, for example those with a viscous coupling or limited slip centre differential, this differential lock is automatic. If the vehicle has axle differential locks, there will usually be controls in the vehicle to engage and disengage these, though with some simple systems you may have to get under the vehicle to engage them manually.

If the vehicle has automatic transmission, there should be a position where it can be locked into low gear; this is essential for engine braking downhill. Depending on the vehicle you may also be able to adjust the ride height, shock absorber firmness and mode of four-wheel drive, or there may be 'electronic brains' making these decisions for you.

High range

High range is for normal paved road conditions or off-road on firm surfaces that do not involve steep inclines, usually, in two-wheel drive or permanent four-wheel drive vehicles, with the centre differential unlocked. High-range four-wheel drive, or for permanent four-wheel drive vehicles with the centre differential locked in, is for use on paved roads in ice and snow or off-road in mild conditions such as wet grass, mud that is not difficult and sand that is not soft.

Low range

> **Warning:** In any difficult situation, such as when stuck or about to descend a steep incline, double check that the low-range gears have not jumped out, leaving the vehicle in neutral.

Low range is for power and control. Low range should always be used in full four-wheel drive – this usually happens automatically. Never use it with freewheeling hubs disengaged or with snow chains fitted to only one axle – the high torque transmitted to only one axle may break something.

Low-range power is required for heavy towing (though you may change up to high range once you have achieved a reasonable road speed), towing out another stuck vehicle, getting through or out of deep mud, snow or soft sand, and climbing steep inclines.

Low-range control is required for engine braking descending steep inclines off-road, crossing rivers and crawling over stones, tree stumps, ditches or large boulders.

On serious off-road vehicles, low-range first gear is too low for most situations, so use it for crawling over tree stumps, ditches and large boulders. Keep your feet clear of the brake and the clutch pedals and let the engine control the speed, especially on the down side of large boulders or tree stumps.

In difficult situations low-range second is the gear to start off in to minimise the chance of wheelspin. Low-range third, fourth and fifth gears give good versatility on sand, mud, off-road snow, difficult tracks and steep inclines.

With vehicles whose low-range gears are not that low, such as Suzukis and Vauxhall Fronteras, you will have to use low-range first gear when I have stated low-range second gear throughout this book.

When changing down the gear-box it can be difficult to get into first gear on the move, and you could get into serious difficulties if you tried to change from second gear into first and failed. If you are likely to require first gear, stop, change into it and remain in it until clear of the difficult section.

In the days of non-synchromesh (crash) gearboxes, double declutching was the standard way to change gears, but it is now a lost art. However, four-wheel drive transfer boxes usually have a dog clutch instead of synchromesh, so you should practise double declutching to be able to move in and out of low range on the move. This is, however, not normally possible on vehicles fitted with an electric range change control.

To change down into low range with the vehicle rolling at around 2-4 mph in second gear, first depress the clutch pedal and shift the transfer box lever into neutral. Release the clutch pedal and dip the accelerator to increase the engine speed to an amount equivalent to the low-range step down ratio (usually a little more than double), then depress the clutch pedal again and shift the transfer box lever from neutral to low range. Finally release the clutch pedal again.

A Jeep negotiating a landslide near Chalt in North Pakistan, using low-range first gear to crawl over the large obstacles.

If you get the engine speed right the gears will go in silently and smoothly. If you were a little out, they will go in with a small clunk. If you were a long way out they will not engage at all, so do not force things. If you get nasty noises, go back to neutral and try again. With practise you will be able to change down into low range at 10-12 mph (16-19 kph).

To shift from low range to high range the reverse procedure is used, but it is much easier. To equalise the engine speed you should slow the engine down by around half speed during the pause in neutral, and use third gear and speeds between 15-25 mph (24-40 kph) (10 mph [16 kph] maximum with electric range change). Change down a gear in the main gearbox as necessary, after you have changed the transfer box from low range to high range. This procedure is useful when towing a heavy trailer.

If the vehicle is new, the transfer box gear lever may be stiff and you may have to be at a complete standstill with the main gearbox in gear. Depress the clutch and push the transfer box lever into low range, with a pause in neutral. If the gears do not go in, roll the vehicle forward a little, in gear, and try again. It may take two or three attempts.

Where possible it is best to change from low range to high range and vice versa with the main gearbox in gear. This way you will feel and hear if the transfer box gears engage, and they will engage positively. If the main gearbox is in neutral, you will not feel or hear the gears engage, and when you try to drive off the transfer box gears may jump out. There are some vehicles on which you cannot change the transfer box gear range unless the main gearbox is in neutral.

Four-wheel drive vehicle controls tend to be built for strength rather than slick changes, and there may be several linkages involved. Moderate force and moderate speed are best for gear-box and transfer box levers. If you have difficulty engaging low range, first gear, or reverse gear, engage a higher gear, engage the clutch momentarily to reposition the gear wheels, then try again. Perform all gear changes as smoothly as possible to reduce the chance of wheelspin.

On loose terrain, when not requiring engine braking, use the highest gear possible without the engine labouring; this will reduce the possibility of wheelspin. Automatic transmission should produce smoother gear changes, but you must think ahead so as to be able to lock into low gear for downhill engine braking.

Do not ride the clutch. It is tempting to keep your foot on the clutch pedal ready for a quick gear change, but you are likely to get clutch slip when you do not want it, such as when you bounce over a hump or pothole; you will also cause premature wear to the clutch plate.

Be gentle on the accelerator to avoid spinning the wheels. Do not knowingly spin the wheels – they will scoop the ground out from underneath, making the situation worse, and if they suddenly grip there could be an immense shock load on the transmission.

Stop the moment you realise that the wheels are spinning, and try to gently reverse out. If this is not possible, get out and inspect the situation for recovery.

Do not brake heavily on loose ground – wheels can lock up and you are likely to spin out of control. If you must brake hard, use 'cadence' ('modulation') braking, that is short, sharp jabs on the pedal as fast as you can, so that the wheels never get a chance to lock up. This is how ABS brakes work. If you are lucky enough to have ABS fitted, it will do what is necessary for you.

The tyres fitted to most four-wheel drive vehicles do not have as much grip on paved roads as normal car tyres, so it is worth getting into the habit of 'cadence' braking on-road. Do not use this method if you already have ABS braking.

Smoothness is also necessary with steering. If you turn the steering wheel sharply when off-road, the vehicle will not turn but plough straight ahead, pushing the sideways-facing front wheels ahead of it. On loose surfaces there is little or no feeling in the steering, so it can be difficult to know if the front wheels are facing straight ahead. Power steering has even

On loose surfaces it is difficult to know in which direction the wheels are pointing – this is even worse with power steering.

less feel; some American and Japanese vehicles in particular are fitted with very light power steering systems, which lack 'feel' even on paved roads.

In deep ruts or when a relatively fast moving vehicle bounces, having the front wheels turned can lead to a sharp change in direction, loss of control and an overturned vehicle. Off-road always be prepared to put your head out of the window to check the direction of the front wheels, but watch out for tree branches or other obstructions that might strike you in the face.

Approach angle

The approach angle is the angle of approach at the front of the vehicle. It is an indication of the angle of slope you can approach without the vehicle body, usually the front bumper, making contact with it.

The approach angle is measured from the front of the vehicle to the front tyre at ground level. The higher the angle the better, providing that it does not exceed the departure angle.

On most vehicles the front wheels are relatively close to the front of the vehicle, so there is little to worry about, unless a spoiler or extra lights have been fitted below the front bumper, or the bumper has been extended in front of the vehicle, to accommodate a winch for example.

You must also think of your vehicle's approach angle when descending a steep slope, and remember that the rear of the vehicle may still connect with the ground if the departure angle is not good enough.

Departure angle

The departure angle is the angle of

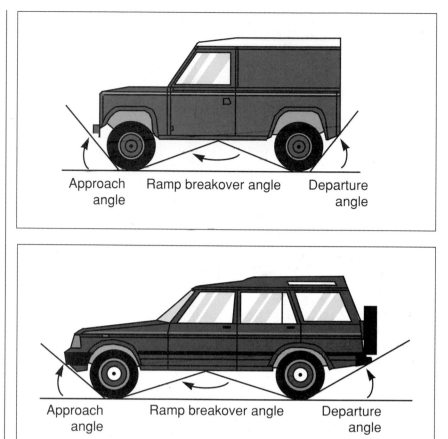

Short-wheelbase vehicles have better angles of approach and departure, and in particular better ramp break-over angle and ground clearance than long-wheelbase vehicles.

departure at the rear of the vehicle. It is an indication of the angle of the slope from which you can depart without the vehicle body making contact with it.

The departure angle is measured from the rear of the vehicle to the rear tyre at ground level. Ideally this angle should be at least equal to the approach angle.

The rear overhang on long-wheelbase vehicles decreases the departure angle.

A tow plate also decreases the departure angle.

On short-wheelbase vehicles this angle is usually excellent, unless fog lamps or towing hitches have been fitted below the chassis or rear bumper, or the bumper has been extended behind the vehicle, for example as a rear step.

On long-wheelbase vehicles the rear body extends well to the rear of the rear wheels, giving a poorer departure angle that may also be made worse by extending the rear bumper away from the body, or fitting fog lamps or a towing hitch below it. A grounded tow hitch may also prevent the vehicle from reversing out when stuck.

Ramp break-over angle

The ramp break-over angle is the angle between the front and rear wheels and the lowest part of vehicle, usually bodywork or transmission between the front and rear wheels. It is an indication of the steepness and height of a ramp or hump that the vehicle can drive over at right angles without the vehicle grounding ('high centred'). A vehicle high centred in this way will lose traction to the wheels that no longer have weight on the ground and, depending on the design of the underbelly of the vehicle, it may incur damage.

The ramp break-over angle is improved by a shorter wheelbase, or an overall larger diameter of wheel and tyre combination.

Turn-over angle

Most manufacturers quote an angle beyond which a vehicle with standard bodywork will tip over. You would feel extremely uncomfortable at half of this angle, but bear in mind that any high load, or a load that moves either within the vehicle or on a roof rack, will reduce this angle.

This turn-over angle is a static figure. If you are traversing a slope sideways, an upper wheel rising over a rock, hump, tree root or stump, or a lower wheel dropping into a hole, can tip the balance. If this happens at any speed, the rebound of the springs, particu-larly if the shock absorbers are worn, may cause the vehicle to turn over.

Overall ride height

The overall ride height depends on the lowest part of the vehicle, other than the wheels. This is usually the differentials and possibly the gearbox, though on some vehicles it may be additional side rails or steps. These components and their position on the vehicle have to be taken into account when traversing deep mud, snow, soft sand, rocks and tree stumps.

On most four-wheel drive vehicles the lowest components are the axle differentials, which are usually to one side of the vehicle but in line. Some vehicles, for example the Vauxhall Fronteras, do not have the lowest components in line, so after clearing a high object at the front, you may have to steer to one side to avoid hitting the rear differential.

Wading depth

The wading depth of a vehicle will depend on the height and location of the air intake, the pressure of the exhaust gases, whether the engine is petrol or diesel, and the direction of flow, if any, of the water in relation to the direction you wish to travel across it. In general 20 inches (0.5 m) is a comfortable limit.

Bumper height or just above is a comfortable wading depth for most vehicles.

Wading depth can be increased by raising the air intake, keeping up a good exhaust gas pressure by using a faster engine speed in low-range gears, creating a small bow wave in front of the vehicle, and having a diesel engine. You can also improve the wading depth by having a plastic sheet across the front of the vehicle, and disconnecting the fan. For a short crossing you can achieve most of the same effect by crossing the water slowly in reverse; never do this at speed with the fan connected, as the fan blades could bend enough to hit the radiator.

Exhaust pressure is important. If the water pressure becomes higher than the exhaust pressure, It can stall the engine. For this reason it is unwise to change gear while in water that comes above the exhaust outlet. If deep wading is envisaged the exhaust outlet can be extended and raised, otherwise increase the engine tick-over speed so that you are unlikely to stall the engine, particularly if you have a catalytic converter fitted.

Electronic air suspension

The electronic air suspension fitted to the Range Rover is likely to become available as an aftermarket accessory for other vehicles in the near future. With this system the overall ground clearance of the vehicle can be raised.

Axle articulation

Vehicles with long-travel springs and increased axle articulation will be more able to keep all four wheels in contact with the ground and thus retain traction in twisty, undulating terrain and across ditches, ramps or ridges. However, for a given amount of axle articulation short-wheelbase vehicles will be more capable than longer-wheelbase vehicles.

Manoeuvrability

Short-wheelbase vehicles have a smaller turning circle than long-

A lack of axle articulation – one wheel is in the air.

wheelbase vehicles, making them more manoeuvrable in tight situations.

Summary

- Be aware of the higher centre of gravity of four-wheel drive vehicles.

- Travel at sensible speeds, and corner, accelerate, change gear and brake smoothly.

- Read the vehicle driver's handbook and acquaint yourself with the extra controls available for four-wheel drive use.

- High range is for paved roads and off-road on firm surfaces that do not involve steep inclines, usually in two-wheel drive or in permanent four-wheel drive with the centre differential unlocked.

- Four-wheel drive or permanent four-wheel drive with the centre differential locked in is for ice and snow, on paved roads or off-road in mild conditions.

- Low range is for power and control. It should always be used in four-wheel drive and should be used in all difficult situations.

Short-wheelbase vehicles are more manoeuvrable in tight situations.

- Learn to double declutch, for changing into low range on the move on vehicles where this is possible.

- On loose terrain, when not requiring engine braking, use the highest gear possible without the engine labouring.

- Do not ride the clutch, avoid wheelspin and if you do not have ABS brakes, learn 'cadence' braking.

- Understand approach, departure, ramp break-over and turn-over angles.

- Visualise the overall ride height and wading depth.

- Increased axle articulation and short wheelbases improve performance.

VEHICLE PREPARATION

- Remove any spoilers, lights, trailer electrical sockets and number plates that are below bumper level.

- Fold up any folding steps.

- Roll up and tie up any mud flaps.

Tie up mud flaps before going off-road.

- Retract any retractable aerials.

- Check that any towing points and rings are strong enough and firmly fixed to a chassis that is not showing any signs of rust.

- Check that battery connections and battery holding brackets are tight.

- Check that axle poppet valves are clean and working, or that remote axles breathers are intact and working.

- If you are not towing, remove any low tow hitches. The standard tow plate on Ranger Rovers and Discoverys is best left on as extra protection for their fuel tanks.

- If you are to be wading, follow the advice given under the section on wading. I prefer to use silicone spray sealant on petrol engine components in hot countries because it forms a solid seal; silicone grease can melt in the heat and flow on to distributor contacts.

- Remove the flimsy covers that are under the engine bay on vehicles such as the Ford Maverick and Nissan Terrano II.

- Bag and/or lash down anything that can move inside the vehicle.

- Check that any recovery aids you might require for the terrain envisaged are easily available.

- I prefer to leave wing mirrors out, as they are useful when reversing. Only fold them back out of the way when necessary to avoid damage.

GET YOUR MIND INTO GEAR

Off-road driving techniques vary not only with the ability and weight of the vehicle, but also with the ability of the driver. Some vehicles have greater capabilities than many drivers can handle and there may often be more than one way of solving a particular problem. Therefore driver training is worthwhile for educating newcomers to both their personal and their vehicle's capabilities.

Alert but restrained driving is essential. A light foot and low gears in four-wheel drive will usually get a vehicle through soft or difficult ground situations. Sometimes sheer speed may be better, but if you lose control at speed you could suffer damage or injury. Remember that careful driving in the first instance can save you time, money and effort. Broken chassis, springs, half-shafts, burnt-out clutches and body damage are caused by the driver, not the vehicle.

Before you do any off-road driving, look under your vehicle and note the position of its lowest points: springs, axles, differentials, transfer box and gearbox. These will often be lower than you think and the differentials are usually off-centre. Remember their clearance and position when traversing obstacles that you cannot get around.

Do not hook your thumbs around the steering wheel. The sudden twist of the steering wheel when a front wheel hits a stone or rut can easily break them or, with modern soft steering wheel covers, tear a thumbnail.

SCOUTING AHEAD

Always travel at a sensible speed, keeping your eyes some 20 yards (18 m) ahead, watching for difficulties. If you are on a track where it is possible that another vehicle may come the other way, have a passenger keep a look out further ahead, while you concentrate on negotiating the awkward areas. Travel only at speeds that allow you to stop comfortably within the limit of clear vision. Always travel slowly to the brow of a hump or sharp bend; there may be a large boulder, hole or steep

Inspect difficult terrain on foot before trying to drive across it.

An oil tanker near Kazuran, Iran – the result of not keeping a good look-out ahead, in this case for underground water tunnels.

Have a marshaller to direct you on sections where you cannot see the problems from the driving seat.

drop into a river bed beyond it.

All difficult sections should be inspected on foot first – this can save you a lot of hard work getting unstuck later. If you are not sure of being able to see the route or obstacles clearly from the driving seat, get a passenger to stand in a safe place where he or she can see the problem clearly and direct you. Arrange a clear system of hand signals with the person beforehand; vocal directions can be drowned by engine noise. Only have one person delegated as a marshaller – more than one can create confusion!

DEALING WITH DIFFERENT CONDITIONS AND SURFACES

Apart from soft sand, most situations where four-wheel drive is needed also require low range, which gives better traction, torque and control. They will normally also require you to stop and inspect the route on foot first, so you can engage low range before starting off again.

On soft sand it is useful to be able to engage low range on the move. On some vehicles this requires plenty of practice in double declutching, and the ensuing confidence in being able to do this smoothly will usually save you from getting stuck. For most situations first gear low range is too low, and you might spin the wheels; use second or third gear, except over large rocks.

On any soft or loose surface pick a route that keeps the vehicle as level as possible, laterally. Wherever there is more weight on one side of the vehicle than the other, upper wheels can lose traction or lower wheels dig in.

When going downhill on a loose surface it is essential to use four-wheel drive and low range with engine braking. Second gear is usually best; first gear is too low, increasing the chance of the vehicle skidding as the engine braking is too high. Use first gear on vehicles with automatic gearboxes, or vehicles with relatively high gears in low range and if the incline is very steep. With permanent four-wheel drive systems remember to engage the lock before entering difficult situations.

If you have been in four-wheel drive on a hard surface, when you change back into two-wheel drive, or with permanent four-wheel drive systems, unlock the centre differential lock. You might find this change and the steering difficult, and if you have manual freewheeling hubs you will not be able to release them. (With permanent four-wheel drive systems the warning light will remain on.) This is due to 'wind-up' between the axles. If you are lightly loaded, you can free this 'wind-up' by driving backwards for about 10 yards (9 m) while swinging the steering wheel from side to side. If, on the other hand, you are heavily loaded, you will have to free it by jacking up one front wheel clear off the ground. Keep well clear of the wheel while doing this – it will turn viciously as it frees up.

Make use of the rhythm of the suspension, touch the brakes lightly as you approach the crest of a hump, and release them as you pass over it; this will stop you from flying. When you come to a sharp dip or rut, cross it at an angle so that only one wheel at a time drops into it. On level ground steer the wheels towards and over the terrain's high points to maintain maximum ground clearance. If you cannot avoid a large or sharp boulder, drive the wheels on one side directly over it, rather than trying to straddle it.

Do not drive on the outside edge of tracks with a steep drop – they are often undermined by water and collapse under the weight. If you have to travel along deep ruts, try to straddle one of the ruts rather than being in both with your transmission dragging the ground in the centre. Cross narrow river beds or ditches at an angle so that you do not get stuck in a dip at 90°, with no room left for manoeuvre.

When on sand, watch out for any changes in colour. If the surface you are driving on is firm and the surface colour remains the same, the going is likely to be the same. If, however, there is a change in colour, you should be prepared for possible softer sand. Moving sand dunes and dry river beds produce the most difficult soft sand. Keep an eye on previous vehicle tracks, as they will give you an indication of trouble spots that you might be able to avoid.

Sometimes you might have to engineer a route, putting stones or sand ladders across drainage ditches or weak bridges, chipping away high corners, or levering aside large boulders. If you have to rebuild a track or fill in a hole completely, do so from above, rolling boulders down instead of wasting energy lifting them from below. Where possible bind them together by mixing with tree branches or brushwood.

If a rock suddenly appears and you cannot stop in time, hit it square on with a tyre, which is more resilient and more easily repaired or replaced than the rest

Do not drive near the edge – it often breaks away under the weight! North-west Pakistan.

Where necessary engineer a route to make it easier to proceed.

of the vehicle. To traverse large boulders, use low-range first gear and crawl over, using the engine for both drive and braking. Avoid slipping the clutch or touching the brakes – you will lose control.

On loose surfaces, do not change gear while going up or downhill – you could lose traction. To remain in control always change to a lower gear before you reach the problem. Always be prepared to stop quickly on the top of a steep hill or sand dune, as the way down the other side may be at a completely different angle. Descend steep hills in low-range four-wheel drive second gear (first gear on vehicles whose low range is not very low), using the engine as a brake. Do not tackle steep hills diagonally; if you lose traction and slip sideways, you may turn over or roll to the bottom. Only cross slopes laterally if it is absolutely necessary. If you must do so, take the least possible angle, make any turns quickly and, if you start tipping over, turn down the slope quickly.

Stuck!

No driver or vehicle is invincible – we all at some time get stuck or have to recover others that are in our way. I once spent 24 hours getting a Unimog out of a Southern Sudan bog and almost as long clearing a Bedford truck whose driver had tried to drive off a ferry against a river bank, in two-wheel drive!

The most important consideration is to admit defeat early. The sooner you admit defeat, the less badly you will be stuck and therefore the easier the recovery will be. Ninety per cent of stuck vehicles are caused by driver error, and a large percentage of driver error is caused by driver fatigue.

A few hours on an off-road fun course is very different from a long day's driving on difficult terrain in the Third World. Apart from low evening sun making it difficult to observe clearly changing ground levels, when you are tired you make poor judgements and are more likely to take short cuts, such as not checking a difficult situation on foot first. Off-road, stop early before you get too tired. Only drive at night in an emergency.

Having become stuck – in a desert it may be for the 20th time that day! – stay calm and think out the recovery. If things look really bad, set up camp clear of the route before it gets dark.

Self-recovery

Apart from mechanical failure or what would be best termed an accident, there are three main reasons for being stuck:

- excessively slippery ground, where one or more wheels spin, although the vehicle itself is not grounded

- being sunk deep enough into soft ground or ruts that the vehicle is grounded, and there is not enough weight on the wheels for them to gain traction

- having one or more wheels clear of the ground, where the terrain being crossed exceeds the limits of the vehicle's axle articulation.

First get out and inspect the situation, unload any passengers and have them push. If the vehicle itself is not grounded, cross-axle differential locks, limited slip axle differentials or electronic traction control are all likely to get you out. If you do not have these aids and you are not too badly stuck, first try using a higher gear with gentle accelerator pressure. If this fails try reverse in low range. If *this* fails try reverse in high range.

If *all* these fail or you were badly stuck anyway, you will have to get down to manual labour. It will be tempting to do as little as possible, but this is usually self defeating and when you try to move the vehicle it may get into a worse situation, requiring more work. Do things properly first time.

There will be one or more answers to each problem, but basically you will have to do one or more of the following:

- dig away the terrain under the vehicle, where it is grounded – this can be difficult as the weight of the vehicle is falling on the digging implements. If the terrain is suitable and relatively level, it may be easier to jack the vehicle up and pack suitable objects under the wheels than to dig out the area under the vehicle where it is grounded. If you are grounded on rock, this will be the only way.

- build up the terrain under the wheels without traction, using

Mud problems on the 'road' to Jam, Afghanistan. The wheels must be cleared and traction aids, such as stones, built up under them.

stones, logs, brushwood, perforated plate, sand ladders or sand channels.

- physically move the vehicle sideways on to terrain where the wheels can achieve traction.

DIRT ROADS (PISTES)

Dirt roads only require two-wheel drive or, with full-time four-wheel drive vehicles, the centre differential locked out. Tyres should be at correct pressures.

Be careful about driving at speed in short-wheelbase vehicles, especially when cornering, braking, or swerving to avoid an obstruction or pothole. They can easily go out of control.

Watch out for stones thrown up by other vehicles (and in some countries small children) that can break your windscreen. Do not overtake when you cannot see through the dust of the vehicle ahead – there may be something coming the other way. Use the horn to warn vehicles that you are about to overtake.

Avoid driving at night; potholes, culverts, broken-down trucks, bullock carts, camels and people are difficult to see and many trucks drive at speed without lights, then blind you with full beam when they spot you. In some countries there are unlit chains and logs across the roads at night as checkpoints.

Bull dust

Bull dust occurs when normally wet areas dry out. It is very light and hangs in the wind, obscuring vision. If you are travelling in the same direction as the wind you might have to keep stopping to let the dust clear, so that you can see your way ahead.

If you cannot see to overtake, drop back, clear of the other vehicle's dust, and wait until the track changes direction so that the wind blows the dust to one side, thus providing clear vision. On dirt roads, culverts do not always extend to the full width of the road, so watch out for these when overtaking.

Summary

- Check that the vehicle is prepared for off-road use.
- Get your mind into gear.
- Note the position of your vehicle's lowest points.
- Scout ahead.
- Drive at a speed where you can stop within the limits of your vision.
- Inspect difficult sections on foot first and engage four-wheel drive if necessary.
- Be gentle with all driving movements.
- Do not drive on the outside edge of tracks with drops.
- On sand look out for changes in surface colour.

Avoid driving at night . . .

A Land Rover driving in bull dust in the Dasht de Laili Desert ('Desert of Green'!), Afghanistan.

- Previous vehicle tracks will indicate trouble spots.

- Where necessary engineer the route first.

- Avoid changing gear on loose surfaces or while ascending, descending or traversing slopes – change to the correct low gear beforehand.

- Use engine braking downhill.

- Only cross slopes laterally if absolutely necessary.

- Do not use four-wheel drive or locked-in centre differentials on firm surfaces, except on slopes.

- Be extra careful with short-wheelbase vehicles.

- Do not overtake if you cannot see clearly past the vehicle ahead.

- Avoid driving at night off-road.

Corrugations

Corrugations are parallel ridges and troughs across dirt tracks caused by the return spring rates of heavy vehicle traffic. The distance between each ridge and the depth of each trough will depend on the most common vehicles using the road, usually heavy trucks. In really bad conditions they can be 10 inches (254 mm) deep and continue for hundreds of miles. To both the vehicle and its occupants they give an effect similar to sitting on a pneumatic drill.

Heavy vehicles have no choice but to travel slowly, while lightweight vehicles can often 'iron out' the bumps by finding the right harmonic speed to skim over the top of the ruts. This is usually 30-40 mph (48-65 kph) – any faster can be dangerous. Going fast over corrugations increases tyre temperatures, causing more punctures. Softly sprung vehicles can go faster more comfortably, but often blow tyres or turn over.

The area of tyre in contact with the ground surface at any time is minimal, so any use of the brakes should be light 'cadence' or ABS braking, and any turns of the steering wheel should be gentle. Short-wheelbase vehicles are very unstable on corrugations and may spin and turn over.

You may be unable to find a comfortable harmonic speed within the realm of safety; then the only sensible answer is to travel at reasonable speed, make regular stops to ease your growing frustration, and be extra vigilant for punctures.

Radial tyres will give a more comfortable ride, but do not lower the tyre pressures – there are usually sharp stones around and soft tyres run hotter.

One is often tempted to try travelling beside the corrugations, but usually thousands of other vehicles have tried that before and given up – hence the corrugations. So take it steady and be patient.

Corrugations will soon find any weaknesses in the suspension and the insulation on your electrical cables. Electrical shorts causing vehicle fires are common, so be prepared. A battery isolator can be indispensable.

It is not unknown for coil springs to move in their seating and leaf spring leaves to break, so inspect all springs regularly. Shock absorber life is also severely reduced. Where sand is involved, always use four-wheel drive with

Shorting electrical cables on badly corrugated roads can cause vehicle fires, as in this instance in Algeria.

any centre differential locked in on corrugations.

Some books recommend the use of four-wheel drive on firm corrugated tracks; their reasoning is that the shock load reversals on half-shafts, as the wheels bounce from one ridge to another, are extreme and can be halved by spreading the load in four-wheel drive. This is, however, not necessarily true with a loaded long-wheelbase vehicle, where the load on the front wheels may be considerably less than that on the rear wheels, and most of these vehicles have much stronger differentials and half-shafts on the rear axle than on the front.

If your vehicle does not have constant velocity joints on the front wheels, if you use four-wheel drive you may damage the joints when going fast enough to iron out the bumps, and their vibration may contribute to steering problems. If you have part-time four-wheel drive on a loaded long-wheelbase vehicle, you may be better off in two-wheel drive, and if you have permanent four-wheel drive leave the centre differential locked out, unless you are on corrugations on sand.

Summary

- Be extra vigilant and drive slowly in short-wheelbase vehicles.
- Try to find the right harmonic speed, so long as it is not so fast as to be dangerous, otherwise be patient, drive slowly and make regular rest stops.
- Regularly check springs and shock absorbers and be prepared for electrical shorts and punctures.
- Do not use four-wheel drive or locked-in permanent four-wheel drive on firm corrugations.

RUTS AND GULLIES

On narrow tracks ruts along the direction of the route become common after vehicles have gone through when the ground is soft. On hills they become the channel for water run-off and after heavy rain may become scoured out to form deep 'V'-shaped gullies.

If the track is wide enough for you to be able to avoid having your wheels in the ruts, do so, straddling them instead. If the ruts are not avoidable, there will be a good chance that the lowest parts under your vehicle may ground or hit stones. Travel at a sensible speed, keeping a good look-out for obstacles. Where these occur, stop and either remove them or fill in the ruts with stones, dry earth or brushwood, so that you can clear the problem.

Use low-range second gear (first gear on vehicles whose low ratio is not that low), with any centre differential locked in, and have some-one ahead of you to give directions. There will be occasions when you cannot see the difficult parts over the bonnet and will not have any feel of which way your front wheels are pointing. In difficult situations only the driver should be in the vehicle.

If you do not have someone with you to use as a marshaller, inspect short distances on foot first, then drive with your head out of the driver's window, observing the front wheel. However, be careful of bushes and tree branches flicking into your face – acacia thorns are bad enough, but razor-sharp palm leaves are worse!

If you keep grounding the differentials on the high ground between ruts, drain plugs that are not recessed may come undone and drop out, so check regularly for this; you may lose the oil, with subsequent seizure.

Another major problem in ruts is that you will not be able to steer. Even in four-wheel drive, turning the steering wheel will have little effect on the vehicle's direction of travel and you may unwittingly drive along with the wheels pointing to one side, though in mud you cannot feel this, especially with power steering. Check regularly out of the driver's window to be sure that the front wheels are pointing straight ahead; otherwise, if they find a position where traction is available, or the side of the rut is broken away, the vehicle may suddenly veer off the track, with possible dangerous consequences.

You may have to drive with the wheels on one side of the vehicle in a rut and those on the other side on higher ground. In this situation the tyre side walls in the rut are at extra risk of damage from

Deep ruts with little ground clearance.

sharp rocks and stones, so be vigilant.

Stuck fast

If you are stuck in ruts on firm ground, try rocking out by quickly shifting from first to reverse gear, but do not try this on sand or mud – you will only dig in deeper. If you cannot rock out, jack up the offending wheel and fill the rut with stones, brushwood or logs. A high-lift jack makes this much easier and can also be used to shunt the vehicle sideways out of the rut.

Be especially careful to avoid the wheels on one side from slipping down deep 'V' gullies. At worst the vehicle can overturn, or it can come to rest with the side of the vehicle trapped against the side of the gully.

Summary

- If the terrain is difficult, inspect on foot first and if possible have a marshaller to give you directions.

- Use four-wheel drive with any centre differential locked in.

- Where possible, straddle the ruts.

- Where necessary, fill in the ruts first.

- When in ruts keep an eye on the direction of the front wheels.

- Check the differential drain plugs regularly.

RAMPS, RIDGES AND DITCHES

Ramps, ridges and ditches should be approached at an angle that allows one wheel at a time to cross the obstacle, where possible keeping the other three wheels under traction. Small ones may be crossed at right angles, but there will be unnecessary shock loads on the vehicle. Where necessary, have a marshaller to give you directions. Larger ones should be crossed in

In this deep gully the vehicle is actually leaning on its side, but still has traction. No damage occurred.

four-wheel drive, with any centre differential locked in. Crossing at an angle the vehicle will cross with a rolling motion, but with less shock loads, unless the ditch is too deep or the ramp or ridge too high. Where this is so, ditches can be bridged with supported perforated plate or sand ladders, or filled in with logs or stones. Make sure that you remove these afterwards, as they will cause the ditch to cease

Crossing a ditch using 'waffles'.

draining the soil and cause local flooding. If it is permitted, ridges can be lowered by removing top soil. Otherwise ramps may be made to and from them with stones, perforated plate or sand ladders.

The main problem with ramps, ridges and ditches is the chance of using up all your axle articulation, or grounding the chassis and finishing up high centred, with diagonally opposing wheels in the air, spinning. The better the vehicle's axle articulation, ramp break-over, approach and departure angles, the more difficult the obstacle that can be crossed. Over short distances, momentum may get you across, though possibly with some damage.

If you have cross-axle differential locks, these should be engaged before crossing. Limited slip differentials and electronic traction control will think the problem out for themselves. Once stuck, a spinning wheel that has drum brakes can be locked on for short distances with the brake adjuster cam.

In theory, when wheels are spinning with open axles 'cadence' braking should not have any affect, but occasionally it does work by stopping the wheel from spinning and you have nothing to lose by trying it. If you have torque-biasing differentials, 'cadence' braking often does work.

If stuck, it is easier to build up the terrain under spinning wheels than to dig away the terrain with the weight of the vehicle on it.

Summary

- Cross diagonally, with a marshaller to give you directions.

- Use four-wheel drive with any centre differential locked in.

- If necessary, fill or bridge a ditch and cut away or make a ramp up to ridges.

INCLINES

Traversing slopes

You will feel uneasy traversing slopes, and this will be your best protection. Even on safe, firm ground and wearing competition seat belts, it can be difficult to use all the controls.

The chances of actually turning over are increased by a high load, especially on a roof rack, which raises the centre of gravity. High loads can of course be unloaded and any loads on or inside the vehicle should be lashed down so they cannot move.

The most likely causes of turning over are slipping sideways and the wheels on the lower side dropping into a hole, or the wheels on the upper side of the vehicle rising over a hump, rock, tree root or tree stump. In both situations, if you are moving fast, the rebound of the springs increases the chance of turning over, especially if the shock absorbers are worn.

The chances of slipping down the slope are increased by wheelspin, wide tyres and, while moving, the action of limited slip or automatic locking axle differentials. Wheelspin leaves little vehicle weight on that wheel, while wide tyres mean less vehicle weight per unit area on each wheel, a disadvantage on loose or slippery slopes. Limited slip or automatic locking axle differentials on loose or slippery slopes cause fish-tailing slides, from which the vehicle may not be able to recover on the down-the-slope movement.

Cross-axle differential locks give even traction, but where too much of the vehicle weight is on the wheels on the lower side of the vehicle, these may scoop out soil from underneath, thus increasing the angle of tilt.

Inspect the slope first, noting any rocks, humps, tree roots, tree stumps or holes to be avoided. If necessary have someone ahead of the vehicle to give you clear hand signals that will enable you to avoid obstacles you cannot see. In difficult situations, passengers should get out and walk, and if the driver's side is up the slope, you can put your head out of the window to observe which way the wheels are pointing, but you will usually be too uncomfortable to do this if you are on the down slope side.

Use four-wheel drive with any centre differential locked in, low-range second or third gear, and travel slowly. Do not attempt to change gear or make any harsh movements of the accelerator that might cause the wheels to spin. If you have to stop, use engine braking as much as possible. If you have to brake and do not have ABS, use gentle 'cadence' braking.

Do not lock in any cross-axle differential locks unless you are actually stuck, and if you do have to use them only lock in the rear differential, never the front, or you will not be able to steer the vehicle.

If the vehicle begins to slip down the hill, or begins to tip over, turn the steering wheel quickly down the slope and blip the accelerator. Once pointing straight down the slope, continue down on engine braking to (hopefully) level ground. The centrifugal force of the quick turn, helped by the blip of the accelerator, will help to keep the vehicle upright until a straight, downhill position is achieved.

It is quite likely, especially with a long-wheelbase vehicle or one more heavily loaded at the rear, that the rear end will slide round more than 45°. In this situation it is more sensible to treat the problem as a failed ascent than trying to turn round. Engage reverse gear and back straight down the slope under engine braking, as explained under the following section on failed ascent of steep inclines.

You will see pictures in books of vehicles traversing slopes with the passengers on the down slope side, supporting the vehicle against it possibly turning over. If any one of them ever stopped to think, they would realise how dangerous and ineffective this practice is. If the vehicle began to slide downhill or tip, they would not be able to stop it doing so. They are highly

Using the 'trapeze' system on the up slope side to help keep the vehicle upright.

likely to slip on loose ground, or trip over rocks, tree roots or tree stumps while trying to avoid the vehicle, and could well end up being hit by the sliding vehicle, or trapped under it if it overturned.

A safer option is to have the doors open on the up slope side, with some passengers having their feet on the vehicle's floor or side steps and their hands holding on to the tops of the doors or roof rack if fitted. This is an approximation of the 'trapeze' system used by racing yachtsmen on yachts. If the vehicle does slip badly or begin to tip over, they can easily jump clear, with little chance of personal injury and no chance of being trapped under the overturned vehicle.

Summary

- Inspect on foot first.
- Use four-wheel drive with any centre differential locked in.
- If necessary, unload high loads, and lash all loads down.
- Travel slowly and avoid any obstacles than can raise an upper wheel, or lower a lower wheel.
- Avoid wheelspin.
- Be careful over the unnecessary use of axle differential locks, and

fish-tailing from limited slip or automatic locking differentials.

- If necessary have a marshaller to give you directions, and unload any passengers.
- If the vehicle begins to slip downhill or tip over, turn quickly down the slope, blip the accelerator and use engine braking straight down the slope.
- Never have anyone outside the vehicle on the down slope side.

Ascending steep inclines

In theory most four-wheel drive vehicles have the ability to climb a 1 in 1 slope (ie 45°) in low-range first gear, but there is rarely enough grip to achieve this other than on a dry paved road.

If the slope is really difficult, again first survey the route on foot. Beyond the top of the slope the descent may be at a different angle and may be steep enough to require a different gear. Note whether you can avoid any stones, tree stumps, tree roots or potholes.

Go straight up the slope. If you take it at an angle, one wheel hitting a bump could turn the vehicle over and any wheelspin or total loss of traction, could cause the vehicle to slide sideways down the slope, possibly turning over.

Use four-wheel drive with any centre differential locked in. If the slope is short you could also lock in any rear axle differential lock. Only lock in a front axle differential if absolutely necessary – you will not have steering. If the surface is hard and dry you can crawl up in low-range first gear, but be careful on the accelerator so as not to spin the wheels.

For most situations low-range second gear will be best (first gear on vehicles whose low range is not that low). If there is room, take a bit of a run at it to gain momentum. Do not try to change gear on the slope. If you appear to be losing momentum, but the wheels are not slipping, press gently on the accelerator.

When ascending steep inclines there is more weight on the rear wheels and less weight on the front, so you have less traction and steering on the front. If you are obviously losing grip, swing the steering wheel a gentle quarter of a turn from side to side; the tyres' side and shoulder treads can often increase the grip.

As you approach the top, lift off the accelerator – you do not want to fly at the top. If you do so the front wheels will be off the ground with no traction or steering and an incorrect landing could turn the vehicle over. Off-road most slopes will require a change of direction at the crest, before descending.

Recovery if you fail

As already recommended, it is wise to admit failure early. When the wheels are spinning without grip, there is a high chance that the vehicle will slip sideways on to the slope. This will make it difficult to straighten up to reverse straight down the slope and the vehicle may slide down sideways and possibly overturn.

Once turned slightly across a slope, the lowest wheels will have more weight on them and may scoop out soft ground beneath, lowering them still further, with an increased chance

Despite using cross-axle differential locks front and rear, the wheels spin without grip and the vehicle starts to slew sideways on to the slope.

of the vehicle turning over.

If you fail on the ascent, it is essential to go back down in a straight line, using engine braking in reverse. Hold the vehicle on the brakes, make a quick change into reverse and gently ease off the clutch and brakes. Do not make any attempt to turn round or descend at an angle to the slope. In reverse you also lose the 'caster' action on the front wheels, so they will tend to turn to full lock. Hold the steering wheel firmly so that the wheels do not go out of a straight line. This is easiest to do using one hand on the top centre of the steering wheel.

Do not use any handbrake while actually descending in reverse. Even two notches can cause the vehicle to slew to one side or spin. If you must brake, use 'cadence', braking if you do not have ABS.

If the engine has stalled, hold the vehicle on the foot brake and engage low-range reverse gear, start the engine and let out the clutch, easing the pressure on the foot brake. Do not allow the engine to bump start, as you may skid and slew out of line as the vehicle starts rolling backwards.

Reverse gear may be too low, so be prepared to press down the accelerator gently if too much engine braking causes the wheels

to skid when gravity causes the vehicle to move faster than the wheels.

When you reach level ground, the low-gear engine braking should slow you down. If you have to use the brakes, use 'cadence' braking if you do not have ABS. Remember that drum brakes are less efficient in reverse.

If you have an automatic gearbox, with your foot on the foot brake select 'N' or 'P', if necessary re-start the engine, engage 'R' then slowly release the foot brake and drive straight back down the slope. Be prepared to press the accelerator gently if the wheels begin to skid. With an automatic gearbox there may not be enough engine braking. If this is so, apply your left foot to the foot brake and use the accelerator to keep the wheels moving.

Summary

- Inspect on foot first.

- Use low-range four-wheel drive, with any centre differential locked in.

- Avoid obstacles and wheelspin, and do not change gear.

- If losing grip, swing the steering wheel gently from side to side.

- Be prepared to stop at the top.

- Admit failure early, stop, engage reverse gear and reverse straight back down the slope, using engine braking, holding the front wheels straight; do not attempt to turn round.

- Do not use the handbrake; if braking is necessary use ABS if fitted, or 'cadence' braking if not.

Descending steep inclines

Warning: Before you descend a steep slope make sure that you can get out at the bottom of it and check that the vehicle is still in gear in both the main gearbox and the transfer box. A steep descent looks much more frightening than the same angle of ascent.

Once again inspect the terrain for problems on foot first. Aim to drive straight down the slope using engine braking. Do not touch the clutch, but be prepared to press the accelerator gently if the vehicle starts slipping because gravity is causing the vehicle to travel faster than the wheels under engine braking. If you have to brake, use 'cadence' braking if you do not have ABS brakes.

In descending there is more weight on the front wheels and less weight on the rear wheels, so the rear wheels are most likely to skid and slide to one side. If you begin to slide sideways try gently pressing the accelerator. You may regain steering if the slope is not too steep and you have a clear run out at the bottom of the slope, while depressing the clutch may regain the steering, as it does on snow and ice.

Low-range second gear is usually the gear of choice (first gear on those vehicles whose low range is not that low), with any centre differential locked in. On short, really steep sections you might use first gear, but normally this is too low and you will have to press the accelerator gently to allow the wheels to keep up with the vehicle. Never try to change gear or use the handbrake down steep slopes.

If you have an automatic gearbox you should use low-range first gear and make sure that it is locked in. You will have less retardation than with a manual gearbox and even with the very latest 'all singing, all dancing' all-electronic controlled vehicles, automatic gearboxes have been known to decide to change up in this situation! Where you do not have enough engine braking with an automatic gearbox, use your left foot on the brakes and your right foot on the accelerator, with enough engine speed to keep the wheels moving.

If the steep descent is on a sand dune, too much engine braking can cause the vehicle to nose into the sand. You may have to use third or fourth gear, low range, on a manual gearbox, second or third gear, low range, on an automatic gearbox, but you may not be able to lock these in.

If the slope is dangerous, with no room to manoeuvre, lower the vehicle on a winch or puller.

Summary

- If necessary, inspect on foot first, making sure that you can get out at the bottom.

- Use four-wheel drive low-range gear, with any centre differential locked in.

- Check that the vehicle is in gear in both the main gearbox and the transfer box.

- Descend the slope using engine braking – do not use the handbrake or change gear on the slope. If you must brake use ABS or 'cadence' braking.

Beaches

Sandy beaches are usually firm enough for a vehicle between high

A Toyota Landcruiser driving along a firm area of beach; here on the Red Sea shore of Yemen the beach is the only road from Hocha to Mocha.

tide mark and 4 yards (4 m) from the sea itself, where there is likely to be an undertow. Beware of the incoming tide, which is often faster than you envisaged and can cut you off from your point of exit. Where there are large puddles or streaming water on a sea beach, beware of quicksand and *keep off.*

Damp sand

Damp sand, after rain perhaps, is easier to drive on, and in many instances flowers bloom overnight as the roots of the plants soak up water and expand, binding the sand together more. This is fine on a one-way trip, but if you have to return the same way later, when the sand has dried out, it could be more difficult.

Firm sand

There are some deserts with large areas of relatively flat firm sand, on which you can travel quite fast in

Also in Yemen, this Landcruiser is driving up a dune – sand is firmer when wet after rain.

high range. If your vehicle does not have constant velocity joints on the front wheels, you should only travel fast in two-wheel drive, and if you have a centre differential lock, it should be locked out.

Soft sand

The key to soft sand is four-wheel drive, with any centre differential locked in, flotation and steady momentum. Any abrupt changes in speed or direction can break through the firmer surface crust, putting the wheels into the softer sand below.

Use as high a gear as possible so that you do not induce wheelspin. Low-range third, fourth and fifth gear will give you a range of speed without the problem of changing down into low range quickly.

If you do not have special sand tyres, speed up gently as you approach a soft section and try to maintain an even speed and a straight line as you cross it. If you find yourself sticking, press down gently on the accelerator. If you have to change down, you must do so smoothly to avoid wheelspin.

In large soft sand areas use flotation tyres, reduced tyre pressure and drive slowly. Never use aggressive tread tyres on sand.

Do not travel in other vehicle's tracks – the crust has already been broken and your vehicle's low points will be that much lower and therefore nearer to sticking. Keeping your eye on other people's tracks will warn you of soft sections, but do not follow them for navigation – they may be 50 years old.

In general, flat sand with pebbles or grass on its surface, or obvious windblown corrugations, will support a vehicle. If in doubt walk the section first. Stamp your feet – if you get a firm footprint, it should support your vehicle; if you get a vague oval, it is too soft. If the soft section is short, you can make a track with sand ladders, but if it is long, low tyre pressures and low-range four-wheel drive will be required.

Do not travel in other people's tracks – here several tracks approach a village near Timbuktu, Mali.

Here in the Algerian desert firm sand plus pebbles will support a vehicle easily. Use high-range two-wheel drive with any centre differential unlocked.

Elsewhere in the desert there is soft sand with sharp stones – here use low range, low speed and normal tyre pressures.

The worst situation is that of sharp volcanic rocks on soft sand. You cannot get up speed and these rocks cut up soft tyres. Low range, low speed and normal tyre pressures will have to be used here, digging out when you get stuck.

Dry river beds can be very soft and difficult to get out of. Drift sand will always be soft. To stop voluntarily on soft sand, find a place on top of a rise, preferably pointing downhill, and roll to a stop instead of using the brakes and breaking the crust.

Many vehicles have too much weight on the rear wheels when loaded, and these wheels often break through the surface crust and dig in, leaving the front wheels spinning uselessly on the surface. A couple of passengers sitting on the bonnet can help for short bad sections, but you must not overload the front continuously or you will damage the front axle.

In the late afternoon, when the sun is low, it is difficult to spot sudden changes in dune strata and many accidents occur with vehicles flying off the end of steep drops; do not travel at this time of day.

Most deserts freeze overnight in the winter months, making the surface crust much firmer. Even if they do not freeze there is always some dew in the surface crust, making it firmest around dawn, so this is the time to tackle the softest sections, especially sand dunes.

Local drivers often travel at night, but unless you know the route very well this will be too dangerous. Start at dawn, then camp around mid-afternoon, before the light gets too difficult and the sand is at its softest. Vehicles in convoy should keep well apart. Having plenty of time to see that the vehicle in front is bogged down gives the following vehicle time to avoid that section, find another way and help with recovery.

Sand dunes

Sand dunes require proper high-flotation sand tyres. You require

In low sun at the end of the day it is easy to fly off the end of a dune. Difficult dunes such as these are best crossed at dawn.

speed to get up a dune, but you must be able to stop on top, for there may be a steep drop on the other side and it may be at a different angle. When descending a steep dune face, use low-range first gear and drive straight down, applying some accelerator to control any slipping and retain steering control.

If the sand is very soft there may be a tendency for the vehicle to nose in. Over a short distance press down on the accelerator, but over a longer distance use low-range third or fourth gear with a manual gearbox, low-range second or third gear with an automatic gearbox, with your left foot on the brake and enough accelerator

Areas of small dunes are best driven round. The firmest sand will be on the up-wind side of them.

to keep the wheels moving.

Dunes are best climbed where the angle is least, so known regular routes, in opposing directions, are often many miles apart to make use of the easiest angles.

Treat dune climbing as any steep ascent. Using low-range four-wheel drive with any centre differential locked in, take a run at the dune to gain momentum, if necessary swinging the steering wheel from side to side to gain extra grip, and remember that the sand will be firmest at dawn.

Areas of small, closely packed dunes are best driven around, as the sand will invariably be soft. Large dunes are spaced out enough to allow driving between them, taking advantage of the firmer areas. In general the sand will be firmest where the up-wind side of the dunes meet the valley floor, so in large dune areas when travelling longitudinally, stay as high up the side of the dunes as possible. Then if you feel your vehicle begin to stick you can gain momentum by aiming downhill and trying again. The bottom of the well between the dunes usually has the softest sand.

On difficult sections only have the driver in the vehicle, and do not play around unnecessarily on sand dunes if you can go around them. There is a big difference between playing around with an empty vehicle near to home and life-threatening situations of turning a loaded vehicle over in a large desert.

Tyre pressures

Only a small percentage of desert sand is really soft, so you are best to use tyres at normal pressures so that you can travel at a comfortable speed on the firm sections and make full use of speed where you have room on soft sections – only lower pressures in an emergency. The best answer is a properly designed tyre for the surface.

Radial tyres are preferable for use in sand. Always check with your tyre manufacturer, but a

On mixed ground use normal tyre pressures, and stop where the sand is firm. This is the Northern Teneré Desert of Niger.

rough guide for radials is that if you drop to 75% of correct pressure for off-road use, you should not exceed 30 mph (48 kph), and for a real emergency dropping to 40% of correct pressure, you should not exceed 12 mph (19 kph). Exceeding these speeds at low pressure can break up the tyres. If you fit wider tyres than the manufacturer recommends, for extremely soft sand use, only drive at low speeds to avoid transmission damage.

Many local vehicles fit balloon tyres on the rear axle, where most of the weight is concentrated, and normal tyres on the front axle. This is fine in two-wheel drive, but should not be used in four-wheel drive unless the sand is very soft. The extra problems of 'wind-up' can cause serious damage.

In wide open sand seas like the Northern Teneré, in the Sahara and some areas of the Arabian 'Empty Quarter', you can often spend hours at a comfortable 40 mph (65 kph) or more. You must, however, make an extra effort to keep wide awake to problems ahead, because to hit a rock, rut or

Lower the tyre pressure only where the sand is soft and does not contain stones.

fly off the end of a hump or sand dune at that speed can wreck the vehicle and kill its occupants.

Summary

- Be extra wary of sand and water together.

- Firm sand can be crossed in high-range two-wheel drive, or with any centre differential locked out.

- The key to soft sand is flotation and steady momentum in low-range four-wheel drive, with any centre differential locked in and using as high a gear as possible.

- Never use aggressive tread tyres, and do not travel in existing tracks or follow them for navigation.

- Sand is firmest at dawn.

- Do not drive in the late afternoon.

- Sand dunes require proper sand tyres at reduced pressures. Tackle them where the angle is least and at dawn.

- Only use reduced tyre pressure when absolutely necessary, and return to the correct pressure as soon as possible.

Recovery from sand

Once you are stuck in sand, do not spin the wheels or try to rock out, as you will only go in deeper and may damage the transmission. First off-load the passengers and, with them pushing, try to reverse out in low range.

The torque on the propeller shafts tends to tilt the front and rear axles in opposite directions relative to the chassis, so if you have not dug in too deeply, when you engage reverse you tend to tilt the axles in the opposite direction, to the direction involved when you got stuck, thus getting traction on the wheels that lost it before. Cross-axle differential locks, electronic traction control or a drum brake locked on a spinning wheel may help here. If you stopped

soon enough in the first instance, this technique will get you out. Although axle differential locks or electronic traction control may help, they may not be helpful in trying to go forward because the wheels may not have any traction.

If the vehicle remains stuck, the only answer is to start digging or jacking up and using sand ladders. It is tempting to do only half of the digging required, but this usually fails and you finish up working twice as hard in the end.

Self recovery with a winch is not easy, as deserts do not abound with trees and burying the spare wheel or a stake deep enough to act as an anchor is harder than digging the vehicle out. A second vehicle on firm ground with a winch or tow rope can help, but you will have to dig out the stuck

vehicle first. So get down to it and either dig it out or jack it up enough to get sand ladders under the wheels.

Reconnoitre the area and decide whether the vehicle must come out forwards or backwards. Dig the sand clear of all points that are touching it, dig the wheels clear, then dig a sloping ramp from all wheels to the surface in the intended direction of travel. Lay down sand ladders, channels or perforated plates in the ramp, to the rear wheels only if things are not too bad, to all four wheels if things are worse. Push the ends of the ladders beneath the wheels as far as possible so that they do not shoot out. If possible, jack up the wheels and place sand ladders under them.

If you are using sand ladders as

Always dig a ramp from the deepest part of the wheel to the surface before inserting perforated plates or sand ladders in the direction of intended travel. Clear away any sand from under the differentials and mark the position of the sand ladders with an upright shovel so that they can be found if they are buried as the vehicle moves on. Only the driver should be in the vehicle – the rest push.

opposed to perforated plates, mark their position in the sand with upright shovels; they often disappear in use and can be hard to find later. Then, with only the driver in the vehicle and all passengers pushing, the vehicle should come out using low-range four-wheel drive.

If the passengers are very fit, they can dig up the sand ladders quickly and keep placing them under the wheels of the moving vehicle. Sometimes, when a ladder is not properly under a rear wheel when a vehicle first mounts it, it can tip up and damage a body panel or exhaust pipe, so an agile person has to keep a foot on the free end to keep it down. Remember to move *quickly* once things are safe, or you will get run over!

New sand ladder designs that are articulated in the centre and lightweight sand channels that tie together in three short sections correct this problem. Do not tie the ladders to the rear of the vehicle in the hope of towing them; they will cause you to bog down again.

Driving the vehicle out backwards is usually the shortest way to reach firm ground, but you will still have to get across or around the bad section. Once out, the driver should not stop again until reaching firm ground, so the passengers may have a long, hot walk carrying the sand ladders and shovels. They may wish to have water bottles with them. With a large convoy a ramp of several ladders can be made up on bad sections and all hands should help.

If the vehicle continues to stick every time it clears the sand ladders, either the terrain is impossible or the vehicle is too heavily loaded. You may have to unload and try ferrying loads a little at a time.

One vehicle travelling alone should carry four perforated plates, four sand ladders or four sets of sand channels, but vehicles in convoy need only carry two each, as they can help each other.

The occupants of vehicles not stuck should take sand ladders back to help those that are. This is the Teneré Desert again.

Heavier vehicles should carry perforated plates.

Summary

- Admit defeat early, do not spin the wheels or try to rock out, and first try to reverse out.

- If this fails, dig the vehicle out and use sand ladders or perforated plates.

- If another vehicle is on firm ground it can tow you out, if you have first dug the stuck vehicle clear. It will usually be easier to get the stuck vehicle out backwards.

- Once clear, the vehicle should not stop to pick up passengers until it reaches firm ground.

Salt flats (sebkhas and chotts)

These are crusts of dried salt-mud covering soft, bottomless salt-mud underneath; there will usually be signs of dried white salt on the surface. They are like quicksand – you sink quickly, and if you cannot be towed out quickly it can be permanent! In areas known for their salt flats, stick rigidly to the known track, preferably convoy with other four-wheel drive vehicles, and have winches or very long tow ropes ready for quick use.

If you are unlucky enough to hit a salt flat, try to drive back to firm ground in a wide arc. *Do not stop and try to reverse!*

Sandstorms

If you have to sit out a sandstorm, turn the rear of the vehicle to face the wind and cover the windscreen and, if possible, all other windows to stop them becoming etched by sand. Many sandstorms are only knee high; you can see to navigate, but you cannot see rocks, ramps, ditches, etc, and can easily hit one. It is best to sit bad sandstorms out.

Momentum in four-wheel drive is also the key to getting through mud, but there are likely to be more unseen problems beneath mud than beneath sand. If mud is not too deep the wheels might find traction on firm ground below, so if there are existing tracks and they are not deep enough to ground your transmission in the centre, such tracks are worth using. Otherwise, slog through in as high a gear as possible, as you would with sand, avoiding any sudden changes of speed or direction.

If the mud is heavy with clay,

Even small sandstorms can etch windscreens.

even ultra-aggressive-tread tyres will soon clog up, so unless you are using exaggerated self-cleaning mud tyres, such as dumper truck tyres, tractor tyres or terra tyres, you will gain by fitting snow chains.

Axle differential locks and electronic traction control are very useful in mud.

Where ruts are too deep and there is not another route, fill them in with dry soil, rocks, stones or brushwood. A corrugated crossing, using sticks, logs or stones positioned at right angles to the rut, is very effective, and the same system can be used on a larger scale across boggy ground.

If you lose traction in ruts, swing the steering wheel gently a quarter of a turn from side to side;

the lugs on the sides of the tyres may then obtain some grip. Correct skids by turning the steering wheel in the direction to which the vehicle is skidding – do not touch the brakes. On level ground it helps if you declutch, and uphill it helps if you gently press the accelerator.

Sheer momentum is usually the only way to climb steep, muddy inclines. Snow chains on the rear wheels or all four wheels are effective, but if these fail, or in extreme conditions, you will have to resort to a winch or puller. Muddy areas are likely to be near trees, one area where a winch is useful.

When descending steep muddy inclines there is a high chance of skidding, so use low-range second gear, engine braking in four-wheel drive with any centre differential lock locked in. With automatic transmission use first gear plus left foot braking, and use the accelerator to keep the wheels moving. Whichever transmission you have, press the accelerator gently when correcting a skid; if you have to touch the brakes use 'cadence' braking unless you have ABS brakes.

If snow chains are used, they must either be on the rear wheels or all four wheels, never on the front wheels only. If you have a limited slip or automatic locking rear differential, only use chains on all four wheels.

If you have lost traction, but the vehicle itself is not grounded, cross-axle differential locks or locked-up drum brakes on spinning wheels can help, as can light application of the handbrake, if it is on the drum brakes, but not transmission brakes. 'Heeling' and 'toeing' (not easy in boots!), or left foot braking if you have automatic transmission, are other alternatives to stop wheels spinning.

If you stick badly, digging out can be heavy work. For deep mud, radial tyres are preferable and can be used effectively at low pressure if there are no sharp stones or tree stumps. If the mud is not deep, cross-ply tyres at full pressure will be more effective, and are

Tyres can cut through mud to find traction on firmer ground below.

less prone to side wall damage.

It is best to jack up the vehicle and fill in the holes under the wheels with stones, logs or brushwood. A high-lift jack makes this easier, but be careful of any jack slipping. If there is a lot of water, dig a channel to drain it away. Perforated plate, placed upside down, that is rough side up, can be useful to give more grip to the wheels in mud, but sand ladders become slippery.

When you get back on the paved road, clear as much mud as possible from the wheels and propeller shafts, as the mud can put them out of balance and cause damage. Then drive steadily for several miles to clear the tyre treads, or you could skid. Think about other road users – try not to leave large lumps of mud on the road. Where permissible, drive on a grass verge for 110 yards (100 m) first to clean the tyres.

Rocks and tree stumps should be traversed in low-range first gear, with any centre differential locked. Keep your foot off the brake and clutch pedals. If you get the centre of the vehicle grounded (high centred), it is easier to jack up one side of the vehicle and build up the ground under the wheels than to dig away the ground under the vehicle while the vehicle's weight is on it. If you expect to travel a lot in mud or bog that does not contain sharp stones, there are special low-ground-pressure terra tyres, designed for this purpose.

If you are grounded in ruts and cannot go forwards or backwards, use the shunting technique described under high-lift jacks; you may have to unload the vehicle first.

Summary

- Steady momentum in four-wheel drive, with any centre differential locked and using as high a gear as possible, is the answer to mud.

- Use existing tracks if they are not deep.

- All-terrain tyres are not that

good in mud. Proper mud tyres, or normal tyres fitted with snow chains, are best.

- Where possible, fill in deep ruts.

- If you lose traction, try swinging the wheel from side to side, but admit defeat early as it will then be easier to dig out.

- Once stuck it is easier to jack up wheels and put traction aids underneath them than to dig out soil with the weight of the vehicle on it.

SNOW AND ICE

To start with you should have at least 50% antifreeze in your cooling system.

Snow is the most deceptive surface – it does not necessarily conform to the shape of the terrain it covers. If there is a track or road, stay in the middle of it where possible to avoid ditches on the side. Drive slowly in four-wheel drive, using as high a gear as possible to avoid wheelspin. If you have permanent four-wheel drive, lock in the centre differential. Try to avoid touching the brakes, accelerating hard or making sharp steering movements. Do everything gently.

Studded snow tyres on all four wheels are good for icy on-road driving, but for deep snow and off-road driving snow chains are better.

If you start to skid, do not touch the brakes – depress the clutch, then, with all four wheels rolling free, you will regain steering.

In deep snow, lowering tyre pressures for flotation can be useful, but if the snow is not deep normal tyre pressures will help the tyres to cut through to the ground below where they will find more traction.

Extra-slippery surfaces can be found where there is water run-off, traffic compaction, shadow areas, for example below bridges, trees, cliffs and high buildings, or in river beds and gorges, and during cold weather following a thaw, rain or sleet and in wide-open areas off-road, where wind polishing occurs.

For on-road driving, there are advantages to being first on the road after a snowfall; it helps if you know the route well, or if the road is clearly marked. The snow will give its best traction to your wheels at this time, and although there may be natural ice in some places, there will not be any caused by the wheel pressure of

The author repairing snow chains at 11,000 feet, a regular problem at this altitude off-road.

preceding vehicles, and you will have more room to pick the best route.

> **Warning:** Check with the vehicle manufacturer the recommended snow chains and regularly check that the chains are taut. The wrong chains, or those incorrectly fitted or loose, can cut brake pipes. This is most important on the front wheels of vehicles with good axle articulation. On the front you may also have to adjust the steering stop so that the chains do not rub against leaf springs or the chassis.

Try to avoid using the brakes; use the engine for braking in four-wheel drive. If you have to brake, use 'cadence' braking (several short pumps) to avoid the wheels locking. Do not do this if you have ABS braking.

Avoid existing tracks unless they are shallow. Downhill use a low gear in four-wheel drive. If you drive into a drift you will have to dig out and it is easiest to come out backwards. Lengths of old floor carpet can be useful as a mat under the wheels to give some grip if you do not have chains.

Carry warm clothing, a good sleeping bag and high-energy carbohydrate survival rations in case you get stuck and have a long wait for help. Also carry shovels and tow ropes.

If the vehicle is not already carrying any load, an extra couple of hundredweight (100 kg) directly over the rear axle will help your tyres to get more grip. Chains are good on sheet ice if you go slowly, but use only the strongest heavyweight chains. Having to keep repairing broken chains in freezing conditions is not a pleasant experience! Braking distances become considerably longer, even with chains fitted.

Although you will have better traction and steering than normal vehicles, you will not have any more control when braking, other than from larger tyres, unless you have fitted chains. Once other vehicles have been on the roads, their compressed tracks will be more slippery. If there is room, make fresh tracks of your own, otherwise take extra care and leave plenty of space for other vehicles going out of control, particularly up or down hills and on bends. Remember that paved roads have a camber that you or other vehicles may slide down; there is a tendency for heavier vehicles, including four-wheel drive vehicles, to do this.

If you are stuck with the vehicle's wheels spinning but not actually grounded, and you do not have cross-axle differential locks or electronic traction control, try locking up any drum brakes on spinning wheels with the adjuster cam, or gently applying the hand brake if this is on the rear drums, then try to drive on. Alternatively try 'heeling and toeing' or, with automatic transmission, have your left foot lightly on the brake pedal as you try to drive off.

Subsequent snowfalls will cover any existing dangerous ice, so even more care is required.

Summary

- Only fit snow chains to all four wheels.

- Inspect difficult areas on foot first.

- Drive slowly in four-wheel drive, with any centre differential locked in, using as high a gear as possible.

- On tracks, stay away from the edge.

- Avoid harsh use of steering, brakes and accelerator.

- If you have to brake, use 'cadence' braking if you do not have ABS.

- Remember that braking distances will increase, so leave room for other vehicles.

- Avoid existing tracks where possible.

- Carry warm clothing, a sleeping bag, survival rations, recovery aids, and have some weight over the rear axle.

Snowdrifts

Snowdrifts give no indication of what they cover. The high ground clearance of most four-wheel drive vehicles is an advantage, but it also means that if you blast in and get stuck, you will probably have got in further and have that much more difficulty getting out again!

Inspect the snow drift on foot first. You should be able to push your way through a short drift, about one vehicle's length, but beyond this, if the snow is above the bottom of the bumper, you probably will not get through without digging a route.

Although your vehicle will often be capable of continuing, your way may be blocked by other vehicles that are stuck. You should have shovels, a long tow rope and possibly a winch to get them out. Hopefully they will then return the way they came, leaving you free to continue. Unfortunately, not every driver that I have rescued has had that good sense!

If you connect two tow ropes, use knots or interlink them through a spliced eye. Never join tow ropes with a shackle; if either rope breaks, the shackle will become a lethal projectile. A double sheet bend knot has some chance of being undone afterwards, but do not use it for snatch (KERR) recovery.

Stuck in snow

If you are forced to stop and await rescue, you will be glad of that sleeping bag and survival rations! Unless you are very close to civilisation it is usually best to stay with the vehicle. If possible, park so as not to obstruct the route. Snow ploughs will push your vehicle clear if they have to, without worrying about damage – opening the route is more important.

Park in gear without the handbrake on – it may freeze up. If possible put a blanket over the engine to keep out wind-blown snow; this may also prevent condensation in the engine and a possible frozen clutch driven plate. Lift the windscreen wiper blades from the glass to stop them freezing to it.

Do not leave your engine running for warmth if you can avoid it. If you fall asleep, drifting snow can help the exhaust gases to suffocate you. If you do have to leave the engine running, regularly clear any snow near to the exhaust pipe outlet and around two doors to prevent suffocation.

If drifting snow gets higher than the vehicle, place a marker on top of it to indicate its location.

Off-road snow

Off-road it is better not to be first. If vehicles have gone through ahead of you, their tracks will show you a possible route and will also make clear where they got stuck.

Off-road driving will be easier at night or in the early morning, when the mud beneath the snow is frozen, so the wheels will not dig in so much.

On relatively flat terrain you should drive in the previous vehicle tracks, apart from where the vehicles have got into trouble. Check anything that looks difficult on foot first. Drifting snow soon covers sharp rocks, ruts or well-worn tracks, ditches, irrigation channels and deep gullies. The meltwater from thawing snow and ice may even be cutting out its own channel below the snow. Be extra vigilant when inspecting on foot. It is very easy to slip into a gully or sharp rocks yourself.

Never drive near to the edge of any track with a drop on one side – you may slide over the edge. If such a track slopes towards the outside edge, and most of them do, you may have to wait until the snow is frozen to its maximum, usually around 0200 hrs, before crossing that section. Do so with only the driver in the vehicle and the driver's door open. Never cross such a section during a thaw.

In general, never traverse an off-road slope that is covered in snow. Where there are sharp inclines, any previous vehicle tracks are likely to become very slippery, if not fully iced up, so where these occur do not drive in them, but make fresh tracks besides them if there is room.

Summary

- Check on foot first.

- Follow other vehicles' tracks.

- Never drive near the edge of a track over a drop. If a track slopes transversely, cross it at around 0200 hrs with only the driver in the vehicle.

Arctic conditions

If you are operating in an area where Arctic conditions are normal, you will want extra charging and battery power, thinner lubricants, special fuels and a heating system for the fuel tanks and fuel lines on diesel vehicles. Most buildings will have outside mains electricity sockets to power vehicle engine heaters, which also use the vehicle's own heater system to transfer some of the heat to the vehicle interior and windows, or else they will have a heated building for parking.

Out in the field, engine and vehicle heaters using independent fuel are cheaper than having the engine running, and depending on the size of the alternator, an engine ticking over may not be able to keep the vehicle's internal heating fan running. These heaters are safe for occupants sleeping in the vehicle.

WATER

Warning: There are some river crossings that should only be attempted if there is absolutely no alternative, particularly for one vehicle alone.

Vehicle preparation

If a turbocharger is fitted, allow it to cool before entering the water. If you cross water regularly and have a catalytic converter fitted, you would be wise to invest in a raised exhaust outlet that can be fitted quickly.

Petrol engines should be sprayed with silicone sealant around the coil, low and high tension leads and distributor, and any holes in the bottom of the distributor (clear these as soon as possible after the crossing). Plastic or rubber gloves, or the bottom half of a plastic drinks bottle over these

A remote axle breather valve.

A remote axle breather valve tube venting high above the engine.

Wading plugs for the clutch bell housing (left) and camshaft drive belt housing (right).

can also help. Silicone sealant is preferable to silicon grease, which can melt and run on to the distributor contacts.

Four-wheel drive vehicles should have poppet valves or breather tubes on the axle breathers, which will keep out water. For the same reason they should not have crankcase breathers below the air inlet system. If stuck in cold water for any length of time, hot axles fitted with poppet valves, and gearboxes will tend to suck water in through oil seals as they cool down, producing a vacuum; the oils will then have to be changed. Likewise, a vehicle stuck in glacier melt water or sea water for more than a couple of hours will need thorough washing and several oil changes to the gearbox, transfer box and engine.

If the axles are fitted with poppet valves instead of remote breathers, you will also have to change the differential and any swivel pin and wheel hub bearing oils, to get rid of salt and silt. To avoid this some vehicles have remote axle breather tubes, venting above the engine, but they should be checked regularly. Poppet valves can easily be converted to this system.

Electrical connections can be permanently damaged by salt water.

Some vehicles have a wading plug that should be screwed into the clutch bell housing, and other vehicles also have a wading plug for the camshaft drive belt housing. On some vehicles these each require different sizes of spanner. These plug the drain holes that ensure any leaking oil does not get

A clutch bell housing drain hole with the wading plug out, and with it fitted.

A camshaft drive belt housing drain hole with the wading plug out, and with one fitted.

and tissues to hand will make life easier if you get stuck.

> **Warning:** Water on beaches, or anywhere with salt and sand together, can be quicksand. Take advice from local inhabitants before crossing.

Before crossing water, stop and inspect it first, if possible by wading through; in cold climates waders are more sensible than wellington boots. Use a shovel or staff to prod for bad sections. Is the bottom solid or moving? Are there any large holes caused by previously stuck vehicles, which must be filled in or avoided? Is there a sensible angle into it and out on the other side? You may flood your engine if the angle in is too steep, and you may not be able to get up the other side if the angle out is too steep. The exit point may also require repairs.

Is the current fast enough to necessitate your aiming upstream to get straight across? How deep is it? Will it come above the exhaust, cooling fan, air intake or vehicle floor? Fast-flowing rivers will be faster and deeper, with more difficult entry and exit where they narrow, so if possible choose a wider place. Moving or stagnant water with an unbroken surface may be deep and is more likely to have a silt bottom into which the vehicle could sink. Moving water with a rippling surface will be shallower, clear of silt and usually denotes a stony bottom, which is better for crossing. If there are dry patches, you can break up your crossing into stages. If the route across has to avoid obstacles, mark it out with stones or sticks according to depth. If the river bed is soft, lower the tyre pressure. Rivers supplied by melting snow or glaciers will be at their lowest level at dawn and highest in the late evening.

Is the entry so steep that you could immediately flood the engine? Difficult or deep water should be crossed in second gear in low-range four-wheel drive

on to the camshaft timing belt or clutch driven plate. They should be removed after wading, not necessarily immediately but within a couple of days.

If the vehicle is regularly used for wading, these plugs can be left in place but taken out weekly to allow any oil to drain out, then put back in place. Some vehicles come with one or more of these plugs permanently fitted, but these should be removed periodically to allow any oil to drain out.

If the water comes above the fan, the fan belt should be disconnected. Not only will this cut down the spray on to the electrics, but it is also essential with nylon or aluminium fan blades that can bend and damage the radiator core. Only remove a fan belt for very short periods, for without it the water pump no longer operates and the engine may be damaged.

If the water comes above the floor, move any articles that could be damaged by it. There is also a possibility of the vehicle floating slightly and therefore losing traction, so have the rear door open but make sure all baggage is well lashed down. If the water reaches above bumper level, fix a waterproof sheet or a couple of large plastic dustbin-size bags across the front of the engine bay. A preattached tow rope or pre-extension of the winch cable, WD40, tools

Inspect the route through a river first! Here in Yemen the vehicle in the foreground is stuck in deep water, while the vehicle behind shows that a better route is possible.

of the water from stalling the engine, while the forward speed should be high enough to create a small bow wave; the waterproof sheet across the front of the vehicle will help to create this. The wave creates a trough behind it, keeping the engine bay and side doors at a lower depth and lessening any spray of water over the engine; if spray comes over the bonnet you are going too fast. Diesel engines are a great advantage in water.

If you only have high-range gears you will have to use low gear and slip the clutch. A fast walking pace is about right for speed, and do not change gear. In deep water you will require first gear to push

(first gear on vehicles whose low range is not that low), and with any centre differential locked. It is worth adjusting the engine tickover speed to a higher setting to minimise the chance of the engine stalling; this is essential if you have a catalytic converter.

Keep the engine speed high to keep enough pressure in the exhaust to stop the back pressure

Rivers supplied by melting glaciers will be lowest at dawn. This is the Lowari Pass to Chitral in north-west Pakistan.

With a plastic sheet across the engine bay, a vehicle crosses deep water demonstrating a good bow wave with a trough behind.

Too steep an approach into water can result in the water entering important parts of the engine.

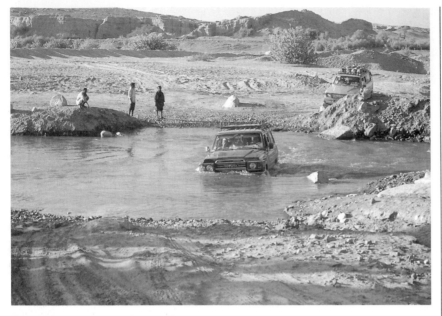

Only cross a river one vehicle at a time.

the wave of water ahead of the vehicle. If you stall in the water, remove the sparking plugs or injectors and try driving out in low-range bottom gear on the starter motor; this works over short distances.

On easy crossings, keep the brakes dry by keeping the left foot lightly on the brake pedal. Once out of any water, dry out the brakes by driving for a few minutes in this manner. Disc brakes are self-cleaning, but drum brakes fill up with water and sediment, so should be cleaned regularly. Do not forget the transmission brake on some vehicles.

A vehicle exiting a river will pour water on to the bank, making it slippery for following vehicles.

If the water is moving really fast and the crossing is more than three vehicle lengths wide, it may only be sensible to cross with a winch and a good anchor point. If fast-moving water is above bumper height, keep the vehicle at 45° to the direction of flow; the full force of water at 90° to the body will force the vehicle downstream.

If a petrol engine stalls or misfires, a quick spray with WD40 over all the electrics may get it firing again; if not, dry out all ignition cable contacts, the rotor arm and contacts inside the distributor cap, if you do not have electronic ignition.

If there is more than one vehicle, only cross one at a time. On a deep crossing the rear of a vehicle will take in a surprising amount of water, which will pour out on exiting the far bank, making this slippery and more difficult for following vehicles. If possible, other vehicles should try alternative exits.

Summary

- Allow turbochargers to cool down.

- Prepare the vehicle for water crossing.

- Inspect on foot first and mark out any sections to be avoided.

- River sections where moving water has a rippled surface will be better crossing points than where the surface is unbroken. If the river is fed by glacier meltwater it will be lowest around dawn.

- Use four-wheel drive low range with any centre differential locked in, and keep the engine revolutions up, driving a bow wave ahead of the vehicle. If the water comes over the bonnet, you are going too fast.

- A fast walking pace is about right for speed.

- In deep fast-flowing water, keep

the vehicle at 45° to the direction of flow.

River beds and flash floods

In many Third World countries river beds are often the standard route for a vehicle track, as they are the only area with relatively level terrain.

Flash floods in river beds kill thousands of people every year, and at certain times of year they are just as common in desert wadis as in mountainous areas. People brought up in the West do not realise that although they are in a river bed under a cloudless sky, heavy rain hundreds of miles away can cause a flash flood many hours later. Therefore always be prepared and never camp overnight in a river bed, although it may often be the only flat ground around.

Most flash floods are seasonal, but freaks can occur at any time. In the Third World there will often be times when a river bed is the only route and you will have to use it in the rainy season. If you are driving up the river bed you can use your own eyes for possible water, but if you are driving down a river bed you will have to ask a passenger to regularly check the route behind you, as your own attention will be on the awkward terrain ahead.

As you drive along, look out for and make mental notes of any places where you can quickly get up the bank out of the river bed, including steep rocks if necessary; be already in four-wheel drive, and if you find flood water coming down, get up the nearest bank. If there is no possibility of doing this where you are, drive down river quickly to the first available such exit.

In most situations flash floods are not very deep, unless contained in a gorge, but they move fast enough to sweep away fully loaded heavy trucks. The flood is usually over very quickly, less than an hour and rarely more than two hours, then you can usually continue on

Here in Afghanistan the river is the main road. Note that the rippling water indicates a stony bottom.

This road in Yemen goes up a wadi – as you drive along look out for possible exits to high ground in the event of a flash flood.

your way; I usually have a meal while sitting one out. The terrain may become extra difficult and even blocked due to the flood water moving large rocks and tree trunks.

In mountainous areas main routes often travel up and down narrow river beds, which usually contain flowing water. Such river beds will alternate between tricky rocks, soft sand or silt, holes caused by previously stuck vehicles and holes scoured out on bends by flowing water. These obstacles are easily seen in the dry, but will often be difficult to discern when covered by water. Always go slowly, therefore, and as always be prepared to inspect on foot first. A well-used route will have local traffic whose drivers know the route well, so follow them.

Summary

- Be alert for flash floods. Keep an eye out for places where you can get out of the river quickly.

- *Never camp in a river bed.*

Crossing narrow, very fast flowing rivers

I have on occasions had to cross short distances of very fast flowing streams, some of them across main roads, particularly in Pakistan's Karakorum Mountains and Morocco's High Atlas Mountains. Where these are obviously fed by glaciers or snow melt, they will be at their slowest, even dry, around dawn, and fastest in late evening. For short distances you may have to allow for being swept downstream a little by gaining momentum and aiming upstream. Use four-wheel drive with any centre differential locked in. It is not wise to attempt this for more than three vehicle lengths. There must be an easy exit on the far side, long tow ropes should already be attached or easy to hand, and at least one other

A flash flood passing the south sluice of the historic Marib Dam in Yemen. Only attempt crossing fast-flowing rivers at dawn and over short distances.

vehicle should be available as back-up.

Drowned vehicles

If it appears that for any reason the bow wave cannot be maintained in deep water and there is a chance of the water being deep enough to reach the air intake or engine manifold, *switch off before the engine stops* – this is absolutely essential with a diesel engine. Water does not compress, so catastrophic damage can occur to a high-compression engine. You should also isolate the battery so that it cannot create a short circuit causing the starter motor to turn over before the injectors or spark plugs have been removed.

You may then instigate recovery without starting the engine. Make sure that the occupants are safe – otherwise rescue them first! – then tow or winch the vehicle on to safe ground, where it will not obstruct other traffic. Chock the wheels, release the handbrake and put the gearbox and transfer box in neutral. Disconnect the battery, open all doors to drain and air the vehicle, and remove and air the contents and floor covering. If off-road or away from help, set up camp clear of any likely traffic.

Check for water and silt in the engine sump, gearbox, transfer box, swivel pin housings, differentials, air intake, carburettor and turbocharger if fitted. Water is heavier than oil so it will sink to the lowest point unless emulsified with the oil – check by loosening drain plugs. If the oil is milky in appearance it will have been emulsified by moving parts. If this is the case, wait several hours, drain off any free water then drain all the oils into separate containers. If there is any doubt, replace with new oils, otherwise let the emulsified oils stand overnight and drain off any more water before re-using them. As soon as you get back to civilisation drain all the oils, brake fluid, power steering fluid and clutch fluid if present, and replace them with new fluids and re-grease all grease points.

Drain any water in the fuel tank from the drain plug and also drain any water from the fuel filter and sedimenter if fitted. Drain and dry out all electrical components in air, not near an open fire; these include the alternator, starter motor, electric winch motor, lamps and fuses. Inspect and if necessary dry or replace the air filter. Clean and dry all inlet manifolds, to the engine.

A Suzuki drowned as a result of not inspecting the route first.

Dealing with water in petrol engines

Remove the distributor cap and rotor arm, dry the distributor body and distributor cap, and all the leads and connections to the sparking plugs and coil. Clean out the carburettor if fitted.

If the electrics are dry and you have another vehicle as a back-up if your batteries run down, turn the engine over in short bursts with the starter motor.

If the electrics and starter motor are not functional or you do not have back-up, use the starting handle if there is one, otherwise jack up one rear wheel, engage second gear high ratio and turn the wheel.

> Stand well clear of the side of the engine that houses the sparking plug sockets!

Water and possibly oil and fuel will eject from these at a pressure high enough to penetrate the skin or blind. Ideally no one should be on that side of the engine, as the ejected fluids can carry some yards/metres. Continue until there is no sign of water in the cylinders. If there is sediment, it would be wise to strip the engine down.

Refit all components when dry and clean, then run the engine until it is warm, checking for any problems. Stop the engine and recheck fuel filters for water and drain or clean as necessary.

Dealing with water in diesel engines

Remove the injectors, then turn the engine over as directed for petrol engines.

> Stand well clear of the side of the engine that houses the injector ports and any point in line with the injector high-pressure pipe outlets.

If in doubt remove the injector high-pressure pipes and keep well clear of the side of the engine where the injector pump is fitted. Oil and water will be ejected from the injector sockets and fuel from the injector pump or high-pressure pipes at even higher pressures than with a petrol engine. Continue until there is no sign of water in the cylinders.

Do not strip the injectors, but dry them out and clean around the injection ports. Dry, clean and replace all components. Injectors should be fitted with new copper washers. If these are not available, clean up the old washers with emery cloth, heat them until red hot with your cooker flame and drop them red hot into cold water to anneal them.

Start the engine and run it until warm, checking for any problems or fuel leaks. Stop the engine and recheck the fuel filter and sedimenter, if fitted, for water and drain if present. If the alternator is functioning correctly and the battery charged, with the engine running check the operation of all lights, gauges, brakes and clutch, recheck all nuts, bolts and drain plugs that have been worked on, and head for civilisation. At all times be vigilant for the possible shorting out of electrical components, causing a fire.

When you reach civilisation have the vehicle hosed out with clean fresh water and fully serviced, including the injector pump and injectors on diesel engines. If the vehicle drowned in sea water it would be wise to have the complete wiring loom replaced, as you will be continuously plagued by minor electrical problems.

Third World ferries

River and lake ferries that do not have proper jetties should be embarked and disembarked in four-wheel drive to avoid pushing the vessel away from the bank, leaving your vehicle in the water!

Weak bridges

Always inspect local bridges before using them. If there are signs that local vehicles cross the river instead of the bridge, that is the safest way to go. If in doubt and the bridge cannot be avoided, unload the vehicle and cross slowly in four-wheel drive, with only the driver in the vehicle. Crossing at speed may cause extra damage to the bridge.

CONVOY DRIVING

When travelling in convoy, vehicles

Embark and disembark from Third World ferries in four-wheel drive with any centre differential locked. Depicted is a Nile ferry in southern Sudan.

should be well spaced out, so that each has room to manoeuvre, does not travel in another vehicle's dust and has room to stop on firm ground should one or more vehicles get stuck. It is wise to use a system whereby any vehicle that gets stuck or needs help has its headlights switched on to main beam. Flashing headlights are not obvious over long distances to drivers ahead checking their rear mirrors.

This is particularly important in

A suspension bridge near Chalt in northern Pakistan. The road is perched on a slope. Inspect bridges on foot first!

Do not drive in the dust created by other vehicles.
Always keep to the allotted convoy order.

deserts. All drivers should keep an eye out for headlights in their mirrors, as these can usually be seen when the vehicle cannot. As vehicles get further apart a vehicle being watched in the mirror appears to become taller, then disappears altogether; but if it switches on its headlights these can be seen.

If the vehicle ahead is stuck, you will recognise this when you catch up with it. Other vehicles should stop where possible on firm ground and their occupants should go to help, on foot if necessary in soft sand. The rear vehicle in a convoy should have a good mechanic and a good spare wheel and tyre in case of a breakdown.

Drivers should keep to the allotted convoy order to avoid confusion and unnecessary searches. The convoy leader should make stops at regular intervals to check that all is well with the other vehicles.

CHAPTER 4

Towing and winching

TOWING ON-ROAD

Four-wheel drive vehicles are ideal for towing, both on and off the road, as they have a strong chassis, engines with high torque at low speed, strong suspension and four-wheel drive.

For on-road towing the rules are much the same as with a two-wheel drive vehicle, but you have the added advantage of four-wheel engine braking on difficult downhill sections; use a lower gear for engine braking downhill. Brake well in advance and smoothly to allow for the extra weight, and also allow more room and more time to accelerate when overtaking. On hot days the extra weight can make the engine overheat on long climbs; using a lower gear will keep the engine cooler.

Load the trailer carefully, both side to side and front to back, and have the recommended weight on the trailer hitch when loaded – this is very important. Have your vehicle's tow hitch adjusted for height so that the trailer tows level or slightly front end down, not rear end down.

If your vehicle can take it (and it may not be possible on vehicles with designed-in crumple zones and safety air bag triggers), fit a second tow hitch on your front bumper. This will make it easier to park your trailer or caravan in a tight spot, or launch your boat. The front tow hitch should be off-centre to the passenger side, so that the driver can see clearly along the side of the trailer.

The standard 2 inch (50 mm) ball hitch is fine for on-road towing, so long as its recommended laden trailer weight is not exceeded. There are ball hitches made to higher laden weight towing specifications, but the clamp on the trailer coupling head is likely to be the weakest part of the system if the trailer should pitch. Trailers with a gross weight above 7,700 lbs (3,500 kg) should have a ring hitch and fully coupled brakes.

For on road use, trailers must comply with all the necessary regulations regarding lights, brake lights, indicator lights, tyres, depth of tyre tread, etc, as well as not exceeding the recommended laden weight that can be towed by the towing vehicle. Anti-sway stabilisers are useful, particularly with longer trailers such as caravans, where the moment of inertia in any swing is greater.

Short-wheelbase vehicles give more control when towing. The tow hitch is closer to the rear axle of the towing vehicle, giving a smaller turning circle and least pitch and roll, but the vehicle is more likely to be pushed around by the trailer. Some towing vehicles will benefit from fitting stronger rear springs or 'helper' springs.

Before starting off, check that all the trailer's lights, brake lights and indicator lights are working, and the tow hitch and trailer coupling are securely locked. As soon as you are moving on firm ground, check that any overrun trailer brakes are working correctly and evenly.

Harsh braking should be avoided – there will be a tendency for the trailer to swing to one side, possibly jackknifing or even turning the towing vehicle over. When the towing vehicle brakes, the weight of the trailer on the towing hitch increases, causing a decrease of the weight on the vehicle's front wheels, which will therefore have decreased braking and steering efficiency. This is worse on a long-wheelbase vehicle as the hitch is further from the axle. If hard braking is required and you do not have ABS, use 'cadence' braking.

When crossing a hump or hill top, the trailer may also tend to lift and lessen the weight on the vehicle's rear wheels, so always slow down in this situation. It can be useful to lightly touch the brakes when approaching the brow of a hill in a straight line, but do not do so on a bend, or you could jackknife.

Remember that your turning circle is increased, and if you turn too sharply the rear of the towing vehicle may come into contact with the front of the trailer.

Reversing

Reversing a trailer is easier if you have a tow hitch on the front of the vehicle, offset to the passenger side so that you can see clearly down the side of the trailer. Having this tow hitch at bumper/chassis level is not a problem at low speed, unless the trailer is so long that its rear end may touch the ground while being reversed.

Longer trailers are easier to reverse than short ones. Start the operation with the vehicle and the trailer in the same straight line, and make sure that any reversing catch that stops overrun brakes from working, if fitted, is engaged.

Slowly begin to reverse the trailer and turn the vehicle in the opposite direction to that in which you wish the trailer to turn; as the rear of the vehicle turns away from the direction in which the trailer is to travel, the rear of the trailer will turn in the desired direction. Do not continue in this way so far that the vehicles jackknife – once the trailer is moving in the desired direction, reverse the steering on the vehicle and follow the trailer into the turn, straightening it up when you reach the correct direction. Continue with any necessary small changes of direction until the trailer is in the required position.

Be prepared to reverse the vehicle steering again if necessary, and, if you go too far in any one direction, reverse whichever manoeuvre you were making and start again.

Starting with a heavy trailer

If the trailer is very heavy, you may have to start moving in low-range second or third gear and change into high range once you are rolling at a comfortable speed.

If you cannot move because the wheels on one side of the vehicle are on mud or wet grass and those on the other side are on firm ground, and you do not have

electronic traction control, use cross-axle locks if fitted and release them as soon as all the wheels are on firm ground.

If you do not have these aids, try locking up the adjuster cam on the spinning wheel, if it has a drum brake; otherwise, if you have an automatic gearbox try left foot braking as you drive off, or 'heel and toe' braking if you have a manual gearbox.

Summary

- Short-wheelbase vehicles are best for towing.

- Do not exceed the recommended laden weight of the trailer.

- Adjust the rear tow hitch to have the trailer tow level or

slightly front end down, not rear end down.

- Allow extra room for braking and get into the habit of 'cadence' braking if you do not have ABS.

- Accelerate, brake and corner gently, and slow down before the brow of a hill.

- With a heavy trailer you may have to start off in low range, then change up to high range once you are rolling at a comfortable speed.

TOWING OFF-ROAD

For off-road towing there are additional problems to be consid-

This poor tow hitch lowers the departure angle, and the electrical socket is vulnerable off-road.

ered. You have a larger turning circle with a trailer, and long trailers such as caravans will have very poor ground clearance at the front and rear, even if the clearance under the axle is high. Trailers get stuck in sand, slip into ditches, overturn on bad tracks, and make life difficult if you have to turn around in an awkward situation.

Transmission 'wind-up' in four-wheel drive will be less of a problem, as the pitching of the trailer will lift the wheels enough to free it. However, speed must be slow. There will be considerable pitch and roll, with the trailer tending to turn the towing vehicle out of line or over in any overrun situation. Have the towing vehicle's electrical connection socket well protected above or within the chassis. The trailer's suspension will not be as sophisticated as that on the vehicle, and the shock absorbers weak or non existent. This is probably why trailers regularly turn over.

Do not use a ball-type tow hitch for serious off-road travel; the ball coupling is not really strong enough. Never use a ball that is integral with a pin, as the pin may be pulled out of the jaw when the trailer pitches. Use a heavy pin hitch or a NATO hitch with the appropriate eyes on the trailer (see Chapter 2). Tow hitches that are able to revolve will lessen the chance of the trailer turning the towing vehicle over in the event of a lateral roll.

The towing vehicle will be constantly aware of drag, push and lateral roll by the trailer. The chances of jackknifing, especially when going downhill or braking, are considerably increased, and on corrugations the vehicle/trailer combination can become uncontrollable at anything but slow speed.

Never load the trailer to more than 75% of the recommended maximum, and where possible have the same wheels and tyres on the trailer as on the towing vehicle. If this is not possible, ensure that you have spare tyres for the trailer. Lowering the tyre pressure may be

An extremely poor tow hitch – the cable and electrical sockets would be ripped off if used off-road.

necessary on soft ground.

In theory, towing a trailer is an advantage because it spreads the total load over six wheels rather than having it all on the vehicle alone, spread over four wheels. In practice this advantage is soon lost on soft ground, where non-driven trailer wheels push a ridge of sand, soil or mud along in front of them. Both vehicle and trailer components can break up on corrugations and a heavy trailer is very difficult to manhandle on soft

This electrical socket is protected within the chassis power take-off (PTO) hole on a Land Rover 110.

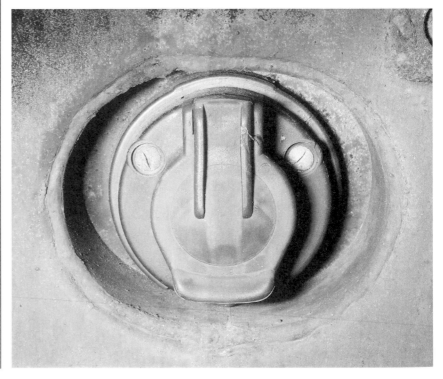

Have the same large tyres on the trailer as on the towing vehicle.

ground, or on any slope, requiring at least two people, preferably three or four. When crossing slopes laterally, trailers tend to slide down, pulling the rear of the vehicle with them.

Wrap the trailer's electrical wiring into a loom and fasten it safely above or within the trailer's chassis, where it cannot snag or catch. Off-road, if you are not on a dirt road or well-used track, disconnect the wiring from the socket on the towing vehicle. This socket is not waterproof except on specialist military vehicles, so disconnect it before wading.

Everything in the trailer must be securely lashed down, with the heaviest items lowest. Open-top trailers should be well covered.

If the trailer is a caravan, cover the front bodywork and window with thick, old carpet to reduce damage from stones and branches thrown up from the towing vehicle's rear wheels. There is no point in leaving the vehicle's rear mud flaps down for extra protection – they are likely to get torn off.

Think twice

If you are considering travelling any distance in really rough terrain, I would advise against towing a trailer. I have seen them turn over themselves, turn the towing vehicle over and bend or break the towing vehicle's rear axle casings. I regularly come across abandoned trailers and have abandoned them myself in the Southern Tenéré Sand Sea on the Agades-Fachi-Bilma route in Niger.

Short-length military trailers on the same high-flotation tyres as the towing vehicle are best, and reduced tyre pressure can be used on soft terrain. Quite apart from the problems mentioned above, with constant bouncing about it is difficult to keep their contents in one piece and recognisable! Very careful packing and padding is required.

Powered trailers, taking power from a vehicle's rear take-off point, are available, particularly ex-military, but they often push the towing vehicle over on turns.

Summary

- Do not use a trailer off-road unless you really have to.

- If you must use a trailer, only use a pin or NATO hitch, not a ball hitch.

- Lash everything securely down and, where possible, have the same wheels and tyres on both the vehicle and the trailer.

- Cover the front of caravans to protect them from damage by thrown-up stones.

- Avoid powered trailers.

TOWING ANOTHER VEHICLE

'A' frames

Vehicles travelling in convoy will find an 'A' frame towing bracket useful for towing an incapacitated vehicle, so long as its wheels can still revolve freely.

A rigid 'A' frame, which has two anchorage points for the front of the towed vehicle and an eye for the towing vehicle, gives the towing vehicle more control, safer braking and it can do the braking for the towed vehicle.

Towed vehicles that have permanent four-wheel drive

Vehicles that have permanent four-wheel drive can be damaged when towed (dead-engine towing).

Vehicles that have selectable neutral settings should have these selected both on the main gearbox and on the transfer box. With the new Range Rovers you will have to insert a 5 amp fuse in position 11 in the under-seat fuse box.

Vehicles that have a steering lock must have it disengaged. On vehicles fitted with servo-assisted brakes, the servo will not be effective if the engine is not running.

If the vehicle is to be towed with the front wheels suspended clear of the road, the propeller shaft should be disconnected from the rear axle.

TOWED RECOVERY

Ideally you would never go off-road without a second vehicle for

Ideally never go off-road without a second back-up vehicle, though I have to confess to several lone crossings of the Sahara Desert, as seen here.

bumper with its ends outside each longitudinal chassis member. Use a chain, or pad the rope or strap, where it is around the bumper. The bridle should be 3 yards (metres) long, to spread the load evenly without a pinching effect on the chassis.

Do not use the lashing down eyes fitted to the chassis of some vehicles, but replace them with stronger JATE rings; the bridle should be fitted to both JATE rings. Do not put a tow rope around a rear axle – the brake pipes along it could be damaged. As a last resort, you could fix a bridle to leaf spring shackles, using sufficiently large 'D' or bow shackles. In this situation, if the rope breaks there will not be any danger from the shackles.

After towing, any knots in a rope will be difficult, if not impossible, to undo, which is why people unwittingly use shackles to connect ropes. However, do not use shackles to join ropes together – if either rope breaks a shackle will become a lethal flying projectile, aimed at the vehicle to which it is still attached. One way around this is to have large spliced eyes on the rope ends, so that ropes can be fed through themselves. Less secure, but fine except for snatch recovery, is to use a double sheet bend knot to connect ropes.

> **Warning:** No one should be between the vehicles or anywhere near the tow rope during a towed recovery. A breaking tow rope whips violently and can be lethal. It is also possible for an attachment point to fail, producing a lethal projectile. Similarly, only the drivers should be in the vehicles, all other passengers being well clear, one of them acting as marshaller from a safe distance and well to one side, to avoid being in line of any broken hitch or shackle.

back-up, though I have to confess to several lone crossings of the Sahara Desert, various sections of the Arabian 'Empty Quarter' and the Sudan north to south.

When more than one vehicle are travelling together, difficult sections should be crossed one at a time, so that other vehicles remain in a safe position from where they can assist with long tow ropes or winches if required. As mentioned in Chapter 2, all rope or winch attachment rings or hitches must

be strong and securely attached to the vehicle. If the vehicle has a chassis, they should be attached directly to it.

If a towing hitch is fitted, use it, but be aware of the danger of a rope slipping off a ball hitch. If you attach a tow rope to a ball hitch, do not use a shackle or metal-lined eye; as already mentioned, if they slip off they will become lethal projectiles.

If no suitable attachment points are provided, fix a bridle to the

Dig out any obstruction or build up under the wheels of the stuck vehicle. It is usually easier to tow it back out the way it went in, so it can be useful to have a second marshaller in front of the towing vehicle (but to one side to avoid any flying projectiles), who can let that vehicle's driver know what is happening. The driver of the stuck vehicle should check that the front wheels are facing straight ahead and, when moving, should hold the steering wheel firmly to stop them running out of line.

In view of the risk of flying projectiles, it is better for the towing vehicle to face forwards, in other words the two vehicles should be back to back. Both should be in low range, and second gear will be best for the towing vehicle, to minimise the possibility of wheelspin. The towing vehicle should slowly take up the strain and the stuck vehicle should also add drive, once the strain has been taken up. When clear, both vehicles should not stop until the stuck vehicle is well clear of the problem area.

If there are sufficiently strong trees around, one or more snatch blocks can be used to increase the pull on the stuck vehicle. Snatch blocks will also be useful where the towing vehicle cannot get a suitable clear run or angle, and can be attached to a suitable chocked third vehicle or tree; use padding or straps to protect the tree.

In a really bad situation on slippery ground, or if the stuck vehicle is heavier than the towing vehicle, it may be necessary to have two or more vehicles in line, connected by tow ropes, in a carefully co-ordinated tandem tow.

Summary

- Ensure that all attachment points are strong enough and securely fitted to a chassis that is not rusty.

- Do not use shackles to connect ropes together.

- Do not use lashing-down eyes, but replace them with JATE rings.

- Dig out any obstruction, or

Direct pull with one vehicle.

Tandem pull with two vehicles.

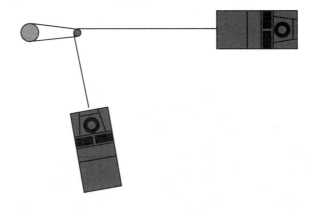

Towing a vehicle up a steep hill, across a river or where the towing vehicle does not have room to tow ahead of the towed vehicle.

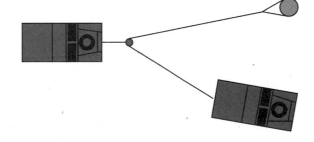

Using a snatch block to give a 2:1 mechanical advantage.

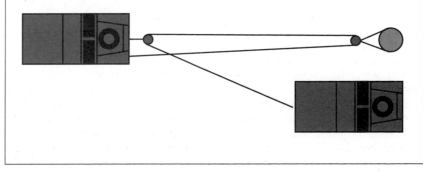

Using two snatch blocks to give a 3:1 mechanical advantage.

build up under the wheels of the stuck vehicle. Then with both vehicles in drive, tow gently out.

KERR (snatch-tow) recovery

This system of recovery is a last resort. It is extremely dangerous, requires special ropes, and all attachments to the vehicles must be in first-class condition, as must be the chassis they are attached to. With this system, breaking attachment points, even parts of the chassis if rusty, become lethal projectiles with enough force to penetrate metal. All passengers and marshallers should be well clear and drivers must realise that both are at potential risk.

Despite this dire warning, many people do regularly accomplish KERR recovery. So long as all attachment points are strong and in good condition and you do not overdo the towing vehicle's speed or rope stretch, it is an acceptable method.

Snatch towing recovery makes use of the elasticity of nylon rope. Do not therefore use chain or inextensible rope as the main rope, or the shock loading is likely to cause structural damage to both vehicles; only use proper KERR rope.

Preferably attach the main rope via bridles to each vehicle (these bridles may be of inextensible material or chain). A safety lanyard to a third strong attachment on the vehicle, such as a tow hitch, is an extra safety factor.

Attach the rope, bridles and safety lanyards and drive the towing vehicle forward until they are just taut; then reverse the towing vehicle back about 2 yards (metres). Lay the main rope out on the ground in a 'snake' formation so that it will pay out cleanly without snagging or knotting, engage low-range second gear on the towing vehicle and accelerate briskly, but not exceeding a fast walking pace.

The tow is ready to start. The KERR rope is laid out in a 'snake' formation, the bridle threaded through the eye of the KERR rope. Do not use a shackle – it could become a projectile if a rope breaks.

The towing vehicle starts off at a brisk walking pace, and the elasticity in the KERR rope pulls the stuck vehicle out.

If the stuck vehicle does not move, do not exceed 2 yards (metres) stretch on the rope. Keep your foot on the brake, as the towing vehicle is pulled back by the stretch in the rope, and release all stretch before anyone goes near to it.

Because of the short distances involved, for safety you would not normally have the stuck vehicle in engine drive; if it suddenly obtained traction it could drive over the rope. You may, however, have to try it as a last resort.

Because you have to release the strain again so quickly, a heavily bogged down vehicle may have to be released by a series of attempts, moving 0.5 yard (metre) each time.

Summary

- Ensure that all attachment points are strong and securely attached.

- Only use proper KERR rope, and for safety attach it via a bridle to two points on each vehicle.

- Accelerate the towing vehicle to a fast walking pace.

- Do not overstretch the rope if the stuck vehicle does not move.

KERR recovery using a hand winch or high-lift jack

When no other vehicle is available, it is possible to employ KERR recovery using a high-lift jack, hand winch or puller.

Engage the handbrake on the stuck vehicle and connect a KERR rope from the vehicle to the high-lift jack, hand winch or puller, and connect the latter to a suitable anchor point. If this is a tree, remember to protect it from damage.

Take up the slack and stretch the rope as much as possible; with a high-lift jack this will only be the length of the rack, but with a hand winch or puller do not exceed 30% for safety. Using this method you will be close to and in line with the rope if it breaks, so put a heavy blanket or tarpaulin over it to minimise any danger.

Drive the vehicle forward, releasing the handbrake at the same time; the energy stored in the rope will help to move the vehicle. You may only manage 0.5 yard (metre) at a time, but repeating this several times may get you out.

Being nylon, KERR ropes have a finite life, shortened by the strain to which they are subjected, abrasion, sand and grit amongst the fibres, and ultraviolet light in direct sunlight. Wash out any grit or sand, thoroughly dry the rope

and store it in a close weave, breathable bag.

WINCHES AND PULLERS AS RECOVERY AIDS

> **Warning:** Immense stresses are involved in winching, so be extra vigilant. Please also respect the environment, tread lightly and use webbing straps to protect live trees.

Vehicle-mounted winches

Vehicle mounted winches are over-rated as recovery aids, being mainly designed to pull loads such as logs or felled trees and launch or retrieve boats.

In any situation the vehicle must be securely anchored, or it will move instead of the intended load, and the pull should be in the correct direction relative to the load. Convenient anchor points are rare, and the vehicle will often be pointing in the wrong direction for the winch to be used effectively.

If you are stuck, the easiest way out is usually backwards. However, most front-mounted winches will not pull in this direction, and

those that can will require extra-long cables.

In most situations, if there is room, towing out with another vehicle will be quicker. In soft sand, digging out and using sand ladders will be quicker and less work than trying to bury the spare wheel deep enough to be effective as an anchor. However, where two or more vehicles are travelling together, where the ground is suitable for ground anchors or there are trees, winches used sensibly with snatch blocks will enable them to traverse extremely difficult terrain.

Most vehicles are no longer designed with winch-fitting in mind, so it is often best to replace the front bumper with an integral heavy-duty bumper that includes a winch mounting. The best designs can be used with high-lift jacks, protect the winch from impact damage, allow easy access to the winch so that you can ensure the cable winds on correctly without damage, and better protect the winch against water ingress during wading up to grill depth.

Winches come in two basic types, as follows.

Capstan winches

Capstan winches have a bollard, usually but not always rotating

A vehicle fitted with a power take-off (PTO)-powered capstan winch.

about a vertical axis. They are driven either mechanically by a power take-off (PTO) from the engine, or hydraulically by an engine-driven hydraulic pump. They can be used continuously for heavy-duty work with the engine at low speed, so long as the engine has an oil cooler fitted.

Capstan winches do not store any rope and have the advantage that any length of rope can be used, so they are useful for rescue operations. Only two or three turns of the rope are around the capstan at any one time, so the pull is constant, and is instantly adjustable by the operator pulling to increase the tension of the rope on the capstan, or by easing the tension to stop the pull. The rope can also be tied off easily to hold a load. Use ropes with little stretch, but not polypropylene, as these are prone to melting if the rope is allowed to slip on the bollard to control the pull.

Capstan winches are not as powerful as drum winches, require two people to operate them safely and the engine must be running. They are not very suitable for self-recovery.

Drum winches

Drum winches have a drum rotating about a horizontal axis with a wire cable of suitable strength stored on and spooled on to the drum. As more cable is wound on to the drum the efficiency of the winch decreases, and most models do not have fine control. They may continue to wind on up to 20 inches (508 mm) of cable after you switch off.

As with capstan winches they should be powered by the engine, either mechanically or hydraulically, for continuous heavy-duty use, where the engine must be running. For intermediate use they can be powered by a vehicle battery, though preferably a separate battery to that used for starting the engine and on a vehicle fitted with a high-output alternator.

An old-type Husky battery-powered drum winch showing good winding.

Electric drum winches are small, lightweight, easy to fit and can be fitted to another four-wheel drive if you change your vehicle. However, the drain on the battery is high and the winch motor will overheat if used for long periods. The engine should be run at a fast tick-over, but in an emergency, even with a drowned vehicle if you are lucky, they can be run for short periods with a dead engine.

Modules that allow remote operation, in some instances by radio control from some distance away, add to operator convenience and safety.

The design of some vehicles, including those with designed-in crumple zones and air bag triggers, requires a low-line winch. However, with these it can be difficult to observe and ensure correct spooling of the cable on the

Remote control is very convenient, together with a little help from the engine.

With this low-line winch it is difficult to observe the correct winding of the cable on to the drum.

drum. They are more susceptible to impact damage from below and more open to the ingress of water and mud, though the top models by Warn and Superwinch have almost eradicated this.

There is a general trend towards winches having integral solenoids built into a bridge over the winch drum. These make installation easier and tidier, but no solenoid is totally waterproof unless fitted into a waterproof box, as on Camel Trophy Vehicles, and the cable cannot be easily observed as it winds on to the drum.

For self-recovery, most vehicles will require a winch with at least 8,000 lbs (3,637 kg) of pull, though 6,000 lbs (2,727 kg) will suffice for a Suzuki. Do not be fooled by advertising pictures of vehicles winching themselves up near vertical gradients! At these angles the battery acid would drain away from most battery plates, the engine oil would drain away from the oil pump and the fuel would drain away from the fuel pick-up pipes! If you have to self-recover up or down a very steep incline, the engine may cut out if the fuel tank is less than half full.

Portable power winches

There are also 'portable' power winches, drum winches powered by the vehicle's battery, and both drum and capstan winches powered by two-stroke petrol

chain-saw engines, which are lighter in weight. These units are designed either to fit on a ball hitch or trailer coupling, or to be connected to the vehicle by a chain.

The main problem with all of these is personal safety and keeping them out of the mud. The operator has to be close to the unit and is therefore vulnerable if anything breaks. This factor is made worse as the units move when they come under tension, and they rarely remain in the correct horizontal or vertical position. The capstan winch is the most portable, due to its light weight, but one feels nervous while feeding a rope on to it while it swings about.

Hand winches

Hand winches are worked by a lever that feeds cable through a gripping jaw. They are small, lightweight, portable and relatively cheap. They can also do anything a power winch can do, but are more versatile, being usable at any angle and able to pull a vehicle backwards or sideways, or right it if it

Hand winches are easy to use.

An old motor cycle tyre will store hand winch cables and stop them scratching the vehicle interior if they bounce about.

has overturned. Moreover they can be used for industrial lifting, including lifting out an engine.

Hand winches do not require a battery or working engine, and are so useful that they are worth carrying as well as a powered winch. If they are overloaded, shear pins will break, but the load will continue to be held. Although they are slow to use, they can be used in forward or reverse, and if there is more than one operator, they are not hard work to use. The cable can be stored in an old motor cycle tyre both to keep it tidy and to prevent it scratching bodywork when carried in the vehicle. The main problem with hand winches is keeping them out of the mud.

There are several sizes and brands, the best known in the UK being 'Tirfor'. However, these use a non-standard 0.323 inch (8.2 mm) cable, whereas 'Brano' units use standard 0.315 inch (8 mm) cables, which are cheaper to replace or to buy longer lengths.

Pullers

Rope pullers are similar to hand winches but use ropes. They do not have so much pull, but their usefulness may be increased by using a snatch block.

In my experience the use of a makeshift Spanish windlass to recover a heavily stuck vehicle is too dangerous. If it breaks, operators are liable to serious injury.

ADDITIONAL ACCESSORIES FOR WINCHING

In addition to the accessories mentioned earlier – woven webbing straps to protect trees, 'choker' chains, 'D' or bow shackles, heavy blanket or coat and one or more snatch blocks – you will also require:

- Heavy industrial gloves to handle cables or capstan winch ropes – cables will always have sharp broken wires somewhere along their length. Pay them out hand over hand.

- Extra-long lengths or cable or rope.

- Chocks for the winching vehicle's wheels, to stop it moving instead of the load.

- Ground anchors when trees are not available as anchor points.

A self-clipping 'choker' chain in use.

Always wear gloves and pay out winch cable hand over hand.

thirds of their length. For heavy recovery several pickets can be used in line, linked by ropes, or several in line at right angles to the direction of pull, with the load spread by a tree trunk or bar across them. Pickets in line should be lashed together from the head of the front picket to ground level on the backing-up picket. In most situations three pickets in line are sufficient.

Buried anchorages – such as a tree trunk or spare wheel buried at right angles to the line of pull.

Flat plate anchors – straight or 'V'-shaped plates with a number of holes through which several 3-foot (1 m) 'T' stakes can be driven.

Picket, flat plate and buried anchors are time-consuming to set up and often require a high-lift jack and a loop of chain to lever them out again. Quicker to use are the following, which are also effective in snow.

These come in several forms:

Augers – 4-foot (1.2 m) stakes with a large screw end that can be screwed into soft ground or bog.

Pickets – 4-foot (1.2 m) wood or preferably angle iron stakes with pointed ends that are driven into the ground for two-

The large screw end of an auger can be screwed into soft ground or bog.

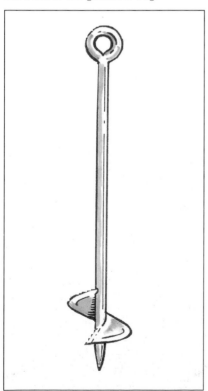

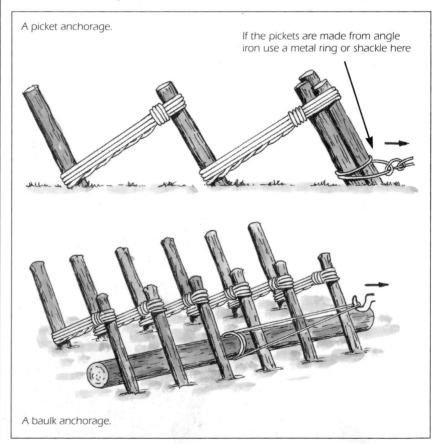

A picket anchorage.

If the pickets are made from angle iron use a metal ring or shackle here

A baulk anchorage.

A triple picket ground anchor.

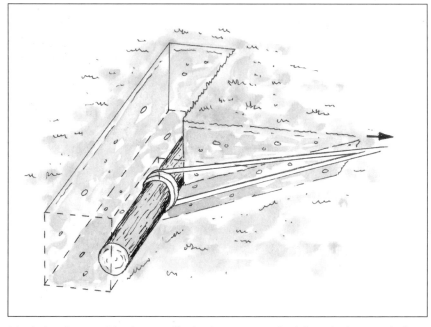

A buried anchorage. A log is more effective than a spare wheel; bury the latter vertically.

A flat plate ground anchor.

Danforth anchors – small boat anchors of the Danforth design that fold up for storage. They are self-burying so long as someone stands on them to begin with as they first bite in.

Dead men – self-burying flat or slightly curved plates with a cable to just below their centre. They originated for chaining out dogs in the Antarctic snow, and were then taken up by mountaineers.

Pull-Pal – a 'high-tech' version of the dead man. An American folding design by Pat Gromillion that is specifically designed for ground anchor use. As with Danforth anchors someone should stand on the plate as it first bites in, until it is firm. Pull-Pals are easy to remove, push them over on their side and they will yank out. A heavy blanket or coat cuts down the speed of flaying cables if anything breaks.

Removing 'T' stakes with a high-lift jack and chain.

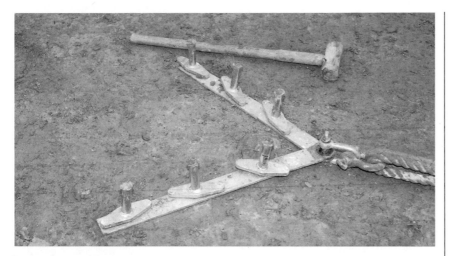

A flat plate 'V'-shaped ground anchor with 'T' stakes.

'Belt and braces' – a triple picket plus flat plate 'V' ground anchor and strap to tow hitch.

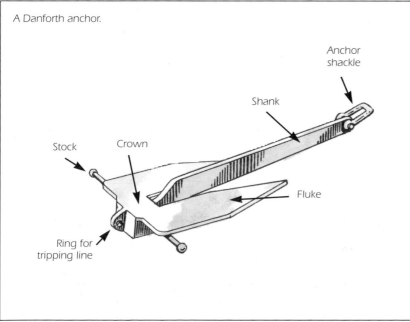

A Danforth anchor.

The Pull-Pal ground anchor.

Place a foot on the Pull-Pal as the strain is taken up and it begins to bite.

Continued strain makes the Pull-Pal bite deeper.

WINCHING

Very few winching situations are straightforward. Inspect the route first and where necessary have a marshaller to direct you.

This is a poor route for winch recovery – the vehicle is leaning on the side of the lowest deep rut.

This is a better route, with the vehicle out of the deepest rut. Use a marshaller to direct, and run the cable over wood on the hump in the track.

There will be many occasions where you will have to use one or more snatch blocks to alter the angle of pull, and others where you will have to winch up a slope but change the direction of pull as you approach the crest. With thought, these situations can all be worked out with snatch blocks, trees, ground anchors and/or more than one vehicle.

There will be times where the change of direction near the crest of a slope, may cause the vehicle to slew round or tip over. A separate hand winch or high-lift jack used as a winch can be positioned to stop this. If you are winching vehicles up or down steep inclines, use multiple ground anchors or,

A winch vehicle secured by ground anchor.

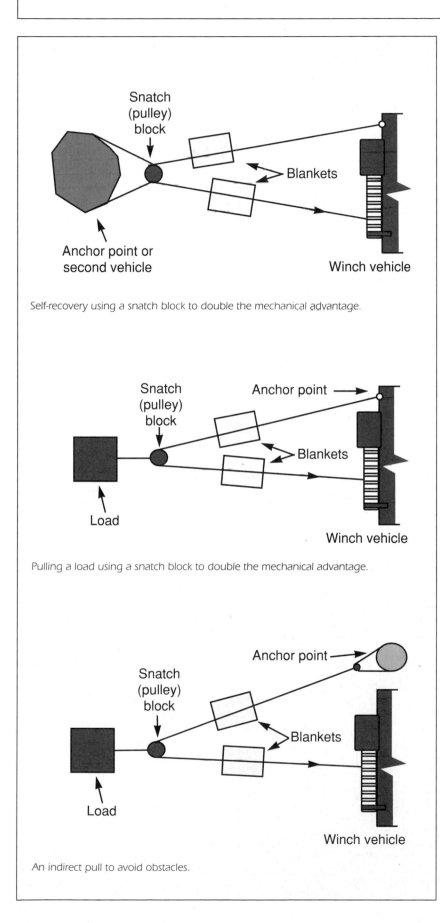

Snatch (pulley) block

Blankets

Anchor point or second vehicle

Winch vehicle

Self-recovery using a snatch block to double the mechanical advantage.

Snatch (pulley) block

Anchor point

Blankets

Load

Winch vehicle

Pulling a load using a snatch block to double the mechanical advantage.

Anchor point

Snatch (pulley) block

Blankets

Load

Winch vehicle

An indirect pull to avoid obstacles.

When the winch vehicle is on near level ground, other vehicles can be winched down very steep inclines.

better still, a ground anchor attached to another vehicle, thus doubling up for extra safety. Where several vehicles are involved, use this system for all but the first vehicle up, or all but the last vehicle down.

Notes on winching

- Winches lower the vehicle's approach angle.

- Check all attachments for strength. Inspect the cable and winch regularly for damage. Always wear gloves to handle the cable and attach it only to safe attachments.

- Keep everyone at a safe distance

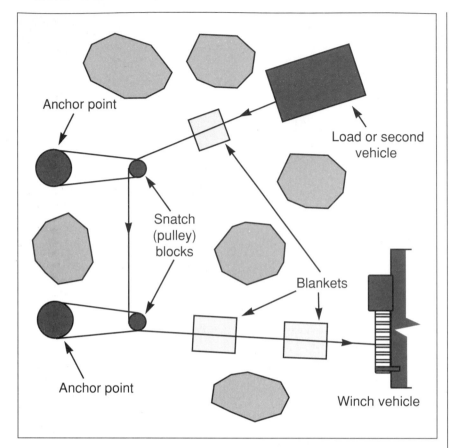

Anchor point

Snatch (pulley) blocks

Anchor point

Load or second vehicle

Blankets

Winch vehicle

Using multiple snatch blocks to avoid obstacles.

the cable does break such weights would become flying projectiles. Blankets, coats, groundsheets or tarpaulins are safer.

• Never step over a cable under tension. Ensure that the electrical winch control cables are kept well clear of the winch cable. If they get caught up in the cable and short out, the winch can become unstoppable unless you isolate the battery.

• Never hook the cable back on itself – use a webbing strap and shackles. Always use shackles to connect the two end loops of webbing straps.

• Do up shackle pins then undo

A Mercedes G Series is gently lowered over the edge.

to the side of the cable and place a heavy blanket or coat over it, halfway along its length, to cut

down damage if anything breaks. I have seen weighted-down sacks used for this, but if

Front-mounted winches lower a vehicle's approach angle – they dig in, then get jammed.

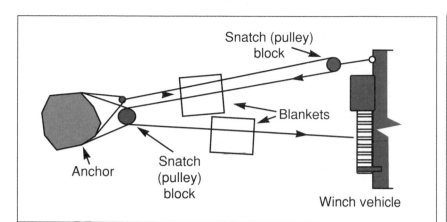

Using multiple snatch blocks to increase the pulling power in self-recovery.

Place blankets, coats or sacks on the winch cable to cut down the velocity if anything breaks.

Never let a winch cable bunch up – it reduces the efficiency and can damage the cable.

Where possible wind straps at least one full turn around the anchor point, especially in order to protect a live tree, and use a bow shackle to connect the ends.

them half a turn – this will make them easier to undo after use. Do up shackle pins tight for long-term use.

• Never engage or disengage the winch clutch when the winch is under load.

• Isolate the winch before putting

Here the strap is higher up the tree to allow the cable to clear the hump.

your hands in or around the fairlead or cable drum.

- Keep hands and fingers clear of the cable and hook when operating the winch.

- Ensure that the cable winds smoothly and evenly on to the drum. If it does not, stop, pay out some cable and start again, guiding it with a gloved hand. A bunched-up cable on one side of the drum must be avoided – it will reduce the efficiency of the winch and easily become damaged.

- When you have finished, unroll the cable, wash it down, particularly if it has been in salt water, and reel it up again accurately.

- Some winch manufacturers supply a 'handsaver' bar to guide the cable hook for the last few feet. This bar has an eye through which it is tempting to thread a finger. Do not do this, as it could get trapped! Hold the bar loosely in the hand or convert it to a 'T' bar.

- If you use a tree as an anchor, use a webbing strap, turned at least once all the way around the tree. This should preferably be at the bottom of the trunk, but may have to be higher if the cable has to clear a hump.

- Snatch blocks are invaluable to double the mechanical advantage, halve the speed for more control, or alter the angle of pull. Several snatch blocks can be used in unison, for further improvements, but they will lower the speed even more.

- Ideally you should not move the winch vehicle while winching, or allow the load to snatch. However, there are

An aerial ropeway – another use for a winch cable.

Using a snatch block to pull at the required angle. Note the weights on the cable.

many occasions during uphill winching when gentle drive to the wheels is a great help.

- Increase engine revolutions to help the battery cope with the load. Give the winch motor a rest to cool down after 10 minutes.

- Never allow the cable to drag over rocks. Over crests run it over a tree branch or plank of wood to stop it cutting in.

- Cables should have machine-swaged fittings. If cable clips are used, the gripping part of the cast clip should be on the 'live' (pulling) side of the cable, and the 'U' bolt that goes through the cast clip should be on the 'dead' side.

- Kinked cables can usually be straightened out by paying them out to a solid anchor and hanging a vehicle down a slope on them for a couple of hours.

A winch cable running over wood to stop it cutting in.

Overland and expeditions

VEHICLE CHOICE

Apart from rare circumstances of expeditions sponsored by a four-wheel drive manufacturer, overlanders and expedition users have to compromise between what they can afford, what can best do the job and whether spares are available en route. Ignoring prices, some vehicles are more useful than others in particular areas.

In 1973 I took eight long-wheelbase Safari Land Rovers into the Hindu Kush and Karakorum Mountains of north-west Pakistan, before the Karakorum Highway was built. In this area of steep mountainsides and regular landslides, the tracks are often built around the smallest available vehicle, thus minimising the work necessary (all done by hand) to keep routes open where possible.

In many places the Land Rovers could not get through – they were either too wide for tracks or bridges, too high to get under rock overhangs or too heavy for the some of the tracks held on to mountainsides by tree trunks! I have since returned several times and made some amazing journeys, mostly following mule tracks, but using small Jeeps.

Research your route thoroughly from at least three separate sources. At least one UK-published four-wheel drive handbook

quotes a well-known all-stone route across the Sahara Desert as being sand. Equally ill-informed writers will unwittingly copy this. The route concerned is the standard route for two-wheel drive vehicles with low ground clearance.

When it comes to worldwide popularity and parts availability, the Land Rover leads, except in the Americas. The most popular four-wheel drive worldwide is now the Toyota Landcruiser, but it does not have such a good parts service as the Land Rover, and because its working life is less, you will not find many old ones

In the Karakorum Mountains, north-west Pakistan – a Jeep on a weak suspension bridge built for smaller traffic.

A Jeep north of Gilgit, Pakistan; the narrow tracks are supported by tree trunks over large drops. Note also the low overhangs.

around that are capable of being cannibalised for parts.

For the Americas no one vehicle stands out. Toyota spares are much more available, but in general in the Americas it would be best to have an American-made vehicle.

Many of the world's militaries use Land Rovers, even in Islamic countries where they were once blacklisted; if you find the right contacts, 'backsheesh' can often find you a spare from a crashed military vehicle, but check the electrics, which could be 24 volts.

Some remote countries use the earliest designs of Jeeps, often put together locally under licence. In these countries small Jeep spares can be the easiest to obtain. Many countries also make Land Rovers under licence, so again spares can be easily found.

For long-distance work most American four-wheel drive vehicles have too low a payload and high fuel consumption. The bigger American four-wheel drive vehicles have the payload, but usually too long a wheelbase, and you would use most of the payload carrying the fuel required.

In many parts of Africa fuel is difficult to find. Overlanders have to use vehicles capable of carrying larger payloads, most of which will be their own fuel. For this use those who can afford them use Mercedes Unimogs, usually ex-military, while those not so well off use ex-military Bedford trucks.

Mercedes Unimogs have exceptional cross-country ability and have step down portal axles, giving higher than normal ground clearance. It is very difficult to get them stuck in sand, though they will stick in mud; their extra ground clearance means that they will have gone that much deeper before sticking, and therefore will be that much harder to recover. Their higher ground clearance also means that they turn over more easily.

Unimog petrol engines are relatively small, so you need to use the gearbox well, but fuel consumption is good. Four-wheel drive can be engaged easily at any speed without double declutching. The chassis is cleverly arranged to give good weight distribution over all four wheels at most angles, but gives a bad ride on corrugations. Mechanically it is overcomplicated – it does not go wrong often, but when it does it is difficult to work on and requires special tools.

Bedford trucks are cheap, simple and in some parts crude. They have good cross-country performance if handled sensibly and slowly, but are too heavy in soft sand. Things go wrong often, but repairs can usually be improvised.

The fuel tank straps break, but the tank can be held with strong rope until repairs can be arranged.

A licence-built Jeep on the road from Chitral to Mastuj in the Hindu Kush Mountains, Pakistan.

The Mercedes Unimog is the best all-round expedition vehicle – if you can afford it.

If you have a 550 engine and a five-speed gearbox, the vehicle will be able to manage some 50 mph (80 kph) plus on the road; it is wise to remove the front propeller shaft before driving at such speeds.

Except in soft sand, diesel-engined Bedfords are economical for their size. With much low-gear and high-altitude work in Afghanistan, I achieved 14 mpg (20 litres/100 km) with a 550 engine powering a full 27-seat bus version, plus camping equipment.

The ideal expedition vehicle, if costs were no problem and all spares have to be carried, would have a payload of about 1 ton, evenly distributed between all four wheels, a short wheelbase (around 100 inches/2,540 mm), forward control, good ground clearance, large wheels for 9.00 in x 16 in (229 mm x 406 mm) tyres, a good power-to-weight ratio and reasonable fuel consumption. The vehicles that most closely fit this specification are the smaller Mercedes Unimogs, the now discontinued Volvo C303 and Land Rover military 1 tonne.

By using several identical vehicles travelling in convoy you can minimise on the weight of spares and tyres to be carried. The idea of using one large vehicle to carry fuel, etc, accompanying several smaller, more agile vehicles does not work. If the heavier vehicle is well bogged down, the smaller vehicles will have difficulty towing it out, and the vast difference in overall journey speed, plus extra spares, causes many problems unless you have a static base camp.

Hard-top vehicles are more difficult for thieves to break into. Taking into account price, availability, spares availability, working life, fuel consumption and resale value, the most common four-wheel drive bought by overlanders and small expeditions is the long-wheelbase hard top or Safari Land Rover.

Australians and Americans complain about the Land Rover's ride, few comforts and small engine, but these people consider a well-graded dirt track to be off-road driving. They have never experienced the corrugations of North and Central Africa and the Middle East. Having spent 28 years bouncing through the roofs of Landcruisers, Chevys, Dodges, Broncos, Pajeros, Suzukis, Troopers and Travelalls, and constantly having to pick up the bits that fall off, I am more than happy to put up with a spartan Land Rover or small Jeep in really difficult country, where they are tough and reliable.

An advantage of Land Rovers is the aluminium alloy body, and the fact that everything bolts on. This means easy repairs in the field, and the inevitable dent can be hammered roughly back into shape and forgotten, with the peace of

Bedford trucks are easily repaired – note the improvised shade.

The Land Rover 101- inch 1 tonne.

Land Rover Series III estates, the most popular expedition vehicles, at the Band-e-Amir Lakes, Afghanistan.

mind that it will not rust. Every vehicle has its faults, and the Land Rover is no exception, but it outperforms all others when the going gets rough.

VEHICLE PREPARATION

When planning a long expedition or overland route in remote areas,

start off with 20% more fuel and water than you calculate will be necessary. This will give you a safety factor to allow for breakdowns, leaking fuel containers, extra fuel used in a bad, soft section, or sitting out a sandstorm. In difficult terrain, using low range, your fuel consumption can double.

When you buy a vehicle, use it for several months before setting off with it on an expedition. This will run in any new parts properly,

and will enable you to sort out any weaknesses and become thoroughly acquainted with the vehicle's handling and maintenance. If you buy a new Land Rover, run it in a wet country before taking it to a hot, dry one. This helps to rust in all the bolts holding the bodywork and roof together and can save you having to tighten up loose ones later, when the vehicle has been bouncing around on rough tracks.

Stone guards are essential for your lights. For sunny countries any shiny parts in your line of vision, for example windscreen wipers, wing mirrors and bonnet or wing steps, should be painted matt black to prevent dangerous reflections. You should also carry new windscreen wiper rubbers for use when you return to a wet climate.

If you intend to sleep in the vehicle, either fit wire mesh anti-thief guards to windows you will need to leave open, or better still fit roof vents protected by a roof rack. Mosquito netting can be fitted to vents or windows with Velcro.

On camper conversions many fittings will not be as strong as the original fittings of the vehicle and will need to be strengthened for rough terrain. Fixed gas piping for cooker units will be dangerous – the connections break up and leak with vibration. Use flexible rubber gas tubing instead. Remember to carry spare tubing and a spare gas regulator.

Some conversions have the gas cylinders fitted under the chassis, where they get plastered by mud and hit by stones. It is better to carry them inside the vehicle (turned off) when travelling, or if necessary on the roof, but well covered against the heat of the sun. Glass-reinforced plastic (fibreglass) roofs and de-mountable campers break up in rough country.

If a spare wheel is carried on the bonnet, supplement the standard bonnet catch with rubber, webbing or spring-loaded catches or straps. Do not carry a spare wheel

Start your expedition with enough extra fuel and water to cover breakdowns.

and can add a few spare wheel nuts as well. If you do carry a complete spare spring, use the same method to bolt it to the chassis, as it will be too heavy for the bumper. If you have coil springs, fit heavy-duty versions and carry a complete spare.

Springs, chassis, steering, bodywork, tyres and exhaust should all be checked and bolts tightened every evening. Check engine oil, tyre pressures and cooling water, and fill the fuel tank, every morning when it is cool. Keep a close eye on electrical wires – corrugations can wear through the insulation, then a shorting lead can flatten the battery or start a fire.

Check all transmission oils, steering box oils and brake and clutch fluid regularly. Keep breather vents on gearboxes and axles clear (they tend to become blocked with dust stuck to oil, so oil seals blow due to the pressure). Also check the breather hole on

on the back door for rough country work, or the hinges will soon break; use the bonnet, roof or, where possible, a swing-away wheel carrier. Spare wheels slung underneath the floor cause problems off-road when you are stuck. The spare wheel can also be useful when jacking up the vehicle, and if it is under the floor it will be very difficult and sometimes dangerous to get out.

For accurate navigation you should know how correct your odometer is for the wheels and tyres you have fitted, since larger tyres will have a longer rolling circumference.

Rebuilt ex-military vehicles are not a good buy for Third World use. Buy the vehicle and do all the work yourself so you know that it was done properly and can understand how to fix it if it goes wrong later. A small vice fitted to a strong bumper or convenient chassis member can aid many repairs. Loctite thread sealer will stop nuts vibrating loose.

If you have leaf springs there is no need to carry the weight of a complete spare. If you carry two main leaves, one for each size of spring (front and rear), you should be able to achieve satisfactory repairs. Fit stronger springs or an extra main leaf, but you must keep

an eye on spring bushes, shackles and spring hangers. The spare leaves can be bolted to the front bumper or rear chassis, using a complete set of shackles and shackle pins, then you have all these spares

Vehicle components require constant checking over rough terrain.

the fuel tank cap; this also blocks with dust, causing fuel starvation.

Fuel and oil

Have a mesh filter in the fuel filler; this may be slow, but it will save you a lot of time cleaning out blocked fuel lines. Start each day with a full tank and always carry spare fuel to avoid being stranded in a bad place at night. If you have a diesel engine, a pair of oil-resistant gloves can make refuelling less messy, and a clear plastic hose will enable you to avoid getting any in your mouth when siphoning. When siphoning fuel from roof cans, there is no need to use mouth suction for each can; start the first can by mouth and, when it empties, put your finger over the bottom of the tube while it is still full, transfer the top end to another full can and the siphon will continue.

Do not let the level of fuel in the tank fall too low, for there will always be some sediment and water to block your fuel lines. With a diesel a low tank could allow air into the system, and you would then have to bleed it.

In some countries fuel stations do not sell oil, or only sell poor-grade non-additive oils, and you have to go to the bazaar to buy good oil. When you buy any, make sure that it is the correct type for your engine or transmission. Check the container's seal to make sure that it has not been filled with something cheaper – never buy oil that is not in a sealed container.

Many gearboxes and axles require extreme pressure (EP) gear oil. This is usually green in colour and smells strongly of sulphur. When you buy this type make sure that 'EP' is written on the container. Non-EP oils are the same colour but do not have the strong smell. It is very important to use the correct oil or you will damage your transmission. Some gearboxes use normal engine oil, so EP oil should not be used where a non-EP oil is specified.

EP oil is hard to find in remote places, so always carry some with you. If you need automatic transmission fluid, power steering fluid or Girling brake fluid, always carry these with you as well, as you will not find them in remote countries. Remember to have some thin oil, for example WD40, for hinges, latches, padlocks, etc. Only use dry graphite on door locks. Remember that even in hot countries you will need antifreeze in many desert and mountain areas at night.

If your axles do not have recessed drain plugs, they can be battered out of shape by thrown-up stones in really bad terrain (even turned undone so that they fall out), so keep a check on them and carry spares.

Repairs

If you have any repairs done by local mechanics in Third World countries, always watch them at work. Make sure you disconnect the battery and alternator before they do any electric welding and watch that they do not replace some of your good parts or inner tubes with old ones. Make sure that you retighten any nuts that were done up by young boys.

If you have to reline brakes or clutch, pay extra for imported western linings; cheap locally made linings will fade quickly. If you have bonded brake linings, the brake shoes can be drilled out for riveted linings. Never let a local mechanic tighten down a cylinder head – always do it yourself. Follow the correct tightening sequence closely and tighten everything down again after 500 miles (800 km).

Check that any oil they have changed has been refilled. In some countries it is wise to check any body, chassis or fuel tank repairs for evidence of false compartments filled with drugs.

Driving over large sand seas means that you end up with a sandblasted front and underside to your vehicle, which will need repainting when you return to a damp climate. A heavy sandstorm can scour the paint completely off your bodywork. With Land Rover's aluminium panels it does not matter, but if you have steel bodywork it is worth covering the front and wings with heavy grease.

In some countries asphalt roads cross sand seas. In these areas be careful not to hit a windblown sand drift across the road at speed. In a really heavy sandstorm cover your windscreen and face it away from the wind, or it will be etched opaque. In scrub or insect country you will need to brush down your radiator regularly if you do not have a chaff/insect screen.

The benefits of air conditioning are questionable for rough terrain. When you have to leave the vehicle often to push or dig it out, the change in temperature drains your strength and willpower. The idea that being cool conserves your water supply only works for a lightly loaded vehicle that never gets stuck; what you save in water has to be carried in extra fuel. Polarising plastic film on the windows will keep the interior of a hard top vehicle cooler, as will aluminium cooking foil on any windows out of which you do not need to see.

Summary

- Choose a vehicle that as far as possible is right for you, right for the terrain envisaged and has spares available en route.

- If several vehicles are to travel in convoy, it makes sense if they can share the same spares, wheels and tyres.

- Get to know how to repair your vehicle before you depart. Protect any weak components and always carry spare fuel and water, plus any special oils or fluids that the vehicle requires.

- Try to avoid local repairers, but if you have to use them keep an eye on all their work.

- Make daily maintenance checks on your vehicle, carry a good tool kit, a good workshop manual and spares for any known weaknesses, in accordance with the following lists.

VEHICLE SPARE PARTS, TOOLS AND EQUIPMENT LISTS

The spare parts to be carried will vary with the type of vehicle, how much extra weight can be carried before extra stress to the vehicle will cause further damage, the vehicle's particular weaknesses, what parts can be improvised, and what, if any, can be easily obtained en route. In most Third World countries spare parts can be sold easily and for a profit.

Get lists of your vehicle's concessionaires and dealers along your proposed route. In many cases they will not have the stock of supplies you were led to believe, but they will usually be able to put you in touch with a bazaar shop or mechanic who can help you.

The following lists assume some experience – without some mechanical expertise an immaculately stocked toolbox is of limited use. They also assume some driving off-road.

German and Japanese vehicles use metric threads requiring metric spanners. American and British vehicles often have a mixture of metric and unified threads requiring a mixture of spanner sizes.

Have spare keys hidden on the vehicle, where they can be retrieved without having to gain entry.

Petrol engine spares

3 fan belts (plus power steering pump belts and air conditioning pump belts if fitted)
1 complete set of gaskets
4 oil filters (change every 3,000 miles/5,000 km)

2 tubes of silicone RTV gasket compound
1 complete set of radiator hoses
Spare heater hose
Spare fuel pipe hose
Spare distributor vacuum pipe hose (if fitted)
2 exhaust valves
1 inlet valve
1 complete valve spring
Fine and coarse valve grinding paste and valve grinding tool
1 valve spring compressor
1 fuel lift pump repair kit (if electric type, take a complete spare pump)
1 water pump repair kit
1 carburettor overhaul kit (if fitted)
2 sets of sparking plugs
1 timing light or 12-volt bulb and holder with leads
3 sets of contact breaker points
2 distributor rotor arms
1 distributor condenser
1 distributor cap
1 sparking plug spanner
1 set of high tension leads (older, wire-type is preferable)
1 ignition coil
Slip ring and brushes for alternator or a complete spare alternator
2 cans of spray-type ignition sealant for dusty and wet conditions
2 spare air intake filters, if you do not have the oil-bath type

Diesel engine spares

Delete from the above list: sparking plugs, contact breaker points, rotor arms, distributor cap and condenser, high tension leads, coil and carburettor overhaul kit, and substitute:

1 spare set of injectors
1 complete set of injector high pressure pipes
1 set of injector copper seating washers plus steel sealing washers where these are used
1 set of injector return pipe washers
Plastic fuel pipe, plus spare nuts and ferrules
A second in-line fuel filter
4 fuel filter elements

3 spare heater plugs, if fitted

Brakes and clutch

All-wheel cylinder seals kits
1 each of all flexible brake hoses
1 brake bleeding kit
1 brake master cylinder seals kit
1 clutch master cylinder seals kit
1 clutch slave cylinder seals kit (or a complete unit for Land Rover Series III or 90/110)

(NB It is important to keep all of these kits away from heat)

1 clutch centre plate

General spares

If you have an automatic gearbox, make sure you have plenty of the special fluid for this, a spare starter motor and a second battery, kept charged.

If you have power steering, carry the correct fluid and spare hoses.

Some Land Rovers have automatic gearbox fluid in a manual gearbox.

2 warning triangles (compulsory in most countries)
1 good workshop manual (not the car handbook)
1 multilingual vehicle parts guide, as supplied by the AA or RAC
1 good torch and a fluorescent light with leads to work it from the vehicle battery, plus spare bulbs and tubes
1 extra tyre in addition to that on the spare wheel. (Only the spare wheel and tyre will be necessary if two vehicles with wheels of the same size are travelling together)
3 extra inner tubes (6 in areas of Acacia thorns)
1 large inner tube repair kit
1 set of tyre levers for tyres
5 spare inner tube valve cores and 2 valve core tools
4 inner tube valve dust caps
1 Schrader tyre pump, which fits into a sparking plug socket thread, or an electric compressor if you have a diesel engine.
Plenty of the correct engine oil

Distilled water or water de-ionising crystals

12-volt soldering iron and solder

Hand drill and drills

Long rope, strong enough to tow your vehicle and upright an overturned vehicle

1 good jack (if hydraulic, carry spare fluid for it)

1 wheel brace plus a ring or socket spanner of the same size

1 (at least) metal fuel can, e.g. a jerry can

1 grease gun and a tin of multi-purpose grease

Correct differential and gearbox oil

1 large fire extinguisher suitable for petrol and electrical fires

1 reel of self-vulcanising rubber tape for leaking hoses (available from yacht chandlers)

1 pair of heavy-duty electric jump leads at least 3.3 yards (3 m) long

10 push-fit electrical connectors (of type to suit vehicle)

2 universal joints for propeller shafts

Correct brake and clutch fluid

1 small can of general light oil for hinges, etc

1 large can of WD40

1 starting handle, if available

2 complete sets of spare keys, kept in different places

1 small Isopon or glass fibre kit, for repairing fuel tank and body holes

2 kits of general adhesive, e.g. Bostik or Araldite Rapid

1 tin of hand cleaner (washing-up liquid will do in an emergency)

Spare fuses, and bulbs for all lights, including those on the dash panel; the charging light bulb is often part of the charging circuit

1 spare radiator cap

Antifreeze, if required

Spare windscreen wipers (keep away from heat)

Inner and outer wheel bearings

Dry graphite lock lubricant

Tool kit

Carry a good tool kit containing the following:

Wire brush to clean dirty threads

Socket set of correct sizes

Torque wrench

Ring and open-ended spanners of the correct sizes

Hacksaw and spare blades

Large and small flat and round files

Selection of spare nuts, bolts and washers of type and thread(s) to fit vehicle

Large Stillson pipe wrench

1 box spanner for large wheel bearing lock nuts

Hammer and club hammer

Large and small cold chisels for large and stubborn nuts

Self-grip wrench, eg Mole-type

Broad- and thin-nosed pliers

Circlip pliers

Insulating tape

Electrical wire (vehicle type, not mains)

2 sets of feeler gauges

Small adjustable wrench

Tube of gasket cement, e.g. Red Hermetite

Tube of Loctite thread sealant

Large and small slot-head and Phillips-head screwdrivers

2 accurate tyre pressure gauges

Hardwood or steel plate(s) to support the jack/axle stands on soft ground

Extras for strenuous off-road use

2 sand ladders per vehicle (4 if the vehicle travels alone)

3 wheel bearing hub oil seals

1 rear transfer box oil seal

1 rear differential oil seal

If you have leaf springs:

1 rear spring main leaf, complete with bushes

1 front spring main leaf, complete with bushes

4 spare spring bushes

4 spring centre bolts

1 set (ie 4) of spring shackle plates

1 set (ie 4) of spring shackle pins

2 rear axle 'U' bolts

1 front axle 'U' bolt

If you have coil springs or torsion bars, carry one spare of each size fitted

1 complete set of shock absorber

mounting rubbers

2 spare engine mounting rubbers

1 spare gearbox mounting rubber

2 door hinge pins

1 high-lift jack (or an extra jack that is not of the hydraulic type, to use on its side when changing springs and/or bushes if you do not have a high-lift jack)

Strong chain plus bolts to fix it, for splinting broken chassis, axle or spring parts

Snow chains if you expect a lot of mud or snow

Paint brush to dust off the engine so you can work on it

Large groundsheet for lying on when working under the vehicle or repairing tyres, to prevent sand from getting between the inner tube and the tyre

2 long-handled plus 2 short-handled shovels for digging out

2 steering ball joints

Spares of any padlocks

Radiator stop-leak compound (dry porridge or raw egg will do in an emergency)

Specific to Series IIA Land Rovers

1 set of rear axle half-shafts, heavy duty

Specific to Series III Land Rovers

4 nylon bonnet hinge inserts (or 2 home-made aluminium ones)

2 windscreen outer hinge bolts (No 346984)

2 windscreen inner tie bolts

2 rear differential drain plugs

1 set of big-end nuts

1 rear axle drive member (Salisbury)

Specific to Land Rover Turbo Diesel and Tdi engines, or any other engines with camshaft drive belts

2 spare camshaft drive belts, stored flat and in a cool place

Now find room for the passengers! Heavily laden CJ5 Jeeps in the Hindu Kush Mountains, north-west Pakistan.

3 pushrods
3 brass cam followers

REGULAR MAINTENANCE CHECKLIST

1. Change oil and renew all oil and fuel filters
2. Clean air filter and change oil bath or air filter element
3. Grease propeller shafts
4. Lubricate all locks with dry graphite
5. Adjust and lubricate all door hinges
6. Inspect undercarriage for cracks, fluid leaks, loose bolts, etc
7. Rotate all tyres, inspecting for cuts and wear
8. Check, clean and adjust brakes
9. Check adjustment of carburettor or injection pump
10. Check and adjust fan belts and accessory belts
11. Check sparking plugs; clean and re-gap or replace as necessary
12. Check ignition timing
13. Check and top up:

front and rear differentials
swivel-pin housings
gearbox
transfer box
overdrive, power steering pump and air conditioning pump (if applicable)
steering box
battery electrolyte
brake and clutch fluid
cooling system
engine crankcase

14. Check that there are no rattles
15. Inspect radiator and heater hoses
16. Check breather vents on both axles, transfer box, gearbox and fuel filler cap
17. Check all lights and direction indicators

Always grease wheel studs before refitting wheels and do not over-tighten them.

Axle stands will add to your personal safety if you can carry them.

TENTS AND BEDS

If you have a roomy vehicle, are not worried about weight and are not constantly on the move, you might as well make yourselves comfortable. This can make a difference to your morale, particularly if you are camping.

Tents

There are a myriad of tents and tent designs on the market, from lightweight emergency bivouacs to heavy, base-camp frame tents and marquees. The main choice is whether you require a tent at all. In fine weather, if you are away from people and domestic animals, it is just as comfortable to sleep out in the open, unless it is raining or snowing.

If any of the party are worried about scorpions or snakes, a sheet of marine plywood on a full-length roof rack makes it comfortable to sleep on, as well as helping to keep the vehicle cool. There are some (expensive) folding tents available to fit on roof racks. Remember that vehicles will rock in any wind.

If you plan to sleep without a tent, take a mosquito net. There are several types on the market, but they are rarely large enough to tuck in properly with no gaps. Some have the advantage of requiring only one point of suspension. A camera tripod or ice axe will do for this, if there is no vehicle or tent nearby.

In America and Germany you can obtain one- or two-person mosquito nets in the form of a geodesic dome tent. These are equally useful to use on the beds of cheaper hotels, as they also keep out bed bugs, ants and other nuisances. Malaria is an increasingly serious problem, so get a net that is impregnated with a safe insecticide. On a long journey carry the correct insecticide to re-impregnate the net.

If you sleep without a tent, note where the sun should rise and position yourself to be in the shade then, or the sun could wake you up earlier than you would like to.

Most tents nowadays are made from synthetic fibres. These are lightweight and strong, but wear quickly and are prone to condensation. If you can carry the extra weight, cotton tents are more comfortable and last longer.

No single-skin tent is fully weatherproof. Tents with a separate flysheet are more so, as well as cooler in the sun and warmer in the cold.

The biggest problem with lightweight tents is that the groundsheet will not last a single trip. Have a plastic sheet or closed-cell foam mat to put under it for extra protection.

Expensive bivouac bags are no better than plastic bags. They may breathe, but you will still get condensation between your sleeping bag and the bag itself.

In Third World countries the ground is often rock hard, so throw away the tent pegs that come with the tent and make stronger ones from heavier iron rod, which can be hammered into hard ground. If you cannot manufacture these yourself, go down to the bazaar and buy the stakes local farmers use to tether their animals.

Tents should never be stored damp, and for transport in the vehicle are best protected in ex-military kit bags.

Air beds, mattresses and camp beds

Air beds are comfortable but heavy, and inflating them is hard work. Thorns and sunlight work against them and you will spend time patching holes. If you do use one, ensure that it is made of rubber not plastic, and only pump it up half full. If you inflate it any harder you will roll around and probably fall off. Perspiration condenses against the surface of air mattresses and on cold nights you will wake up in a puddle of cold water, unless you have put a blanket or woollen jumper between yourself and the mattress.

Camp beds are narrow, collapse frequently, tear holes in groundsheets and soon break up. Cold air circulates beneath the bed, and since your body weight compresses the bedding, only several layers of blankets under you will give you proper insulation.

Open-cell foam mattresses are comfortable but often too thin. Have two thicknesses, or else put a closed-cell foam mat, such as a Karrimat, on the ground and an open-cell mattress on top of it. If you fit a washable cotton cover that fully encloses them, they will last longer. Closed-cell foam mats come in many sizes to order. They also come in a 3 mm (0.118 inch) thickness, suitable for putting under a groundsheet for protection against sharp stones, or on ice, where otherwise the tent groundsheet could stick to the ice and be torn when pulled free.

Foam mattresses are best wrapped in strong waterproof covers during transport. One of their advantages is that the perspiration that collects in them evaporates quickly when aired, so they are easy to keep fresh and dry. Remember to air them every second day.

The most popular mattresses nowadays are self-inflating ones. As with air beds, in really cold climates you will be warmer if you put a blanket or sweater between your sleeping bag and the mattress.

Sleeping bags

On a long overland trip you can combat changing temperature conditions with a combination of two sleeping bags. First get a medium-quality, nylon-covered, down sleeping bag and, if you are tall, make sure it is long enough for you. This bag will be the one you use most often for medium cold nights.

Second, get a cheap all-synthetic bag, that is one filled with artificial fibre. These cheap, easily washable bags are best for use alone on warmer nights and outside the down bag for very cold nights. Make sure that the synthetic bag is big enough to go outside the down bag, without compressing

Afghan horse stakes and strong home-made tent pegs – on typical Third World ground!

the latter when it is fully lofted up.

In polar and high mountain areas the golden rule is never to be parted from your own sleeping bag, in case a blizzard or accident breaks up the party. This holds true when travelling anywhere that is cold.

Space (survival) blankets, plastic sheets and bags

Space blankets – aluminised plastic sheets – very much advertised by their manufacturers, are no better than a polythene sheet or bag. Body perspiration condenses inside them, making the sleeping bag wet, so that the person inside gets cold.

In hot or desert areas, however, used in reverse to reflect the sun, they are very good during the heat of the day to keep yourself, a tent or vehicle cool. A plastic sheet or space blanket can be spread over a ring of boulders to make an effective bath, and plastic sheets are ideal for making desert stills.

Also over-rated are Pertex lightweight towels – if weight is a problem, cut down a normal towel.

Summary

- Have a good mosquito net, mattress and sleeping bag or bags.

- Foam mattresses are preferable to air beds.

- Cotton tents last longer and do not suffer from condensation. Double skin tents are warmer in the cold, cooler in the heat and more weatherproof.

- Have stronger tent pegs for rock-hard ground.

CLOTHING

Even in the Sahara Desert and the 'Empty Quarter' a bright sunny day can become freezing cold and wet. I have experienced snow and ice in the Hoggar Mountains and on the Tassili Plateau – wherever you go you should be prepared for the worst.

The layer principle, whereby several thin layers are worn that can be added when cold or removed when hot or working hard, is well proven, and weatherproof outer garments will also be windproof.

Cotton is more comfortable than synthetic fibres in the heat, but has no warmth when wet. Wool and synthetic fibres with wicking properties retain warmth and comfort when you are wet or perspiring, but synthetic fibres of this type must be washed frequently, or they soon smell.

In hot climates clothes should be light enough to dry quickly when washed overnight, and you will be glad of long trousers and long-sleeved shirts where sunburn is a problem. In Moslem countries too much naked flesh and shorts (even on men) are frowned upon.

In cooler climates, particularly at night, an insulated 'Duvet' jacket is a welcome luxury. Down jackets are lightweight and warm when dry, but those filled with synthetic fibres retain much of their warmth when wet and are easily washed. Fibre pile jackets are warmer than fleece jackets.

Don't forget warm gloves and head cover, and for a protective outer shell breathable waterproof/windproof membrane jackets and overtrousers, such as those made of 'Goretex' fabric, are best. They are easily washed and lighter in weight, less messy and less smelly than oiled cotton. The jacket should have a roomy hood with a wire hoop that can be positioned against the wind, and a double full-length zip, so that you can wear it half open if you are overheating.

If you are working hard your sweat will condense (or freeze, if it is cold enough) on the inner surface of these garments. So if rain or wind chill are not a problem, remove them if activity is making you sweat.

Overtrousers should have long zips on each leg, so that you can don or remove them over boots.

Boots

In most countries you will be glad of a comfortable pair of lightweight hiking boots. There is nothing to be gained from expensive designer brands – lightweight leather boots are fine in wet areas and those made partly of Goretex fabric are comfortable in hot countries, as they allow your feet to breathe. In snow, full climbing boots or Canadian insulated hunt-

Even in the Sahara Desert you will require warm clothing.

ing boots will keep your feet warm.

You should think about having to wade rivers on foot for inspection before crossing. In warm countries you will be quite happy to do this in sandals or old shoes, though in some areas you may have to think about Bilharzia or similar problems. In cooler climates wading will be uncomfortably cold and wellington boots do not come high enough up the legs. The only sensible answer is a pair of waders and some thick socks.

Summary

- Aim to be comfortable, but not overweight.

- Have a pair of lightweight walking boots and clothing for cold and wet weather, as well as warm.

- In a cold climate you will be glad of a pair of waders, for checking out rivers on foot before crossing.

FURNITURE AND UTENSILS

Fragile items and paperwork, which must be protected from dust and water, are best kept in Pelican or Underwater Kinetics cases, which have silicone gasket seals. These come in many sizes, with foam inserts that can be customised to fit fragile equipment. Cases containing clothes can be sealed with strips of foam. Film stock is usually an important part of your journey and must be kept cool in hot countries.

During the day a refrigerator can be used if you have a second battery. If you are one vehicle alone, it is best to switch the refrigerator off at night, or use the type that can also be run on gas. If you do not have a refrigerator, a polystyrene insulated box will help.

If folding chairs are covered with light cotton, this will rot

Use a folding table to keep sand out of your food.

quickly in intense sunlight. Look for nylon or terylene-covered chairs. Full-size ammunition boxes are good for protecting kitchenware and make good seats. A folding table will enable you to prepare food without getting it full of sand.

Billies, pots and pans, plates, mugs, cutlery, etc, should be firmly packed inside boxes, with cloth or thin foam separating metal utensils and cutlery, or they will rub against each other and become covered in black metal filings. Even stainless steel will exhibit this problem, though not to quite such an extent.

A pressure cooker guarantees sterile food and can double as a large billy. Kettles with lids are preferable to whistling-type kettles, which are difficult to fill from cans or streams. For melting snow and ice, it is best to use billies. Where possible do not waste fuel melting snow – melt ice.

Dull-grey aluminium billies are better than the shiny aluminium type, which crack and split with repeated knocks and vibration. Big, strong aluminium billies are best bought at Army and Navy auctions or surplus stores. In the Third World good alternatives will be readily available in local markets.

A wide range of non-breakable cups and plates is available; soft plastic mugs leave an aftertaste, so get melamine. Large mugs with wide bases will not tip over easily. Insulated mugs become unhygienic, as dirt and water get between the two layers and cannot be cleaned out. Metal mugs are hot to touch and can burn your lips. Melamine mugs become stained by tea or coffee, but there are cleaners available, although Steradent tablets are a cheaper substitute. Heavyweight stainless steel cutlery is more durable than aluminium for a long expedition.

Head torches, such as those made by Petzl, are useful to keep both hands free when camping, or for vehicle maintenance.

Buying

When buying equipment be especially wary of any shop that calls itself an expedition supplier, but does not stock the better brands of equipment. All the top-class equipment suppliers will give trade discounts to genuine expeditions, or group buyers such as clubs or educational establishments. Some, such as Field and Trek and Cotswold Camping, have special contract departments for this service.

Summary

- Protect valuable items and paperwork in waterproof cases.

- Pack all metal utensils carefully, to avoid them rubbing against each other.

- A folding table enables you to keep sand and grit out of food.

- Wide mugs are less likely to get knocked over.

- Head torches are useful when camping.

FOOD, WATER AND COOKING

Always have high-energy, carbohydrate, emergency rations in the vehicle and carry tinned meats and fish for when you cannot get decent supplies. From my experience dehydrated foods are not good enough if you have to perform physical work, including trekking.

Gas is the easiest and cleanest fuel to use for cooking. Liquid petroleum gas (LPG), such as Calor Gas, is usually called butane gas in the UK, and by various oil company names worldwide, such as Shellgas or Essogas. Though available worldwide there are different fittings on the cylinders in different countries that are not interchangeable. Where you use a pressure reduction valve there will be a rubber tube connection; make sure that you carry spare lengths of the correct size rubber tubing.

Gas cylinders are heavy and refilling can be difficult. Camping Gaz cylinders supplied in Europe are intended to be factory refilled, but in some countries, for example Algeria, Morocco and Yemen, they are available with overfill release valves so that you can fill them yourself from a larger domestic butane gas supply.

In Asia enterprising campsite managers and gas suppliers have discovered ways of filling normal gas cylinders from their own supply. Stand well clear while they do this – the process involves pushing down the ball valve with a nail, then overfilling from a supply of higher pressure. This can cause flare-up problems when the cylinder is first used with standard cooking equipment, so if you use such a source of supply, release some of the pressure by opening the valve for a couple of minutes, well away from any flame, before lighting up.

Lighting stoves is a problem in cold climates or at altitude. Local matches never work, unless you strike three together, so take a good supply of the 300 match size, such as Cook's Household Matches. The best answer is a butane cigarette lighter, kept in your trouser pocket where it will be warm. Remember to carry plenty of refills (not all in your pocket).

There are many good camping gas stoves available, but when cooking for large groups outside I prefer to use the large cast iron industrial gas rings used by builders to melt bitumen. These are wide, heavy and stable when very large billies are used, and they do not blow out in the wind.

In cold areas, use propane gas instead of butane gas. If gas supplies are a problem, there are good twin-burner stoves that use unleaded petrol or kerosene. There are also single-burner, multi-fuel stoves that will operate on diesel fuel.

Water

Canvas and goatskin water bags do not work and waste precious water. Suffice to say that local desert lorry drivers now use tied up inner tubes! When conditions are below freezing, water in jerry cans outside the vehicle will freeze and expand. This may burst the jerry can, and also means that you will not have drinking water readily available. Keep at least one can inside the vehicle.

Water purification is one of the most important aspects of expedition health. There are three ways to make water safe to drink: boil it for at least 20 minutes; sterilize it with chemicals; or filter and then sterilise with chemicals.

Boiling vigorously for five minutes renders most water safe, but if you have enough fuel boiling for 20 minutes is the only way to be absolutely sure, especially at altitude.

There are two types of water filter, those that rely on a very fine ceramic filter and those that have activated carbon and additional chemical sterilization, usually with iodine or silver salts. The latter will render any water safe, but there are some organisms that will pass through the finest filters, so if you use ceramic filters you should also sterilize the water afterwards.

Separate chemical sterilization comes in two forms, chlorine-based and iodine-based. The commonly available chlorine-based tablets will not purify turbid water, nor fully guard against amoeba, giardia and other organisms, so they are not of much use in the Third World. Iodine-based products will work in turbid water and will guard against all these organisms, but a few people are allergic to iodine. In its simplest form, common Tincture of Iodine, three drops per quart/litre, is the answer, or you can buy more expensive Potable Aqua tablets, using one tablet per quart/litre for

10 minutes. These tablets are supplied to the US Armed Forces.

Remember that sterilized water also requires a sterilized container. Filtered or boiled water should only be put into a sterilized container, and chemical sterilisation should be performed in the container to be used.

EQUIPMENT CHECKLIST FOR VEHICLE CAMPING

Good compass, maps and guidebooks

GPS if required

Selection of plastic bags for storage/waste disposal, etc

Cling wrap and aluminium foil for food

Large bowl for washing up and washing clothes

Water jerry cans – strong ex-military type

Fire extinguisher

Large supply of paper towel, toilet paper, scouring pads, plus some 'J cloths' and tea towels

Large supply of good matches in waterproof box and/or disposable lighters

Salt, instant coffee, tea bags, powdered milk

Tinned meats that do not contain much water

Washing-up liquid (also good for greasy hands)

Good vegetable cooking oil or, better still, ghee substitute, which is solid at room temperature, so easier to transport

Frying pan, or suitable billy lid

Pressure cooker

Selection of strong saucepans or billies

Kettle with lid (not the whistling type that is hard to fill from a can or stream

Can opener – good heavyweight or wall type that can be fixed to vehicle

Stainless steel cutlery

Plastic screw-top jars for sugar, salt, etc (Nalgene are best)

1 large sharp bread knife

2 small sharp vegetable knives

1 large serving spoon and soup ladle

Plates and/or bowls for eating out of, and wide-bottomed mugs that do not tip over easily

Lightweight folding chairs and table

Battery-powered fluorescent light(s)

Combined anti-mosquito and insect spray repellent

Good sleeping bag or sleeping bag combinations, for the climate expected, plus mattresses

Thin nylon line to use as clothes line, plus pegs

Washing powder for clothes

Plastic tubing to fill water tank or jerry cans

Water purification filters plus tablets or iodine as back-up (keep all away from heat)

2 tubes of universal glue-cum-sealant, eg Bostik

Chamois leather

Sponges

Phrase book/dictionaries where necessary

Torches plus spare batteries

Scissors

Small dustpan and brush

Soap, shampoo, toothpaste, towels

Medical first aid kit plus multivitamins. (Be careful about using oil of cloves to mask toothache – you could develop a serious abscess without realising it)

Rehydration salts

Anti-malarial tablets and salt tablets, where required

Anti-histamine for dust allergies

High factor sunscreen lotion/cream

MASTA type anti-AIDS kit, containing sterile syringes and needles

Mosquito nets or fitted mosquito netting, if passing through areas with mosquitos

Sewing kit and safety pins

Personal clothing, sunglasses, medicaments and spectacles if you wear them

Hidden strong box, and money belt, for passports, visas, travellers cheques, cash, vaccination certificates, car papers, insurance

Now is not the time to discover that something important is missing! Comfort is being added to this beautiful campsite in the South Teneré Desert, Niger.

papers, UK and International driving licence, permission-to-drive letter if you do not own the vehicle, photocopies of travel and medical insurance policies and six spare passport photographs.

Where possible, keep things carefully packed in strong boxes. These can be very adaptable as they can also be used for sitting on when camping, or as a base for sleeping on inside the vehicle.

Many other things can be taken along, but most of these are personal belongings. They include: dental floss, waterproof watch, tissues (good for many other reasons than blowing your nose), clothing (including a tie for men for formal occasions that may crop up and dealing with embassies – store the tie rolled up in a jar with a lid), a dress for ladies (for that same occasion), jacket, swimming costume, moisturising cream, toothbrushes, comb, Swiss Army knife, camera, film, photographic accessories, sunglasses plus spares, prescription medicines, spare prescription spectacles if worn, airmail writing paper, envelopes, sellotape, ballpoint pens and felt tip marker pens (keep pens away from heat).

COMMON PROBLEMS, BUSH MECHANICS AND RUNNING REPAIRS

Overloading

Overloading is a major cause of broken-down vehicles, and the easiest to avoid – simply calculate your payload against the manufacturer's recommendation for the vehicle.

Overturned vehicles

Short-wheelbase vehicles have a

Avoid overloading! This Toyota is returning from Saudi Arabia through Raydah, Yemen, loaded high with goods.

habit of breaking away or spinning on bends and corrugations, often turning over in the process. Therefore drive these vehicles with care. Given the nature of the terrain they cover, overturned vehicles are not unusual off-road. Usually it happens at slow speed and no one is injured, nor even windows broken.

If your vehicle overturns, first make sure the engine is turned off and the battery disconnected. Check for human injury, then completely unload the vehicle. Once unloaded, vehicles can usually be righted easily using manpower, though a second vehicle or winch can make things easier in the right conditions. Once the

An overturned Land Rover on the 'road' to Jam, Afghanistan.

on one side wider than the other, it will be easier to remove the tyre over the narrowest side, starting with both beads in the well of the wheel. Several books infer that you should not do this, but it is much easier to perform and will not do any damage.

Narrow tyre levers are more efficient than wide ones. Sweep out all sand and grit, file off any sharp burrs on the wheel and put everything back together on a ground sheet, to stop any sand or grit getting in to cause further punctures.

If necessary, when refitting the tyre use liquid soap and water or bead lubricant; a Schrader valve tool will hold the inner tube valve in place. Pump the tyre up enough to refit the bead on the rim, then let it down again to release any twists in the inner tube. Then pump the tyre up again to rear tyre

vehicle is righted, check for damage, sort out all oil levels and spilt battery acid. Remove the sparking plugs or injectors and turn the engine over several times to clear the cylinders of oil before running again.

> **Warning:** Do not have anyone on the side of the engine where the sparking plugs or injectors have been removed, as fuel and oil can be ejected at very high pressure.

Punctures

Punctures are common in off-road travel. Rear wheel punctures often destroy the inner tube, so several spare inner tubes should be carried. Wherever possible I prefer to repair punctures with a known good tube and get the punctured tube vulcanised when I next visit a larger town. However, you should always carry a repair kit in case you use all your inner tubes. Hot patch repair kits do not work well enough on light truck inner tubes.

If you cannot break a bead, try driving over it or using a jack and the weight of the vehicle. If you still cannot break the bead, pour strong, warm soapy water into the

crack and allow it to soak in, then try again. If the wheel has the rim

Acacia country, near Timbuktu, Mali. Acacia thorns are a regular cause of punctures.

With offset wheels it is easier to remove the tyre over the rim on the narrowest side.

Narrow tyre levers are more efficient.

pressure. If the wheel has to be fitted on the front later, it is easy to let out some air.

Damaged steel-braced radial tyres often have a sharp end of wire projecting internally, causing further punctures. For off-road or Third World use, these wires can be cut down as short as is possible and the tyre then gaitered, using thicker truck inner tubes. The edges of the gaiter should be bevelled and the tyre must be at full pressure to stop the gaiter moving about. On paved roads gaitered tyres behave like a buckled wheel, so they are dangerous.

Most light truck tyres can be re-cut when worn. Re-cut tyres are useful to use in areas of sharp stones or Acacia thorns, where tyres damage easily. However, they are not legal on light vehicles on the public highway.

Wheelbraces get overworked in off-road use, so also have a good socket or ring spanner available to fit the wheel nuts, and grease the studs before fitting the nuts. With

Using a socket supported by a jack to help undo a stubborn wheel nut.

Once you get this far the rest is easy.

Use a Schrader valve tool to hold the inner tube valve in place until the tube is blown up.

a hot wheel after a puncture, you may need an extension tube on the wheel brace to undo the wheel nuts; but do not retighten them this way or you will cause damage.

If you cannot get a wheel nut undone, use a correct size socket spanner whose socket cup is shorter than the length of the nut, or fit a packing piece within the socket. Support the socket on a jack, apply your weight to the socket spanner in the correct direction to undo it and at the same time sharply strike the head of the socket with a club hammer. Remember that some vehicles have left-hand threads on the wheel nuts on one side of the vehicle.

Fuel problems

Bad fuel is common – extra fuel filters are useful for all vehicles, and essential for diesel engines. The main problems are water and sediment. When things get bad, it is quicker long term to drain the fuel tank, decant the fuel and clean it out. Always keep the wire mesh filter in the fuel filler in place.

Do not let the fuel tank level fall too low, as this will produce water and sediment in the fuel lines. With a diesel engine you may then have to bleed the system. If fuelling up from 40-gallon drums, give them time to settle and leave the bottom inch, which will often be water and grit.

In remote areas it is common for fuel stations to be out of fuel for weeks, then, when fuel arrives, all the tanks are filled at once. If possible you should give the tanks in the fuel station time to settle, before you fill up, or again you could have sediment and water in your system. I once fuelled up eight Land Rovers in Timbuktu in this way and had to clean all fuel systems several times each day for the next week!

If you have petrol in jerry cans in a hot, dry climate, always earth them to discharge any static electricity before opening them. Also earth the vehicle before putting the fuel can to the fuel tank filler

When filling up with fuel from 40-gallon barrels, allow time for the water and sediment to settle first.

spout. Static discharge is a major cause of petrol vehicle fires in hot dry climates.

Fuel starvation is often caused by dust blocking the breather hole in the fuel tank filler cap. Electric fuel pumps are unreliable, so if your vehicle has one carry a complete spare. For mechanical fuel pumps, carry a reconditioning kit. In hot countries or in low gear at altitude, mechanical fuel pumps on petrol engines often get hot and cause vapour lock. Wrap the pump in bandages and pour water on it to cool it. If this is a constant problem, fit a plastic pipe from the windscreen washer system to the bandaged fuel pump and squirt it regularly.

Low-pressure fuel pipes can be repaired using epoxy resin adhesives, bound by self-vulcanising rubber tape, but high-pressure injector pipes must be brazed or completely replaced. Carry spares of these and spare injectors.

Diesel engine problems are usually fuel or water, and you should know how to bleed the system correctly. If this fails to correct the problem, check all pipes and joints, fuel pump and filter seals for leaks;

hair-line cracks in the high-pressure injector pipes are hardest to find. Fuel tank leaks are best repaired with glass-reinforced fibre kits.

Blocked fuel pipes should be blown out with a tyre pump. Ideally this should be done in the direction of flow, but I have known instances where one has had to blow out in the reverse direction, when something relatively large is the cause.

On corrugations the filter on the fuel pipe pick-up in the fuel tank may break off. It can be replaced temporarily with fine cloth, wired over the end of the pipe.

Electrical problems

These are another constant problem. With petrol engines it is worth changing the ignition system to an electronic system. Carry a spare distributor cap, rotor arm, sparking plugs, points, condenser and coil; all tend to break up or short out in hot countries. Replace modern high-tension leads with the older copper-wire-type and carry a spare set. A broken high-

tension lead can be connected with a nail or screw that has had the head cut off and filed to a point, such that it has a point at both ends, and covered with plenty of insulating tape.

Keep a constant check on sparking plugs and contact breaker points. If you are losing power, first check the gap and wear on the points. Spray all ignition parts with silicone sealant to keep out dust and water.

Keep battery connections tight, clean and greased. Replace battery slip-on connections with the clamp-on type, and keep battery plates covered with electrolyte, topping up only with distilled water or de-ionised water. Batteries are best checked with a battery hydrometer, and there are special instruments for checking the sealed-for-life batteries.

Cracks in the distributor cap or rotor arm can be cleaned out and filled in with Araldite, GRP resin or bitumen from the road surface that has been heated up to make it liquid. If the distributor cap clips are broken, the cap can be held in place with stretched self-vulcanising rubber tape. Leave any breather holes clear, if you are not wading.

A cracked battery case can likewise be repaired with Araldite or molten bitumen from the road.

If the ignition key is lost or the switch broken, the relevant electric cables can be hand-connected to run the vehicle, but the whole unit will have to be cut off if it includes a steering lock. On some Third World-issue Japanese vehicles the whole key unit can be removed easily and the rest of the unit turned with a screwdriver.

Alternators and batteries should be disconnected before any arc welding is performed on the vehicle. Never run the engine with the alternator or battery disconnected.

On some vehicles the red charging warning light on the dashboard is connected in series with the alternator field circuit. Thus bulb failure will prevent the alternator from charging the battery, so this bulb should be checked first before suspecting an alternator fault. Carry spare bulbs for all lights, and also make sure you carry spare fuses and fan belts.

GENERAL REPAIR IMPROVISATIONS

Nuts and bolts

Always use a torque wrench on aluminium cylinder heads or other aluminium components.

Clean the threads of nuts and bolts with a wire brush before trying to remove them.

Fuel and oil

For an emergency fuel tank use a jerry can on the roof with a hose connected to the fuel lift pump. Drive slowly and never let the can get lower than half full.

In an emergency, you can run a diesel engine on kerosene (paraffin) or domestic heating oil, by adding one part of engine oil to 100 parts of the fuel to lubricate the injector pump. In hot climates diesel engine crankcase oils are good for use in petrol engines, but petrol engine crankcase oils should not be used for diesel engines.

A broken carburettor or diesel pump linkage can be worked remotely from within the vehicle using a long piece of string! I once drove a jeep all day in this way in the Karakorum Mountains before I could get a repair made up. (Some books will tell you that wiper blades can also be worked with string, but this would only work if the linkage to the wiper motor is completely severed.)

If you burst an oil gauge pressure pipe, remove the 'T' piece, remove the electric pressure sender from it and screw this back into the block. You will then still have the electric low-pressure warning light.

Don't mix two different types of engine oil if you can help it.

When filling up with engine oil, bring the level up to halfway between the high and low marks on the dipstick and no further.

Steering relays that do not have a filler hole can be topped up by removing two opposite top cover bolts and filling through one of the holes until oil comes out of the other.

When replacing wheel hub bearing oil seals, also replace the metal mating piece.

Leaks

Replace wire hose clips with flat metal Jubilee clips. Carry spare hoses, although these can be repaired in an emergency with self-vulcanising rubber tape. Heater hoses can be sealed off with a sparking plug.

Bad radiator leaks can be sealed with epoxy resin or glass-reinforced fibre. For small leaks add some Radweld, porridge, or raw egg to the radiator water. Bad leaks can be minimised by removing the filler cap, so that the system is no longer pressurised, but frequently top-up the system.

Check for any pinholes in the rubber connecting hose between the air filter and the engine inlet manifold.

Temporary drain or filler plugs can be whittled from wood and sealed in with epoxy resin.

Silicone RTV compound can be used for most gaskets other than cylinder head gaskets. Silicone RTV compound or PTFE tape is useful when putting together leaking fuel line connections.

Paper gaskets can be re-used if smeared with grease.

If you develop a hydraulic brake fluid leak and do not have spares, travel on slowly, using the engine as a brake. If the leak is really bad you can disconnect a metal pipe upstream of the leak, bend it over twice and hammer the end flat, or fit an old pipe to which this has already been done. Rubber hoses can be clamped

using a round bar to minimise damage.

Transmission

If you cannot get into gear, first check for stones caught up in the linkage.

If you lose your clutch, you can still change gear by adjusting the engine speed, as with double de-clutching. It is best to start the engine with the gearbox already in second gear.

The new, lighter clutch pedal on the latest Land Rover Defenders can be achieved on Land Rover 90s and 110s by fitting the double coil 'over centre' assisting spring, part number ANR 3400.

Broken and bent parts

Lengths of strong chain with long bolts plus wood or tyre levers can be used as splints on broken chassis parts, axles or leaf springs.

With four-wheel drive vehicles, if you break a rear half-shaft you can continue in two-wheel drive by removing both rear half-shafts and putting the vehicle into four-wheel drive. Engage freewheeling hubs and any centre differential lock, if you have them. Release the clutch gently on starting – it is very easy to get wheel spin due to the low load on the front wheels.

If the front or rear differential is broken, remove both of the half-shafts on that axle and the propeller shaft concerned, and engage four-wheel drive if it is the rear that is disconnected. If a permanent four-wheel drive jams in the centre differential lock position, remove the front propeller shaft and drive on slowly.

Bent track rods should be hammered back as straight as possible to minimise tyre scrubbing and the possibility of a roll. Drive slowly.

The age-old trick with stubborn track rod ends and steering arm is to soak with penetrating oil then put a heavy hammer head against one side of the unit and strike the opposite side of the unit a sharp blow with another hammer.

If the track rod end has the nut facing downwards, it helps if you put a jack underneath it and jack it up a little before using the hammers.

Electrical matters

If one vehicle in a convoy has a defunct charging system, swap that vehicle's battery every 62 miles (100 km).

For repair work at night, or camp illumination, small fluorescent lights have the least drain on the battery.

Overheating

If the engine is overheating, switching it off will cause uneven cooling, with possible damage. It will cool down quickest going downhill in gear, using the running engine as a brake. If you stop with a hot engine, unless it is showing signs of seizure, keep the engine ticking over fast; this will cool it down more quickly and evenly than if you stop it.

Spare fan belts can be made up from thick string, but they will not last long. Tights or stockings would only last for a few miles/kilometres. You should always carry spares of all necessary belts, even in the UK.

Air conditioning causes the radiator water temperature to rise. One way to create the opposite effect if the water temperature is getting too high is to switch off the air conditioning and to turn on the heating – not very pleasant in tropical heat, but it may save your engine from damage.

Wheels and tyres

Never drive a low-pressure tyre over sharp rocks.

Off-road a wheel can be changed without a jack. Run the wheel on to a mound of earth or rock and place an axle stand, stones or logs under the axle. Apply the handbrake, put the vehicle into gear in low-range four-wheel drive, then remove the

Do not use tyres at low pressures over sharp rocks.

rock or dig away the ground beneath the wheel.

Once a wheel has been refitted, fill in the hole with rocks or logs, or cover it with a sand ladder and dig away under the axle supports.

Build a shelter around the vehicle to keep out sand while you are working on it.

If you get wheel shimmy on returning to paved roads, first check for mud, buckled wheels, gaitered tyres and loose wheel bearings. If it is none of these, check the swivel pins, which can usually be dampened by removing shims.

Emergency winches can be made up by using driven wheels on one axle without tyres, or with spare brake drums or smaller wheels bolted on the outside of the wheels across one axle. Rope wrapped around one wheel should then go through a shackle connected to the anchor point and back, to be wrapped around the other wheel. In this way any change in rope length due to one wheel slipping is self-adjusting. Use high range – low range will have too much torque.

Hub winches of this type used to be on sale in America and I have seen several home-made units used in the Sahara.

Working practices

In sand, always work on a groundsheet and do not put parts down in the sand. In sand storms, make a protected working area around the vehicle using groundsheets.

Four-wheel drive vehicles are high off the ground, so it is often easier to work on the engine if you put the spare wheel on the ground and stand on it. If your bonnet can be hinged right back, tie it back so that the wind does not drop it on to your head.

Spanners left out in the sun can become *very* hot to pick up!

Carry any spare parts containing rubber well away from heat, including the sun's heat on the bodywork.

General

Steering locks are best removed; if not, leave the key in them permanently in dusty areas. A spare set of keys should be hidden safely somewhere under the body or chassis.

Some spares can be purchased on a sale and return basis with a small percentage deducted if returned in good condition.

The most important thing about survival is to avoid the need for it in the first place!

Know your vehicle's capabilities, and do not overload it. Know how to maintain and repair it. Carry adequate spares and tools. Be fit and get sufficient sleep. Start your journey with 20% more fuel and water than you have calculated as necessary, to cover extra problems such as bad terrain, leaking containers, extra time spent over repairs, sitting out a bad sandstorm or being stuck in a river.

Know accurately where your next supplies of fuel and water are. In hot climates, carry plastic sheet to make desert stills and carry space blankets. In cold climates carry warm clothing and sleeping bags. Carry more than one compass and know how to navigate properly. Use magnetic compasses well away from vehicles and cameras.

Do not rely on electronic navigation aids, or the batteries that power them. Do not leave the piste unless you really do know what you are doing. In deserts, travel only in the local winter months. Know how correct your odometer is for the wheels and tyres you are using. Make notes of distances, compass bearings and obvious landmarks as you go along, so you can retrace your route easily if you have to.

Observe correct check-in and check-out procedures with local authorities. Preferably convoy with other vehicles. When lost, do not continue. Stop! Think! And if necessary, retrace your route.

Back-up plans

If you are a large party, you should arrange a search and rescue plan before you start out. This would include the use and recognition of radio beacons or flares for aircraft search. Many countries do not allow you to use radio communication, but where they do you can carry portable satellite communication.

For most people an air search is highly unlikely, and high-flying commercial passenger aircraft overhead are unlikely to notice you, whatever you do. A search, if it does come, will be along the piste or markers. Usually this will only involve other vehicles travelling through being asked by the local authorities to look out for you when you fail to check in.

Local drivers will not understand or appreciate coloured flares, so your best signal for outside help is fire. At night, if you hear a vehicle, cardboard boxes or wood are quickly and easily lit, but during the day you need lots of thick black smoke. The best fuel for this is a tyre.

Bury most of a tyre in the sand to control the speed at which it burns (keep it well away from and down wind of the vehicles or fuel) and start the exposed part burning with a rag soaked in either petrol or diesel fuel. As the exposed part of the tyre burns away, you can uncover more from the sand to keep it going, or cover all of it with sand if you wish to put out the fire. Avoid inhaling the sulphurous fumes.

Headlights switched on and off at night can be used while the battery still has charge.

A need to survive

Once you are in a 'need to survive' situation, the important things are morale, health and water. Concentrate on getting your vehicle(s) moving again; this will keep you occupied and help to keep up morale. Health is important. If you are sick your morale will fall and diarrhoea causes dehydration.

Survival is a life-threatening situation. You should have a good medical kit, including antibiotics, and know how to use them. This is not a situation for debating the ethics of the unnecessary use of antibiotics. At the first sign of trouble, so long as the patient is not allergic to them, use them.

Water

In a 'sit it out and survive' situation, with all manual labour kept to a minimum, food is unimportant and dehydration staves off hunger, but water is *vital*.

The average person can survive for three weeks on water alone. Food is not so important in a hot climate; in high temperatures a person without water but resting in the shade can live for two to three days. If a person rests during the day and travels at night, this period is reduced. Life expectancy increases in cooler conditions, but it is generally accepted to be a maximum of ten days.

The average consumption of water in a hot, dry climate should be eight litres a day. This can be lowered to four litres a day in a real emergency. Diarrhoea increases dehydration, so should be controlled by medicine where necessary. Salt intake should be kept up but not overdone; licking your bare arms will replace some lost salt.

The minimum daily water requirements to maintain the body's water balance at rest in the shade are as follows:

Mean daily temperatures (°C)	Litres of water per 24 hrs
35	5.3
30	2.4
25	1.2
20 and below	1.0

It must be stressed that this is for survival. There will be gradual kidney malfunction and possibly urinary tract infection, with women more at risk than men.

Most important of all is the purity of any water that is drunk. In the Third World it is wise to treat all water sources as suspect and either boil or sterilize it.

The Sahara Desert is hot and arid – so be prepared.

Filtered water should also be sterilized.

Sources of water

Deserts – rock pools and wells; any river bed with healthy-looking bushes will have water, if you can dig deep enough; desert stills.

Forests and jungles – rivers, water holes and wells; some plants with collection-shaped receptacles; collecting the transpiration of a tree limb or large bush by sealing a plastic bag over it and collecting the water that descends to the lowest point.

Dew – collected from the vehicle body or plastic sheets by wiping with a sponge or cloth and squeezing it into a container.

Snow and ice

Water supplies can be improved by making as many desert stills as

A desert still.

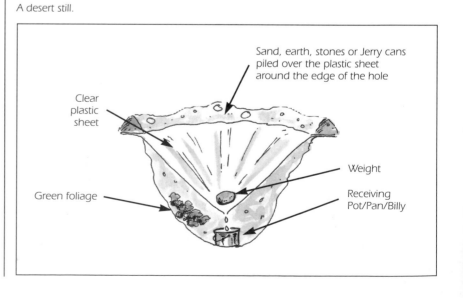

Sand, earth, stones or Jerry cans piled over the plastic sheet around the edge of the hole

Clear plastic sheet

Weight

Green foliage

Receiving Pot/Pan/Billy

possible. To make a still, dig a hole about 0.3 yard (metre) deep and 1 yard (metre) in diameter, place a clean saucepan or billy in the centre of the hole and cover the hole with a 2-yard (metre) square plastic sheet weighted down with stones, jerry cans or tools at the edges. Place one stone or similar object in the centre to weigh it down directly over the billy.

Overnight, water vapour from the sand will evaporate and condense on the underside of the plastic sheet. In the morning, running a finger down from the edge to the centre of the sheet will cause the condensation to run down and drip into the pan. All urine should be conserved and put into shallow containers around the central billy,

> **Warning:** Do not use the leaves of the Sodom Apple (*Calatropis procera*), a bush with orange-sized green fruits, which are common in many deserts, as they are poisonous.

as can any non-poisonous green foliage. The water so collected should be boiled or sterilized before drinking.

If you have antifreeze in your radiator, do not drink the water from this, as it is highly poisonous. Even if you have not put antifreeze in the radiator yourself, there is still likely to be some or inhibitor additives left in it from previous use, or from the factory when the vehicle was first manufactured. Radiator water can be put into the desert still in the same way as urine, and the resulting condensate should be boiled or sterilized before drinking.

Water from bad or brackish wells and seawater can be made drinkable in the same way. Note, however, that solar stills can take a lot of energy to create and will yield little water in return. Until the situation is really desperate, they are probably not worth considering as a viable means of collecting water.

The will to live is essential. Once you give up, you will be finished. If you find a person in such a situation and do not have a doctor to handle them, feed them water (to which has been added 1 level teaspoon of salt and 2 tablespoons of sugar per litre of water), a teaspoonful at a time, every few minutes for a couple of hours. It is essential to try to stabilise them in this way before trying to take them on a long, tough drive to hospital. Sachets of salts for rehydration are available for your medical kit. If the patient is unconscious, rehydration salts may be administered rectally.

Shelter

Except in forest and jungle it is always best to remain with the vehicle, so you will have this as shelter. In hot climates you will sweat inside the vehicle during the day, so make extra shade with tarpaulins suspended between vehicles or between the vehicle and the ground.

In heavy snow and a strong wind a snow hole will be warmer than the vehicle or a tent.

In forest and jungle there will be plenty of greenery around with which to make a shelter, but a waterproof sheet will be more waterproof. Mosquito nets will often be essential. Beware of sheltering under trees with dead limbs, or under coconut palms.

Survival in hot dry climates

To minimise water loss, avoid manual work during the day; work at night or in the early morning. Build shade and stay under it as much as possible, keeping well covered with loose cotton clothing. 'Space blankets' with the reflective side facing out give the coolest shade. Keep warm and out of the wind at night.

Unless you are well off the piste with no chance of a search, you should stay with your vehicle. If someone must walk out, pick one or two of the strongest, most determined persons to go. They

Do not use or touch the Sodom Apple or milkweed (Calatropis procera) – it is very poisonous.

Create shade by suspending tarpaulins between vehicles.

must have a compass, torch, salt, anti-diarrhoea medicine, loose all-enveloping clothes, good footwear, good sunglasses and as much water as they can sensibly carry.

In soft sand a jerry can of water can easily be hauled along on a rope from the waist. On mixed ground tie the jerry can to a sand ladder, one end of which is padded and tied to the waist. Those who walk out should follow the desert nomad pattern of walking in the evening until about 2300 hours, sleep until 0400 hours, walk again until 1000 hours, then dig a shallow hollow in the sand and lie in it under a space blanket, reflective side out, until the sun has lost its heat.

If the walkers have a full moon they can walk all night; in this way fit people would make 37-43 miles (60-70 km) on 10 litres of water, less in soft sand.

Short-term use of potassium (Slow-K) helps to sustain mental alertness. Immodium is best as a diarrhoea 'blocker', but Lomotil contains atropine which can cause problems with focusing the eyes.

Survival in cold climates

This is all about keeping warm. You must keep the cold out and keep your own body heat in. In the Arctic you soon learn that if you are cold when you get into a sleeping bag, it will be several hours before you warm up enough to relax. It is best to do something physical to warm you up first. If you have to dig a snow hole, you will certainly be warm enough by the time you finish. Once in a sleeping bag, food and hot drinks, but not alcohol, will help keep you warm.

Shelter is important, so stay with the vehicle. If you have to leave it, make sure that you have sunglasses or goggles against glare, and that your head is covered. A considerable amount of body heat is lost through the head, and once it gets too cold your brain stops functioning sensibly.

Overwork is counter productive. Too much sweat will wet your inner clothing so that it loses much of its insulation, and once you stop your activity you will soon feel cold. Too much sweating also leads to dehydration, which makes you vulnerable to fatigue.

Modern synthetic fibre garments are best to wear, but during strong physical activity sweat may condense, and even freeze, against the inner surface of your outer garment. So unless wind chill or rain are present, take the outer garment off while working.

If available, food, either hot or cold, and hot drinks will help keep your body heat up. High-energy carbohydrate snacks such as glucose, sweets and chocolate bars are particularly useful. If you do not have hot drinks, sip cold drinks or snow occasionally to fend off dehydration.

If any one becomes incoherent or you rescue someone with hypothermia, the first priority is to get them into shelter, remove wet clothing and preferably get them into a sleeping bag if one is available. Otherwise a large plastic bag is more useful than aluminium-coated 'space blankets'. If the victim is coherent, give hot drinks and hot food or high-energy carbohydrate snacks. Do not give alcohol, which causes peripheral vasodilation, bringing body heat to the skin but lowering the body core temperature. Do not allow the victim to smoke, as nicotine causes vasi-constriction, reducing the blood flow to hands, fingers and toes.

Victims should be warmed up by the body heat of others, in close contact. Use mouth-to-mouth/nose resuscitation or cardiac massage if necessary. Do not give up easily if the victim appears to be dead, as many have been resuscitated successfully after quite long periods. If you can get the victim back to civilisation, but medical help is not readily to hand, put the victim in a *warm* bath to warm up slowly.

Snow holes

To build a snow hole you require a depth of about 2 yards (metres) of snow, so a good-sized snow drift is essential. Start digging at the base and dig upwards. Once you are at least a yard (metre) in, make a chamber large enough for the party.

Next block the lower entrance hole, but cut a small ventilation hole out through the roof and regularly check that it is clear. By having the snow hole above the entrance, warmer air will be trapped there. Keep shovels inside

A snow hole.

with you, so that you can dig yourselves out if it collapses.

Do not try to build an igloo – in most areas of the world the snow is of the wrong type, even in Eastern Greenland!

Survival in forests and jungles

Forests and jungles are the only area where, if you have not been rescued for several days, it may be sensible to abandon the vehicle and attempt to walk out. In this instance you will have travelled in on a now well-marked route, so it will be more sensible to retrace that route rather than to make any attempt at travelling across country. You are not likely to have problems obtaining water, but you should sterilize all drinking water.

The most important considerations, apart from the will to survive, will be health, dry clothing, comfortable footwear and avoiding biting insects. Any cuts, large or small, can turn septic quickly and be slow to heal; they should be cleaned and treated at once.

Keep up your salt intake, use antibiotics and anti-diarrhoeals at the first sign of trouble, and if necessary use Slow-K to retain mental alertness.

Tropical jungles

In tropical jungles a mosquito net and some method of being able to sleep off the ground (hammocks are not always suitable) are essential, and sleeping bags should be kept in waterproof bags when not in use.

Footwear must be comfortable to walk in when wet, and it is advisable if possible to keep a dry set of clothes in a waterproof bag for use only at night. Put your wet clothes back on as soon as you get up in the morning. They will be uncomfortable for a few minutes, but any dry clothes would soon be just as wet.

In leech country a heavyweight cotton sock worn between socks and boots and tied with a drawstring just below the knee offers good protection, except from leeches dropping down on you from trees! The only place I know where such socks can be bought off the shelf is in Malaysian Borneo, where they are called 'leech socks'.

If you have delicate skin, talcum powder applied between the crutch, and anywhere else that rubs when moving, will make life more comfortable.

FINAL POINTS

Have a full medical and dental check-up and catch up on all necessary vaccinations before departure.

Vehicles on ferries or being shipped to Third World countries (even those inside containers) are regularly broken into en route. Sometimes you can see this happening, but the authorities do not allow you to interfere and stop it. Do not therefore leave valuable articles in vehicles that you cannot guard personally.

Finally, aim to be as self-sufficient as possible. Carry spare food and clothing to suit a changing climate and social conditions, and have the tools, spares and ability to maintain your vehicle. Without these, despite the occasional kind person, you will be conned and exploited to the extent that the journey can become a major ordeal. However, with adequate care and preparation, the journey will be an experience of a lifetime.

THE EXPEDITION ADVISORY CENTRE AT THE ROYAL GEOGRAPHICAL SOCIETY

The Royal Geographical Society in London has always been the world's premier meeting place for serious expeditions, with a library containing more than 160 years of reports on expeditions and a map room second to none in this field. When I began leading expeditions this is where I was able to research my projects and destinations.

In 1980 the Expedition Advisory Centre was formed by the Royal Geographical Society and the Young Explorers Trust. Currently sponsored by Shell International Petroleum Company, the great success of the Centre is due to the dedicated work of its staff, led by Shane and Nigel Winser.

The EAC is mainly concerned with those planning scientific expeditions overseas, mostly at undergraduate level and, through its association with the Young Explorers' Trust, those leading school or youth expeditions. The Centre also helps those planning adventurous activities abroad, including mountaineering, caving, canoeing and underwater expeditions, as well as to a lesser extent independent and overland travellers.

The Centre's services include:

- Access to past expedition reports
- The Expedition Planner's Handbook and Directory, which covers just about everything you need to know about equipment suppliers, funding bodies, scien-

tific agencies and how to organise, run and report an expedition

- A wide range of more specialised publications written by experts in their fields
- Specialist advisors with recent experience of particular expeditions
- Country Fact Sheets
- Services for those wishing to join an expedition or recruit members for their own expedition

Every year, over a weekend in November, the EAC organises a two-day 'Planning a Small Expedition' seminar at the RGS London Headquarters. Experts give presentations on everything from leadership, through staying healthy, to communications and sources of research. The first day features logistics workshops including Mountaineering, Caving, Polar, Diving, Tropical Forests, Hot Deserts and Savannas. The second day includes field work workshops, all of which include case studies of recent expeditions.

As well as the seminar speakers, other expedition specialists are on hand to pass on their knowledge. Equipment suppliers and book shops have their latest offerings on display, and there are registers for those recruiting expedition members, or those wishing to join an existing expedition. The EAC's specialist publications are also on sale. Centre staff also take a smaller road show of 'Expedition Planning Workshops' around UK universities in the weeks preceding the main seminar.

The EAC also organises a one-day biennial 'Independent Travellers' seminar at the RGS London headquarters in May. Seasoned travellers present talks on everything from how to stay healthy through to organising, funding and recording adventurous travel, illustrated by case studies of recent trips. Many other experienced travellers, travel writers and photographers are in attendance, swopping tales and ideas and passing on advice to less experienced travellers. There are displays by equipment, clothing, insurance, flights and adventure holiday specialists, together with those by book shops.

Both the 'Planning a Small Expedition' and the 'Independent Travellers' seminars have become very popular and are well worth attending by prospective expedition personnel and travellers. Book early to avoid disappointment.

APPENDIX 1

Off-road driving tuition

Military authorities and Land Rover have run off-road driving courses for as long as they have had vehicles for off-road use, but these were not open to the general public. In 1986 David Bowyer set up the UK's first non-military and non-factory-based off-road driving centre and school, spawning a new industry. At his specially landscaped, non-damaging course in Devon, tuition is available in each driver's own or company vehicle, or a vehicle belonging to the school. Extended courses are available in recovery, KERR recovery and winching.

Many well-established centres also organise corporate days, prod-

Learning to understand axle articulation at David Bowyer's off-road centre.

uct testing and adventure safaris in the UK and overseas. Groups of owner-driver vehicles cover off-road routes encompassing a variety of conditions and scenery, while having the expertise of experienced leadership.

There are now a remarkable number of off-road centres around the UK and across Europe. Land Rover have opened up their special training facilities to the public and Vauxhall offer free tuition to purchasers of their off-road vehicles through selected off-road centres.

I had to learn the hard way in the field, but now these schools exist you can learn the techniques quickly and enjoy yourself at the same time. The low cost of tuition will save you money in vehicle damage and lessen the chance of hurt pride if you get seriously stuck somewhere.

There are also many sites

Keith Hart introducing four-wheel drive in the classroom at David Bowyer's off-road centre.

Testing driving skills on the seesaw with Ronnie Dale.

where you can pay a fee to drive your own vehicle off-road legally, for practice or fun. Tuition may or may not also be available, but experienced marshalls are on hand with vehicles equipped to recover yours if you get stuck.

OFF-ROAD CENTRES

The sites listed here may or may not offer off-road driving tuition, and only a few of them offer courses on winching and recovery.

The addresses given are not necessarily those of the site used. Some centres have several sites available and some sites are only for fun days, using your own vehicle.

Before choosing a centre, always telephone first. The site may be fully booked on the day you require, or temporarily closed.

The number of centres is increasing so fast that it is highly likely some may cease operating during the life of this book.

* Denotes member of the Off-road Training Association

ALL-TERRAIN OFF-ROADING
Ewenny Farm
Upper Maryland
Chelmsford
Essex CM3 6EE
Tel 01621 774030

THE BARONY COLLEGE
Park Gate
Dumfries & Galloway DG1 3NE
Tel 01387 86251

BASKERVILLE CHALLENGE 4x4 CENTRE
The Garrison
Brilley
Whiteney on Wye
Hereford & Worcs HR3 6HF
Tel 01497 831357

BRANDS HATCH 4x4 OFF-ROAD SCHOOL
Fawkham
Longfield
Kent DA3 8NG
Tel 01474 872367

BUCKMORE PARK 4x4 OFF-ROAD DRIVING CENTRE
Maidstone Road
Chatham
Kent ME5 9QG
Tel 01634 861295

CANTERBURY OFF-ROAD CENTRE
Rushbourne Manor
Hoath
Canterbury
Kent
Tel 01227 728268

CHEVIOT 4x4 CENTRE
Yearle Farm
Wooler
Northumberland
Tel 01668 82287

CHINNOCK OFF-ROAD COURSE
(near Yeovil, Somerset)
Andy Raison
15 Matts Lane
Stoke-sub-Hamdon
Somerset TA14 6QE
Tel 01935 825314 (evening)

CLUB OFF-ROAD
5 Quarryside
Mirfield
West Yorkshire
Tel 01924 469376

COLZIE HILL RECREATION
Auchtermuchty
Fife KY14 7EQ
Tel 01337 27075

COUNTRY SPORTS
Penny Spring Farm
Detling
Kent
Tel 01622 739439

DON COYOTE
Lamancha Village
Nr Edinburgh
Lothian
Tel 0131 443 2881

DAVID BOWYER'S OFF-ROAD CENTRE*
East Foldhay
Zeal Monachorum
Crediton
Devon EX17 6DH
Tel 01363 82666

DRIVE-IT-ALL
Enstone Airfield Complex
Church Enstone
Chipping Norton
Oxfordshire OX7 7NP
Tel 01608 678339

EAST MIDLANDS 4x4
    TRAINING CENTRE
Manor Farm
Kneeton Road
East Bridgford
Notts NG13 8PJ
Tel 01949 20003

EDGEHILL SHOOTING
    GROUND
Nadbury House
Camp Lane
Warmington
Oxon
Tel 01295 878141

FOLLY 4x4
The Hollies
Kings Road
Market Lavington
Nr Devizes
Wilts SN10 4PZ
Tel 01380 812434

FRESH TRACKS
(Office address:)
Haultwick Farm
Ware
Herts SG11 1JQ
Tel 01920 438758

FRONTIER TRAILS
Home Farm
Cholderton
Nr Salisbury
Wilts SP4 0DW
Tel 01980 654162

GOLDING BARN 4x4
Golding Barn Estate
Small Dole
Nr Upper Beeding
West Sussex
Tel 01903 812195

GOTWICK WOOD OFF-ROAD
    CENTRE
Gotwick Wood Farm
Holtye Road
East Grinstead
East Sussex
Tel 01342 315504

GRAHAM CLARKE
The Steadings
Dunkeld House Hotel
Dunkeld
Tayside
Tel 01350 728700

GRAVELMANIA
CY Repair Services
6 Curzon Drive
Manor Way Industrial Estate
Grays
Essex RM17 6BG
Tel 01375 371655

HERITAGE MOTOR CENTRE
Gaydon
Warwickshire
Tel 01926 641188

HIGHLAND DROVERS*
Kineardine
Boat of Garten
Highland PH24 3BY
Tel 01479 83329

HIGHLAND OFF-ROAD
    ADVENTURE CENTRE
New House, Plot 3
Strathnacro
Glenuquart
Invernesshire

IAN WRIGHT OFF-ROAD
    DRIVING SCHOOL
7 Church Row
West Peckham
Maidstone
Kent
Tel 01622 817509

INTERNATIONAL OFF-
    ROADERS
BRT House
40 Bridge Street
Chepstow
Gwent NP6 5ET
Tel 01291 628889

LAKELAND SAFARI
Duddon View
Castle Way
Broughton-in-Furness
Cumbria LA17 7UW
Tel 01229 716943 (24 hrs)

LAKELAND VILLAGE OFF-
    ROAD DRIVING
The Lakeland Village
Newby Bridge
Ulverston
Cumbria LA12 8PX
Tel 015395 30090

LANDCRAFT*
Plas-yn-Dre, Top Floor
High Street
Bala
Gwynedd LL25 7LU
Tel 01678 520820

THE LAND ROVER
    EXPERIENCE
Lode Lane
Solihull
West Midlands B92 8NW
Tel 0121 700 4619

LANDWISE
Rothiemurchus Estate
By Aviemore
Highland PH22 1QH
Tel 01479 810858

LEISURE PURSUITS
Chartin House
Hammerwood Road
Ashurst Wood
East Grinstead
West Sussex RH19 3RX
Tel 01342 825522

LLAMA OFF-ROAD EVENTS
10 Woodend Place
Tettenhall Wood
Wolverhampton
West Midlands WV6 8JU
Tel 01902 756589

MANBY SHOWGROUND
    PERFORMANCE DRIVING
    CENTRE
Sunny Oak
Little Cawthorpe
Louth
Lincolnshire LN11 8ND
Tel 01507 604375

MID-NORFOLK OFF-ROAD
    CENTRE
Wood Farm
Runhall
Norwich
Norfolk NR9 4DW
Tel 01362 850233

MOORLAND OFF-ROAD
ADVENTURE SPORT
1 Beckside Cottage
Brook Lane
Thornton-le-Dale
Pickering
North Yorks YO18 7RW
Tel 01751 476537

MOTOR SAFARI
Treetops
Mold
Clwyd CH7 4SS
Tel 01352 770439/770769

NEWTON FARM
Wormit
Newport-on-Tay
Fife DD6 8RL
Tel 01382 541651

NEWTON HILL COUNTRY
SPORTS
The Sandford Country House
Hotel
Newton Hill
Wormit
Nr Dundee
Fife
Tel 01382 541460

NORTH DOWNS SPECIALIST
ACTION SPORTS
Warren Barn Farm
Slines Oak Road
Woldingham
Surrey CR3 7HN
Tel 01342 325913

NORTH HEREFORDSHIRE
OFF-ROAD DRIVING
SCHOOL
The Vauld
Marden
Hereford & Worcs HR1 3HA
Tel 0156 884372

NORTH YORKSHIRE OFF-
ROAD CENTRE
Bay Ness Farm
Robin Hoods Bay
Whitby
North Yorks YO22 4PJ
Tel 01947 880371

OFF-ROAD LEISURE
Arkwright Road
Willow Brook North Industry
Corby
Northants
Tel 01536 403500

OFF-ROAD MOTIVATIONS
Andover Garden Machinery
Salisbury Road
Andover
Hants SP11 7DN
Tel 01264 710113

PAUL READ'S 4x4 FUN FARM
22 Gordon Hill
Enfield
Middx EN2 1QP
Tel 0181 366 0487

PRO-TRAX
Vince Cobley
32 Southfield Road
Gretton
Nr Corby
Northants
Tel 01536 770096

*(Vince also organises the Warn
Challenge Events)*

QUEST 4x4
Bury St Austens Farm
Rudgwick
West Sussex RH12 3AN
Tel 01403 822439

READING TRAIL PARK
Island Road
Smallmead
Reading
Berks
Tel 01635 268394

RED DRAGON OFF-ROAD
18 Ragged Staff
Saundersfoot
Dyfed
Tel 01834 813917

RONNIE DALE OFF-ROAD
ADVENTURE DRIVING
SCHOOL*
Whiteburn
Abbey Street
Bathans
Duns
Borders TD11 3RU
Tel 01361 840244

ROUGH TERRAIN
TRAINING*
36 Hinton Road
Woodford Halse
Daventry
Northants NN11 6TR
Tel 01295 788414

ROUGH TRACKS
Nr Chatham
Kent
Tel 01634 261176

SHANDON COUNTRY
PURSUITS
Stuckenduff Farm
Rhu
Strathclyde G84 8NF
Tel 01436 820838

SOUTH WEST ALL TERRAIN
(SWAT 4x4)
Beach House
Church Steps
Fore Street
Kingsbridge
Devon TQ7 1PZ
Tel 01548 857335

SPECTRUM CORPORATE
SERVICES
Unit 3, Swinton Meadows
Business Park
Meadow Way
Swinton
Mexborough
South Yorks S64 8AQ
Tel 01709 578686

SWALESMOOR OFF-ROAD
DRIVING CENTRE
5 Spring Row
Long Causeway
Denholme
Bradford
West Yorks BP13 4AE
Tel 01274 833114

TRAK 1 OFF-ROAD RACING
Barn Elms Farm
Bradfield
Nr Reading
Berks
Tel 01895 258410/811303

TUFF TERRAINS
Abbeycwmhir
Llandrindod Wells
Powys
Tel 01597 851551

TUFF TERRAINS IRELAND
Castle Leslie
Glaslough
Co Monaghan
Ireland
Tel 00 353 47 88364

TUF GOING
Freightmaster's Estate
Coldharbour Lane
off Ferry Lane
Rainham
Essex
Tel 01268 764830

TUF TRAX
Westerings
Station Road
West Haddon
Northants NN6 7AU
Tel 01788 510575

VENTURE 4x4
Eastern Grove
Squares Grove
Three Holes
Wisbech
Cambs PE14 9JY
Tel 01945 772270

WARWICKSHIRE COLLEGE
   OFF-ROAD DRIVING
   SCHOOL*
Moreton Morrell
Warwickshire CV35 9BL
Tel 01926 651367

WEARDALE OFF-ROAD
   CENTRE
Cloves House Farm
Wolsingham
Co Durham DL13 3BG
Tel 01388 527375

WILD ROVERS
38 Chatsworth Road
Hazel Grove
Stockport SK7 6BT
Tel 0161 449 0725

WILD TRACKS
Chippenham Road
Kennett
Nr Newmarket
Suffolk CB8 7QJ
Tel 01638 751918

YORKSHIRE OFF-ROAD & 4x4
   TRAINING CENTRE
Ghyll Grange
Brunthwaite
Nr Silsden
West Yorks BD20 0NJ
Tel 01850 301839

YORKSHIRE 4x4
   EXPLORATION
West Pasture
Crakehall
North Yorks DL8 1TT
Tel 01609 770710

4x4 ADVENTURE
Caeau
Botwnnog
Pwllheli
Gwynedd LL53 7SW
Tel 01758 83688

4x4 DRIVE
The Castle House
Rock Park
Wirral L42 1PJ
Tel 0151 645 8124

4x4 OFF-ROAD EXPERIENCE
Whitbread Hop Farm
8 The Links
Addington
West Malling
Kent ME19 5RX
Tel 01732 843018

APPENDIX 2

Competitions and clubs

In the UK land is at a premium, and with the exception of historical byways it is illegal to drive a vehicle off the public road, so one has to use private land. If you are not a landowner yourself, join an off-road centre safari or a four-wheel drive club, which will have organised events at weekends on private or military land, and evening meetings for films and lectures.

The Association of Rover Owners Clubs has member clubs around the country, each a separate entity arranging its own events and newsletters. A National Event is organised once a year.

The All Wheel Drive Club covers all makes of vehicle, including two-wheel drive Buggies and the preservation of military vehicles. It is a nationwide organisation holding local weekend events and evening meetings around the country. Members also compete in events in France and further afield. Many Land Rover and Range Rover owners are members of both of these organisations, and there are also other clubs that are not associated with any 'umbrella' organisation.

The main club events are Non Damaging Trials, Trials and Safaris, while some meetings also include Winching and Trailer Manoeuvring. Non Damaging Trials are particularly suitable for the road-going vehicle that you use every day. They follow a marked-out course that does not have any awkward trees or rocks that might damage your vehicle.

Trials are over more difficult terrain and may include awkward trees, rocks, steep inclines and deep water, so vehicles can get bent, but speeds are very slow so personal injury is unlikely. Trials courses are marked out with canes, the idea being to complete all sections without going off route or touching any of the canes.

Safaris are speed events; you do not race as such, but are timed individually over a set course and complete a number of runs, sometimes including runs at night.

Recently there has been an upsurge of interest in 'green laning', which is the vehicular use of old lanes that historically should remain open for all vehicular use. Some of these have been illegally blocked by land owners and others are the cause of much debate amongst other interested users, including ramblers, horse riders, cyclists and motor cyclists. This is a contentious issue, so one should 'green lane' only in the company of experienced club members or off-road centres, who have fully checked the legal position of the lane before using it and have the know-how and equipment to get the vehicles out again if conditions become too difficult or impassable.

A Land Rover Special negotiating a caned route – a bounce raises a wheel.

A Jeep Wrangler clears the water trough, tow strap ready!

A Land Rover takes it gently through the woods.

Various large, commercial Speed Rallies occur around the world, where vastly expensive high-speed, Kevlar-bodied, high-tech super cars stand the best chance of winning.

The really strongly motivated can compete for places in the Camel Trophy, the ultimate four-wheel drive competitive challenge. From thousands of hopeful applicants, some 40 from each participating country are chosen for a long, hard weekend of evaluation, including physical fitness, swimming, bridge-building, map-reading and psychological assessment, as well as driving and winching, all intentionally with little sleep. Eventually two finalists and a reserve are selected to compete in an international final, and they deserve their satisfaction.

A major problem with the Camel Trophy is that very few of those who apply ever get to take part in it. More down-to-earth competitions have recently evolved such as the Warn Challenge. Sponsored by Warn Winches and organised by Vince Cobley, co-winner with Dave Fletcher of the Warn Transylvania Trophy 1993, the Warn Challenge is open to all,

whether novice or expert, using road-legal vehicles.

A series of events are held around the country over the year, with the first two from each round going forward to a grand final in April. Each event is designed to be non-damaging, but testing driving skills, ingenuity, fortitude, team work and team spirit over a series of set stages and tasks including navigation, challenging driving, winching, wading and the construction and use of aerial rope-ways and rafts.

Entries are arranged into teams of three vehicles, at least one of which is fitted with a winch. The stages are arranged so that team-work plays a major part in getting all three vehicles through. The judges' scoring is based on skills, planning and execution, rather than vehicle prowess.

The aim of the Warn Challenge is to promote controlled off-roading, and to help to pass on safe winching techniques and practises during an adventurous weekend event. With the current difficulties over 'green laning' this type of event is likely to be the future of off-roading in the UK.

The Warn Challenge is open to any make of vehicle and any make of winch. There are also international 'Warn Adventures', where the vehicles entered must be fitted with a Warn Winch. The 1995 Warn Adventure was held in Morocco.

For full details contact:
VINCE COBLEY
PRO-TRAX
32 Southfield Road
Gretton
Northants NN17 3BX
Tel/fax 01536 770096

Gently does it on the Warn Challenge!

The Warn Trophy is about teamwork.

UK CLUB GUIDE

* Member clubs of the Association of Rover Clubs Ltd

Ae 4x4 CLUB
Anne Smith
Closs Cottage
Closs
Boreland-by-Lockerbie
Dumfriesshire DG11 2LQ
Tel 01576 6291

ALL WHEEL DRIVE CLUB
SAE to PO BOX 6
Fleet, Hants GU14 9YL

ANGLIAN ROVER OWNERS'
    CLUB LTD
Dave Thompson
14 Black Swan Lane
Luton
Beds LU3 2LU
Tel 01582 507905

THE ASSOCIATION OF
    ROVER CLUBS Ltd*
Andrew J. Stavordale
65 Longmead Avenue
Hazel Grove
Stockport SK7 5PJ
Tel 0161 456 8224

ARC OVERSEAS LIAISON
    OFFICER*
Fran Luxton
Woodbine Cottage
Lameton
Nr Tavistock
Devon PL19 8RZ
Tel 01822 610650

101 FORWARD CONTROL
    CLUB AND REGISTER*
Mr H. Smith
13 Gloucester Gardens
Braintree
Essex CM7 6LG
Tel 01376 552331

BRECKLAND LAND ROVER
    CLUB LTD*
Wendy Chandler
8 Acorn Road
North Walsham
Norfolk NR28 0HA
Tel 01692 404453

BUCHAN OFF-ROAD
    DRIVERS' CLUB
Robert Farquhar
44 Craigpark Place
Ellon
Aberdeenshire AB41 9FG
Tel 01358 22668

BUX 4x4
John Butler
Home Farm
High Street
Ludgershall
Bucks HP18 9PF
Tel 01844 237479

BUXTON AND DISTRICT
    LAND ROVER CLUB
Mrs C. Ollerenshaw
29 Dale Road
Buxton SK17 6LN
Tel 01298 71558

CHELTENHAM &
    COTSWOLDS LAND ROVER
    CLUB*
Ian Wood
21 Olbury Road
Cheltenham
Gloucestershire
Tel 01242 230793

A Land Rover being lowered over the edge by winch during a Warn Trophy event.

CHILTERN VALE ROVER
    OWNERS' CLUB*
Colin Argent
21 Meadow Way
Codicote
Hitchin
Herts SG4 8YL
Tel 01438 821581

CLEVELAND 4WD CLUB
Eric Graves
71 Barrington Crescent
Thorntree Estate
Middlesborough
Cleveland

CLUB DISCOVERY
Ray Grates
West Farm
Witham-on-the-Hill
Bourne
Lincs PE10 QJN
Tel 01778 33484

CLUB HIGH FRONTIER
Steve Pyne
Home Farm
Cholderton
Nr Salisbury
Wilts SP4 0DW
Tel 01980 654162

CLUB 4x4 (LEIGH)
Mike Fishlock
School Bungalow
Manchester Drive
Leigh-on-Sea
Essex SS9 3HP
Tel 01702 712577

CORNWALL & DEVON LAND
    ROVER CLUB*
Jean French
5 Pinewood Close
Plympton
Plymouth
Devon PL7 3DW
Tel 01752 338279

CUMBRIAN LAND ROVER
    CLUB*
Peter Anstiss
11 Alder Close
Newton-with-Scales
Preston
Lancs PR4 3TQ
Tel 01772 685735

Construction and use of an aerial ropeway
is one of the Warn Trophy tasks.

THE DEESIDE FOUR-WHEEL-
    DRIVE CLUB
Lorraine Allan
c/o Banchory Lodge Hotel
Banchory
Kincardineshire AB3 3HS
Tel 013302 2625

DORSET LAND ROVER AND
    RANGE ROVER OWNERS'
    CLUB*
Norman Legg
119 King John Avenue
Bear Wood
Bournemouth
Dorset BH11 9SA

EAST DEVON OFF-ROAD
    CLUB
Peter Broom
Armidale
Fenny Bridges
Honiton
Devon EX14 OBG
Tel 01404 850960

EAST ESSEX 4x4 CLUB
67 Lawling Avenue
Heybridge
Essex CM9 7YD
Tel (Rob) 01621 819709 or
    (Elaine) 01376 502078

EAST MIDLAND OFF-ROAD
    CLUB
Martyn Jacques
Woodstock
Gainsborough Road
Winthorpe
Newark
Notts NG24 2NN
Tel 01636 79421

EAST NORTHANTS LAND
    ROVER OWNERS' CLUB*
Dave Vaughan
1 Woodavens Close
Northampton NN4 9TX
Tel 01604 763626

ESSEX LAND ROVER CLUB*
Dave Bygrave
The Knoll
Bygrave Road
Ashwell
Nr Bladock
Herts SG7 5RH
Tel 0146274 2418 (evening)

EX-MILITARY LR
    ASSOCIATION
Mark Cook
50 St Andrew Street
Leighton Buzzard
Beds LU7 8DS
Tel 01525 372016

FORWARD CONTROL
    REGISTER IIA and IIB*
C. B. Heron
28 Front Street
Daisy Hill
Sacriston
Co Durham DH7 6BL
Tel 0191 371 2527

FOSSE & WATLING LAND
    ROVER CLUB
Tel 01455 848228/615731

4 COUNTIES OFF-ROAD
    CLUB
Lauren Rawlinson
136 Springfield Avenue
Banbury
Oxon OX16 9JD
Tel 01295 264946

FRIENDSHIP 4x4 ROMILEY
J. A. Bradley
35 Urwick Road
Romiley
Stockport
Cheshire SK6 3JS
Tel 0161 430 2609

FYFIELD LRC
Mike Sassoon
Broom Hills
Ongar Road
Fyfield
Nr Ongar
Essex CM5 ORB

FYLDE OFF-ROAD CLUB
David Brown
52 Woodlands Road
Lytham St Annes
Lancs FY8 4BX
Tel 01253 796198 (9am–5pm)

GLAMORGAN OFF-ROAD
    CLUB
Tom Baker
95 Coldbrook Road
East Barry
S Glamorgan CF63 1NG
Tel 01446 740881

GLOSSOP & DISTRICT 4x4
    GROUP
Peter & June Threlfall
40 Winster Mews
Gamesley
Glossop
Tel 01457 868248

GOLDING BARN 4x4
Golding Barn Estate
Small Dole
Nr Upper Beeding
West Sussex
Tel 01903 812195 (John
    Morgan)

GREENHOUS 4x4 OFF-ROAD
    CLUB
A. M. Frearson
Greenhous Hanley
Victoria Road
Hanley
Stoke-on-Trent
Staffs ST1 3JE
Tel 01782 202200

HANTS & BERKS ROVER
    OWNERS'*
Gary Langton
1 Hillside Court
16 Solent Road
Drayton
Portsmouth
Hants PO6 1HH
Tel 01705 388929

HERTFORDSHIRE LAND
    ROVER FANATICS
Mick Fox
143 Boundary Way
Garston
Watford
Herts WD2 7SR
Tel 01923 462753

HIGHLAND 4WD CLUB
Colin Stewart
Main Street
Newtonmore
Highland PH20 1DA
Tel 0154 03 251 (day)

HUMBERSIDE LAND ROVER
    CLUB
Ian Brimble
37 Oaklands Drive
Hessle
Humberside HU13 0LT
Tel 01482 641260

ISLE OF DOGS FWD CLUB
Jon Dunning
69 Taeping Street
Clippers Quay
Isle of Dogs
London E14 9UT
Tel 0171 515 6453

ISLE OF MAN 4WD CLUB
B. P. Waring
58 Groudle Road
Onchan
Isle of Man
Tel 01624 627826

ISLE OF WIGHT 4x4 CLUB
Mike Penketh
75 Church Road
Wooton
Isle of Wight PO33 4PZ

INVICTA LRC
Membership Secretary
31 Mary Road
Deal
Kent CT14 9HW
Tel 01304 380958

THE JAPANESE 4x4 CLUB OF
    GT BRITAIN
Ray Gardner
41 Whitehorn Avenue
Yiewsley
Middx UB7 8JY
Tel 01784 455639

LANCASHIRE & CHESHIRE
    ROVER OWNERS' CLUB*
Ian Foster
31 Slimbridge Close
Breightmet
Bolton BL2 5NT
Tel 01204 396449

LAND ROVER REGISTER
    (1947–1951)*
Richard Lines
45 Park Road
Yeadon
Leeds LS19 7EX
Tel 01132 506546

LAND ROVER SERIES ONE
    CLUB*
David Bowyer
East Foldhay
Zeal Monachorum
Crediton
Devon EX17 6DH
Tel 01363 82666 (business hours
    only)

LAND ROVER SERIES II
    CLUB*
PO Box 1750
Bridport
Dorset DT6 5YJ

LAND ROVER SERIES III
    CLUB
Frank King
16 Holly Street
Cannock
Staffs WS11 2RU
Tel 01543 423326

LEE VALLEY LAND ROVER
   OWNERS' CLUB
Harry Stalick
24 Love Lane
Chigwell
Essex IG8 8BB
Tel 0181 504 3873

LEICESTERSHIRE AND
   RUTLAND LAND ROVER
   CLUB*
M. J. Smith
1 Yarwell Drive
Wigston Magna
Leicester LE89 1OF
Tel 0116 881041

LIGHTWEIGHT LAND ROVER
   CLUB*
Sue Foster
31 Slimbridge Close
Breightmet
Bolton BL2 5NT
Tel 01204 396449

LINCOLNSHIRE LAND
   ROVER CLUB*
Kevin Martin, Club Secretary
11 Lincoln Road
Nocton
Lincoln LN4 2AE
Tel 01472 398019

LLAMA OFF-ROAD CLUB
David James Round
10 Woodend Place
Tettenhall Wood
Wolverhampton
West Midlands WV6 8JU
Tel 01902 756988

MIDLANDS OFF-ROAD CLUB
Bruce Harris
34 Mayfield Road
Hurst Green
Halesowen B62 9QW
Tel 0121 422 9465

MIDLAND ROVER OWNERS'
   CLUB*
John Blackwell
14 Matlock Close
Brownsover
Rugby
Warwickshire CV1 1LB
Tel 01788 569902

MID WALES FOUR WHEEL
   DRIVE CLUB
Carol Tweedle
'Llwyn'
Harford
Llanwrda
Dyfed SA19 8DS

MID WEST OFF-ROADERS
   CLUB
Much Marcle
Nr Ledbury
Hereford & Worcs HR8 2NB
Tel 01684 561957 or 01531
   660302

NATIONAL OFF-ROAD
   ASSOCIATION
Keith Felstead
62 Clapgun Street
Castle Donington
Derbys DE7 2LF
Tel 01332 811130

NEWCASTLE AND
   NANTWICH ROVER
   OWNERS' CLUB*
Garry Thompson
70 Cambridge Drive
Clayton
Newcastle
Staffs ST5 3DQ
Tel 01782 617224

NORTH DEVON OFF-ROAD
   CLUB
Ray Smith
99 Chanters Road
Bideford
Devon EX9 2QP
Tel 01237 473279

NORTH EAST ROVER
   OWNERS' CLUB*
Gary Campbell
1 Hawthorne Road
Blyth
Northumberland NE24 3DT
Tel 01670 362256

NORTHERN OFF-ROAD
   CLUB
Beverley Bairstow
14 Ailsa House
Fairhaven Green
Idle
West Yorks BD10 9ND
Tel 01274 610405

NORTH LAKES 4x4 CLUB
Geoff Tomlinson
Holme Lea
Quarry Field
Stockdalewath
Dalston
Carlisle CA5 7DP

NORTHERN IRELAND FWD
   CLUB
Ian Henderson
12 Abbot View
Newtownards
Co Down BT23 3XT
Tel 01247 811584 (evening)

NORTH WALES LAND ROVER
   CLUB*
Dave Cuthbert
25 Sunningdale Avenue
Colwyn Bay
Clwyd LL29 6DF
Tel 01492 534417

NOTTINGHAM LAND ROVER
   CLUB*
Annie Bentley
19 Manns Leys
Cotgrave
Nottingham
Tel 01152 894282

PEAK & DUKERIES LAND
   ROVER CLUB*
Alan Reaney
96 Ridgeway Road
Gleadless
Sheffield S12 2SY
Tel 0114 655108

PENNINE LAND ROVER
   CLUB*
Ivor Hill
2 Westbourne Road
Pontefract
West Yorks WF8 4JY
Tel 01977 707895

RANGE ROVER REGISTER
   LTD*
Les Booth
667 Lower Rainham Road
Rainham
Kent ME8 7TY

RED ROSE LAND ROVER
    CLUB*
B. L. Hart
75 Coniston Road
Fulwood
Preston
Lancs PR2 4AY
Tel 01772 709391

ROCHFORD & DISTRICT
    LAND ROVER OWNERS
Paula Fenily
17 Plumberow Mount Avenue
Hockley
Essex
Tel 01702 206055

SCOTTISH LAND ROVER
    OWNERS' CLUB*
Alan Walker
77 Albert Avenue
Crosshill
Glasgow G42 8RA
Tel 0141 423 8671

SCOTTISH OFF-ROAD CLUB
Bob Webster
1 Hallyard Farm Cottages
Kirkliston
Edinburgh EH29 9DZ
Tel 0131 333 4291

SOMERSET & WILTSHIRE
    ROVER OWNERS' CLUB*
Martyn Bourne
9 Burrowfield Square
Bruton
Somerset BA10 OHR

SOUTH DOWNS LAND
    ROVER CLUB
David Stevens
32 Langney Green
Langney
Eastbourne BN23 6HY
Tel 01323 460513

SOUTHERN COUNTIES
    OFF-ROAD CLUB
Jane Dooley
149 Slepe Crescent
Parkstone
Poole
Dorset BH12 4DL
Tel 01202 734949

SOUTHERN ROVER
    OWNERS' CLUB*
Tracey McCartney
5 Regency Way
Crook Log
Bexleyheath
Kent DA6 8BT
Tel 0181 301 5451

STAFFORDSHIRE &
    SHROPSHIRE LAND ROVER
    CLUB*
Vanessa Johnson
4 Waltham House
Overend Street
West Bromwich
West Midlands B70 6ER
Tel 0121 553 4070

SUFFOLK 4-WHEEL DRIVE
    CLUB
Louise Wall
9 Otago Close
Whittlesey
Peterborough PE7 1YL
Tel 01733 202746

SURREY LAND ROVER CLUB
Mike Boyd
102 Easter Way
South Godstone
Surrey RH9 8HH

TWIN AXLE CLUB
Andrew Stirling
4 Littleworth Cottages
Etherington Hill
Speldhurst
Kent TN3 OND
Tel 01892 862676

WHITE ROSE 4x4 CLUB
D. Stevens
63 Oak Street
Crofton
Wakefield
W Yorks WF4 1JN
Tel 01924 864639

WOKINGHAM ALL TERRAIN
    CLUB
43 King Street Lane
Winnersh
Wokingham
Berkshire RG11 5AX
Tel 01734 771665

WYE AND WELSH ROVER
    OWNERS' CLUB*
Peter Slingerland
Old Bakery
The Square
Ruardean
Glos GL17 9TJ
Tel 01594 544058

VIKING FWD CLUB
The Club Secretary
21 Marstown Avenue
South Wigston
Leicester LE18 4UH

WEST WALES 4x4 GROUP
Jennifer Barber
Trenaa
Beulah
Newcastle Emlyn
Dyfed SA38 9QB
Tel 01239 810050

YORKSHIRE ROVER
    OWNERS' CLUB*
Dave Barker
Rivendell
2 Huby Banks
North Yorks LS17 OAH
Tel 01423 734412

SINGLE-MARQUE CLUBS

AUSTIN CHAMP REGISTER
John David Mastrangelo
Springfield Farm
Horton
Nr Chipping Sodbury
Wilts BS17 6PE

THE AUSTIN GIPSY
    REGISTER
Mike Gilbert
24 Green Close
Sturminster Newton
Dorset

CLUB DISCOVERY
West Farm
Wutham-on-the Hill
Bourne
Lincs PE10 0JN
Tel 01778 33484, fax 01778
    33466

THE HAFLINGER CLUB
John Pettit
8 Fitzroy Avenue
Harlbourne
Birmingham B17
Tel 0121 429 5307

HAFLINGER OWNERS' CLUB
James Jarvie
Wester Auchenrivoch Farm
Banton
Kilsyth
Glasgow G65 0QZ

THE UK JEEP CLUB
65 Grosvenor Crescent
Arksey
Doncaster
S Yorks DN5 0SX
(Please send SAE)

THE JEEP REGISTER
Chris Bailey
Hornby Farm
Oakley Park
Llandinam
Newtown
Powys
Tel 01686 688714

LADA NIVA OWNERS' CLUB
David Woodman
103 Offa Lodge
Vale Park
Chirk
Nr Wrexham
Tel 01691 777252

LADA NIVA SOUTH-EAST
   OWNERS' CLUB
Paul Sutton
163 Borough Road
Petersfield
Hants GU32 3LP
Tel 01730 263911

LAND CRUISER 4x4 CLUB
Joe Boatwright
Tel 01793 497366

LEICESTER RHINO CLUB
Tracey Smith
75 Church Street
Thurmaston
Leics LE4 8DQ
Tel 0116 692169

LONDON & SOUTH EAST
   RHINOS
Joe A. Nunes Pereira
16 Seymer Road
Romford
Essex RM1 4LB
Tel 01708 747873
or Rob Ford
Tel 0181 597 2426

MITSUBISHI MOTOR
   OWNERS' CLUB
Brenda Newland
Colt Car Co
Watermoor
Cirencester
Glos GL7 1LF
Tel 01285 655777

NATIONAL NIVA OWNERS'
   CLUB
Geraint Rowlands
Golwyg-Y-Myndd
8 Cleveland Avenue
Tywyn
Gwynedd LL36 9EG

NATIONAL NIVA OWNERS'
   CLUB (SCOTLAND)
Iain McLean
Thistle Flat
Plumscarden
Elgin
Moray IV30 3USD

NORTH EAST SUZUKI 4x4
   CLUB
Gail Hall
5 Prudhoe Avenue
Fishburn
Co Durham TS21 4DA
Tel 01740 620400

PINZGAUER OWNERS' CLUB
The Castle House
Rock Park
Wirral L42 1PJ
Tel 0151 645 8124

REDWOOD RHINO CLUB
Wendy Stanton
54 Thackers Way
Deeping St James
Peterborough PE6 8HP
Tel 01778 341427

SOUTH WEST ENGLAND
   RHINO CLUB
Jeff Bolt
2 Ottery St Mary Cottages
Tavistock
Devon PL19 8NR
Tel 01822 617146

SUZUKI RHINO CLUB
Suzuki GB Plc
PO Box 56
Tunbridge Wells
Kent TN1 2XY
Tel 01892 535110

TOYOTA ENTHUSIASTS'
   CLUB
Billy Wells
28 Park Road
Feltham
Middx TW13 6PW
Tel/fax 0181 898 0740

TOYOTA OWNERS' CLUB
c/o Toyota (GB) Ltd
The Quadrangle
Station Road
Redhill
Surrey RH1 1PX
Tel 017377 68585

UMM OWNERS' CLUB
Glen Jones
8 Elworth Road
Elworth
Sandbach
Cheshire CW11 9HQ
Tel 01270 768522

WARWICKSHIRE RHINO 4x4
   CLUB
Paul Chare
4 Inchford Road
Solihull B92 9QA
Tel 0121 704 2089

APPENDIX 3

Available vehicles

AMPHI-RANGER 2800 SR

A German amphibious, seawater-resistant 4x4 built specifically for in-water use, while continuing to be a good on-road vehicle. The 3 mm (0.12 inch) thick aluminium hull also acts as a protective skid plate underneath, where it is 4 mm (0.16 in) thick.

The propeller is tucked up behind the rear bumper on land, but is lowered for use in the water. In water, steering is by the front wheels, with an optional laterally swivelling propeller.

Available as hard or soft top, pneumatically operated differential locks, front and rear, are available as optional extras.

Wheelbase:	98.4 in/2500 mm	
Engine:	177 cu in/2.9 l	244 cu in/4.0 l
Cylinders:	V6 petrol	V6 petrol
Output:	145 bhp/	157 bhp/
	107 kW	115 kW
	@ 5600 rpm	@ 4200 rpm

The Amphi-Ranger 2800 SR amphibious vehicle.

Torque:	164 lb ft/	220 lb ft/
	222 Nm	298 Nm
	@ 3000 rpm	@ 2400 rpm
Transmission:	five-speed manual/	
	four-speed automatic	
Four-wheel drive:	part-time	
Front suspension:	independent on coil	
	springs	
Rear suspension:	independent on coil	
	springs	
Brakes (front/rear):	disc/disc	
Handbrake:	drum brake on rear	
	axle	
Wheels:	5.50 x 16	
Base tyres:	215/75 R 16 C –	
	31 x 10.5 R 15 T	
Turning circle:	39.4 ft/12.0 m	

ASIA MOTORS ROCSTA

A sturdily built Korean vehicle, based roughly on the early CJ Jeep and using Mazda derived engines. Early imports fell down on suspension and understeer, but these have now been improved.

On-road the vehicle is skittish and can be hard work. Off-road, within the limits of leaf sprung suspension and lack of axle articulation, it performs as well as its competitors.

Forward visibility over the low bonnet is excellent if you are not tall enough to loose vision through the top of the windscreen, but the pillars and roll bar limit side vision.

The Asia Motors Rocsta.

The gear change is slick, but one's hands tend to hit the dashboard. Winding down the windows is a problem and the plastic trim at the rear is vulnerable off-road.

A solid if not exciting vehicle, with an independent front suspension model due in 1995/6.

Wheelbase:	84 in/2132 mm	
Engine:	110 cu in/1.8 l	134 cu in/2.2 l
Cylinders:	4 petrol	4 diesel
Output:	78 bhp/	62 bhp/
	57.3 kW	45.4 kW
	@ 5500 rpm	@ 4050 rpm
Torque:	98 lb ft/	93 lb ft/
	133 Nm	126 Nm
	@ 3000 rpm	@ 2500 rpm
Transmission:	five-speed manual	
Transfer box:	two ratio	
Four-wheel drive:	part-time – manual	
	freewheeling hubs	
Front suspension:	live beam axle on leaf	
	springs	
Rear suspension:	live beam axle on leaf	
	springs	
Brakes (front/rear):	disc/drum	
Handbrake:	on rear drums	
Wheels:	6.00J x 15	

Base tyres: 215/75 R 15
Turning circle: 31.5 ft/9.6 m

AUVERLAND A3

Spartan specialist vehicles, built with out-and-out off-road ability in mind, regularly come and go, but the French Auverland has stood the test of time. Using the Peugeot XUD9 diesel engine, a Peugeot gearbox and Auverland's own transfer box and live axles on long-travel coil springs, fitted with a limited slip rear differential as standard, this vehicle's off-road performance ranks with the best; though obviously on-road its performance suffers and the engine is underpowered.

Wheelbase:	88.5 in/2250 m
Engine	116 cu in/1.9 l
Cylinders:	4 diesel
Output:	66 bhp/48.6 kW @ 4600 rpm
Torque:	88 lb ft/119 Nm @ 2070 rpm
Transmission:	five-speed manual
Transfer box:	1.00:1/2.02:1
Four-wheel drive:	part-time
Final drive:	rear limited slip differential
Front suspension:	live beam axle on long-travel coil springs
Rear suspension:	live beam axle on long-travel coil springs
Brakes (front/rear):	disc/drum
Wheels:	6.50 x 16
Base tyres:	650/205 16
Turning circle:	32.8 ft/10 m

CHEVROLET/ GMC

Chevrolet/General Motors Corporation are changing their four-wheeler nomenclature for 1995 – there are so many improvements that they are new models. The compact sport utility Chevrolet S-Blazer becomes simply the Chevrolet Blazer, and the full-size Chevrolet K-Blazer becomes the Chevrolet Tahoe. In the same way

GMC's compact is now called the GMC Jimmy and the full-size GMC Jimmy is now called the GMC Yukon. The up-market Blazer/Jimmy is sold as the Oldsmobile Bravada.

These vehicles are the typical American approach to four-wheel drive. Based originally on strong pick-up designs, they come in either two- or four-wheel drive, with several options of suspension stiffness (choose the off-road package, the stiffest, for off-road use). They are mostly part-time four-wheel drive – full-time four-wheel drive will be available in mid-1995 on the four-door models.

The new Dexron III automatic transmission fluid will never require replacement under normal service and GM are moving over to using the same key for both doors and ignition.

The Insta-Trac part-time four-wheel drive system has a front half-shaft disconnect to allow changing between two- and four-wheel drive 'on the fly', and a four-wheel drive low gear.

Chevrolet Blazer/GMC Jimmy

Long- and short-wheelbase two- and four-door models, with more aerodynamic bodies, increased cargo capacity and shoulder room, but the spare wheel is now under the floor on the four-door models. The chassis is now boxed to increase stiffness and there are five weights of suspension. The straight-line steering is much improved and variable-ratio steering feels more precise.

Five-speed manual gearboxes are available in two-door models, while four-speed automatic is standard. The standard engine is a throttle-injected 4.3-litre V6 petrol, with a more powerful port-injected 4.3-litre V6 option on the Jimmy.

Wheelbase:	100.5 in/2553 mm	
	107 in/2718 mm	
Engine:	262 cu in/4.3 l	262 cu in/4.3 l
Cylinders:	V6 petrol	V6 petrol
Output:	195 bhp/ 144 kW @ 4500 rpm	200 bhp/ 147 kW @ 4500 rpm
Torque:	260 lb ft/ 353 Nm @ 3400 rpm	260 lb ft/ 353 Nm @ 3600 rpm
Transmission:	five-speed manual/ four-speed automatic	
Transfer box:	4WD – LO Gear	
Four-wheel drive:	part-time with Insta-Trac full-time option on long-wheelbase models	
Final drive:	3.08:1/3.43:1/3.73:1	
Front suspension:	independent on torsion bars	
Rear suspension:	live beam axle on leaf springs	
Brakes (front/rear):	disc/drum with ABS	
Handbrake:	on rear drums	
Wheels:	7 x 15	
Base tyres:	P205/75 R 15 – P235/75 R 15	
Turning circle:	35.2 ft/10.7 m 39.5 ft/12 m	

Chevrolet Tahoe/GMC Yukon

Midway between the Suburban and the compact Blazer/Jimmy vehicles, the full-size Tahoe/Yukon sports utility vehicles continue with the old body shape, but now have a turbo-diesel option and many improvements. A long-wheelbase four-door option will be available mid-1995.

The new 6.5-litre V8 turbo-diesel uses a drive-by-wire Electronic Fuel Injection system. A normal accelerator pedal is pressed, but a computer decides the cleanest, most efficient way to produce the amount of power requested. The diesel engine is mated to a stronger automatic transmission.

There is an option of twin rear doors or a split tailgate with lift-glass and Remote Keyless radio transmitter entry system (RKE).

Wheelbase:	111.5 cu in/2832 mm	
Engine:	348 cu in/5.7 l	397 cu in/6.5 l
Cylinders:	V8 petrol	V8 turbo diesel
Output:	200 bhp/ 147 kW @ 4000 rpm	180 bhp/ 133 kW @ 3400 rpm

Torque:	310 lb ft/ 420 Nm @ 2400 rpm	360 lb ft/ 488 Nm @ 1700 rpm
Transmission:	five-speed manual/four-speed automatic	
Transfer box:	4WD – LO Gear	
Four-wheel drive:	part-time with Insta- Trac	
Final drive:	3.42:1/3.73:1	
Front suspension:	independent on torsion bars	
Rear suspension:	live beam axle on leaf springs	
Brakes (front/rear):	disc/drum with ABS	
Handbrake:	on rear drums	
Wheels:	6.5 x 16	
Base tyres:	LT 245/75 R 16 C	
Turning circle:	41.5 ft/12.6 m	

Chevrolet/GMC Suburban

America's 'Superwagon', the giant amongst station wagons, has no competition in its four-wheel drive form, which also has independent front suspension on torsion bars.

Available in ½ and ¾ ton (508 and 762 kg) versions, these vehicles can tow 6,500 lbs (2,948 kg) and 10,000 lbs (4536 kg) respectively. Four-wheel drive is Insta-Trac part-time with four-wheel drive low gear.

The vehicle is a full nine-seater, and the passengers get a more comfortable ride than in most vans because they are well behind the front axle and it is aimed at the luxury market, with various luxury interior fittings.

The 6.5-litre drive-by-wire turbo diesel is available with a stronger automatic gearbox.

K 1500

Wheelbase:	131.5 in/3340 mm
Engine:	350 cu in/5.7 l
Cylinders:	V8 petrol
Output:	200 bhp/147 kW @ 4000 rpm
Torque:	310 lb ft/420 Nm @ 2400 rpm
Transmission:	four-speed automatic
Transfer box:	4WD LO-Gear
Four-wheel drive:	part-time with Insta- Trac
Final drive:	3.42:1/3.73:1/4.10:1

Front suspension:	independent on torsion bars
Rear suspension:	live beam axle on leaf springs
Brakes (front/rear):	disc/drum with ABS
Handbrake:	on rear drums
Wheels:	7 x 15
Base tyres:	P235/75 R 15 X – LT235/75 R 16 E
Turning circle:	46.4 ft/14 m

K 2500:

Engine:	454 cu in/7.4 l
Cylinders:	V8 petrol
Output:	230 bhp/169 kW @ 3600 rpm
Torque:	385 lb ft/522 Nm @ 1600 rpm

Diesel:

Engine:	395 cu in/6.5 l
Cylinders:	V8 turbo diesel
Output:	190 bhp/140 kW @ 3400 rpm
Torque:	385 lb ft/522 Nm @ 1700 rpm

CHRYSLER

Chrysler Jeep

The original World War II Jeep was the forerunner of modern four-wheel drive recreational vehicles, and many copies of it are still being built under licence around the world. The trade name has been owned by a plethora of manufacturers over the years and is now owned by Chrysler, who have been very successful in bringing the marque back to popularity.

The spartan short-wheelbase models (the Wrangler) remain very popular and, despite their outdated suspension, have good off-road performance; but it is the Cherokee models that have struck public admiration, both in looks and price. In the UK they have taken the large estate car market by storm.

All models suffer from an accelerator that is too light for off-road use. Some Command-trac models have a system to disconnect a front half-shaft when in two-wheel drive, but in engineering terms

there is little to recommend it.

Chrysler Jeep Cherokee

The Cherokee is more of a family estate than an out-and-out off-roader, and is of modern car-type 'monocoque' construction, rather than having a separate 'ladder' chassis. Probably for structured rigidity, the roof line is low and the sills high, making entry and egress awkward, and one cannot hose out the mud after off-roading. The rear passenger doors are small.

With the smaller engine there is Command-trac part-time four-wheel drive, but with the 4.0-litre engine one gets Command-trac plus Selec-trac, which also gives full-time four-wheel drive in high range, with a centre differential to eliminate 'wind-up'.

Four-wheel drive selection is a bit of a lottery, but the transfer box range change improves with use. A worrying factor is the use of open front axle universal joints to the front wheels, instead of constant velocity joints, for a vehicle with this performance.

On-road the vehicle handles well, but with the massive power of the 4.0-litre engine it is easy to get into a power slide in two-wheel drive. It is therefore best to use permanent four-wheel drive, with the centre differential unlocked, except on motorways, where two-wheel drive is more economical and there is less feedback through the steering wheel.

Off-road the poor ramp break-over angle and poor axle articulation limit the performance. Steering is too light to know

The Chrysler Jeep Cherokee.

where the wheels are pointing, the automatic gearbox cannot be locked into first gear for engine braking, and the limited slip differential does not appear to improve things much.

Some of the fittings are prone to failure.

Wheelbase:	101.4 in/2576 mm	
Engine:	153 cu in/2.5 l	153 cu in/2.5 l
Cylinders:	4 petrol	4 turbo diesel
Output:	122 bhp/	116 bhp/
	90 kW	85 kW
	@ 5300 rpm	@ 4000 rpm
Torque:	148 lb ft/	207 lb ft/
	200 Nm	281 Nm
	@ 3200 rpm	@ 2000 rpm
Transmission:	five-speed manual/four-speed automatic	
Transfer box:	two ratio	
Four-wheel drive:	part-time Command-trac	
Final drive:	4.11:1	
Front suspension:	live beam axle on coil springs	
Rear suspension:	live beam axle on leaf springs	
Brakes (front/rear):	disc/drum with ABS	
Handbrake:	on rear drums	
Wheels:	7J x 15	
Base tyres:	215/75 R 15	
Turning circle:	32.6 ft/11.2 m	

4.0-litre engine:

Engine:	244 cu in/4.0 l
Cylinders:	6 petrol
Output:	184 bhp/135 kW @ 4750 rpm
Torque:	214 lb ft/290 Nm @ 3950 rpm
Transmission:	four-speed automatic
Transfer box:	two ratio
Four-wheel drive:	Selec-trac – the same as Command-trac plus two-wheel or full-time four-wheel drive in high range
Final drive:	3.55:1 – rear limited slip differential

Chrysler Jeep Grand Cherokee

The Jeep Grand Cherokee has taken over from the Jeep

Wagoneer. With 4½ in/114 mm extra wheelbase at 105.9 in/2690 mm, the vehicle is available with the 4.0-litre V6 engine or a 317 cu in/5.2-litre V8 engine, giving 220 bhp/162 kW at 4800 rpm and 285 lb ft/386 Nm of torque at 3600 rpm. There are live beam axles on coil springs front and rear.

Three four-wheel drive arrangements are available: Command-trac and Selec-trac as on the Cherokee, plus Quadra-trac full-time four-wheel drive with a viscous coupling centre differential. This is in effect a fully automatic four-wheel drive system, that locks itself in when necessary. No driver input is required or desired, except to move the transfer box control into low range for nasty terrain.

Chrysler Jeep Wrangler

The Wrangler is an icon of the past – obvious Second World War Jeep heritage combined with just enough modern comforts to make it a butch statement vehicle.

The padded roll-bar is standard, reminding careless drivers that the high ground clearance, short wheelbase and narrow track best suited to off-road manoeuvrability can also result in overturned vehicles.

Many of the fittings are tacky, the suspension is leaf spring all round, and the power steering is so light as to be disconnected from reality. The four-wheel drive system is Command-trac, part-time, and when it was converted to right-hand drive they forgot about the windscreen wipers.

On-road it is what you would expect from cart-sprung suspen-

The Chrysler Jeep Wrangler.

sion, and you really have to be careful with all the power of the 4.0-litre engine.

Off-road the limited axle articulation, intrusive front spring hangers and rear bumperettes, together with poor ramp break-over angle, negate its performance, and the limited slip rear differential seems to have little effect. However, if fitted with oversize tyres, the 4-litre engine will pull the vehicle through most situations.

Wheelbase:	93.4 in/2372 mm	
Engine:	153 cu in/2.5 l	244 cu in/4.0 l
Cylinders:	4 petrol	6 petrol
Output:	122 bhp/	154 bhp/
	90 kW	135 kW
	@ 5300 rpm	@ 4750 rpm
Torque:	148 lb ft/	214 lb ft/
	200 Nm	290 Nm
	@ 3200 rpm	@ 3950 rpm
Transmission:	five-speed manual/three-speed automatic	
Transfer box:	two ratio	
Four-wheel drive:	part-time Command-trac	
Final drive:	4.11:1 – rear limited slip differential	
Front suspension:	live beam axle on leaf springs	
Rear suspension:	live beam axle on leaf springs	
Brakes (front/rear):	disc/drum	
Handbrake:	on rear drums	
Wheels:	6.5 x 15	
Base tyres:	205/75 R 15	
Turning circle:	32.9 ft/10 m	

Colt Shogun – refer to Mitsubishi Shogun

DAIHATSU

The earlier Daihatsu Fourtraks sold in different countries as the Rocky, Taft, Wildcat, Berton Free Climber, Feroza or Toyota Blizzard became popular as solid, reliable, hard-working vehicles at a good price, though their on-road performance could be hard work and they are not that impressive off-road. The Sportraks followed, but the new independent front suspension with coil springs at the

The Daihatsu Sportrak.

rear versions are quite a lot more expensive.

On-road the vehicle rolls around somewhat, though slowly and predictably, and off-road the poor ramp break-over angle due to a protection plate under the transfer box causes it to be high-centred often.

Depending on your body build, the electrically engaged high-range four-wheel drive button, which is beside the rear window heater button, is likely to be obscured behind the steering wheel; considerable damage could be inflicted if the wrong button was pressed at high speed.

Sportrak:

Wheelbase:	85.6 in/2175 mm
Engine:	97.6 cu in/1.6 l
Cylinders:	4 petrol
Output:	95.2 bhp/70 kW @ 5700 rpm
Torque:	94.5 lb ft/128 Nm @ 4800 rpm
Transmission:	five-speed manual
Transfer box:	two ratio
Four-wheel drive:	part-time – automatic or manual freewheeling front hubs
Front suspension:	independent on torsion bars

The Daihatsu Feroza.

The Daihatsu Independent.

Rear suspension:	live beam axle on leaf springs
Brakes (front/rear):	disc/drum
Handbrake:	on rear drums
Wheels:	6.0 x 15
Base tyres:	195 SR 15 – 225/70 R 15
Turning circle:	32.2 ft/9.8 m

Fourtrak Independent:

Wheelbase:	86.8 in/2205 mm 99.6 in/2530 mm
Engine:	168.7 cu in/2.8 l
Cylinders:	4 turbo diesel, intercooled
Output:	102 bhp/75 kW @ 3400 rpm
Torque:	181 lb ft/245 Nm @ 1900 rpm
Transmission:	five-speed manual
Transfer box:	two ratio
Four-wheel drive:	part-time – automatic freewheeling front hubs
Front suspension:	independent on torsion bars
Rear suspension:	live beam axle on coil springs
Brakes (front/rear):	disc/drum
Handbrake:	on rear drums
Wheels:	6.0 x 15
Base tyres:	215 R 15 – 255/70 R 15
Turning circle:	33.5 ft/10.2 m 37.4 ft/11.4 m

FORD

Ford Bronco

The Ford Bronco is what the Americans call full-size. Based on Ford's F-Series pick-ups, it is not a car-like vehicle with off-road capabilities, but a tough heavy-weight contender; its ride is more truck-like than car-like.

The interior is roomy and the four-wheel drive, transfer box, automatic or manual freewheeling hubs and ABS are up-to-date with those of the Explorer. What lets it down is Twin Traction Beam independent front suspension when off-road.

There are three ways of having four-wheel drive: with the standard automatic freewheeling hubs you just come to a stop and shift into four-wheel drive, and the rest is automatic. You can have manual freewheeling hubs, but you can also have push-buttons on the dashboard for hub engagement and low range. Once the hubs are engaged you can shift 'on the fly' between two-wheel and four-wheel drive in high range at normal speeds.

Engines come in 5.0-litre or 5.8-litre petrol, with multi-port injection.

There is Keyless Remote Entry and a limited slip rear differential is optional.

Wheelbase:	104.7 in/2659 mm	
Engine:	305 cu in/5.0 l	354 cu in/5.8 l
Cylinders:	V8 petrol	V8 petrol
Output:	205 bhp/ 151 kW @ 4000 rpm	200 bhp/ 155 kW @ 3600 rpm
Torque:	275 lb ft/ 373 Nm @ 3000 rpm	325 lb ft/ 441 Nm @ 2800 rpm
Transmission:	five-speed manual/ four-speed automatic	
Transfer box:	two ratio	
Four-wheel drive:	part-time	
Final drive:	3.08:1/3.55:1/4.10:1 – optional limited slip rear differential	
Front suspension:	independent Twin Traction Beam on coil springs	
Rear suspension:	live beam axle on leaf springs	
Brakes (front/rear):	disc/drum with ABS	
Handbrake:	on rear drums	
Wheels:	6.5 x 15	
Base tyres:	P235/75 R 15 SL	
Turning circle:	36.8 ft/11.2 m	

Ford Explorer

America's best-selling compact sport utility, though it would not be called compact in Europe, the Ford Explorer is based on the Ranger pick-ups. It is available with two- or four-wheel drive, two wheelbases and optional limited slip rear differential. You can have automatic freewheeling hubs with a dash-mounted electronic transfer box shift, or manual freewheeling hubs with mechanical transfer box shift.

Wheelbase:	102.1 in/2593 mm
	111.9 in/2842 mm
Engine:	244 cu in/4.0 l
Cylinders:	V6 petrol, multiport injection
Output:	160 bhp/118 kW @ 4000 rpm
Torque:	225 lb ft/305 Nm @ 2500 rpm
Transmission:	five-speed manual/ four-speed automatic
Transfer box:	1.00:1/2.00:1
Four-wheel drive:	part-time Control-trac – automatic or manual freewheeling front hubs
Final drive:	3.08:1/3.27:1/3.73:1 – optional rear limited slip differential
Front suspension:	independent on torsion bars
Rear suspension:	live beam axle on leaf springs
Brakes (front/rear):	disc/drum with ABS
Handbrake:	on rear drums
Wheels:	6 x 15
Base tyres:	225/70 15

The Ford Explorer.

Turning circle:	34.8 ft/10.6 m
	37.3 ft/11.4 m

Ford Maverick/Nissan Terrano II

A combined effort by Ford and Nissan (though mostly by Nissan), this vehicle is intended to be an 'all-rounder'. Modern computer design input is obvious, and for what it is meant to be, the on-road handling is very good, though off-road it does not live up to the manufacturer's hype.

Depending on which badge you choose, there are differences in trim, or which engines are available on which models, and each manufacturer has their own range of accessories. As the basic vehicle is identical, you can choose what extras you get for the price.

Put together at Nissan's Motor Iberica Plant at Barcelona in Spain, though some engines have both Mexican and Japanese input, the build quality is good, apart from the silly tray under the engine bay, which falls off when you go off-road.

Very few owners would take this vehicle truly off-road, but if they do, approach, departure and ramp break-over angles are not up with the best. Axle articulation is limited and the rear wheels rub against the wheel arches on full compression.

The diesel engine is more suited to off-road use than the petrol engine, though the torque comes in a little late. The long-wheelbase model is less skittish on-road, and obviously the short-wheelbase model has better off-road performance.

Wheelbase:	96.5 in/2450 mm	
	104 in/2650 mm	
Engine:	146 cu in/2.4 l	165 cu in/2.7 l
Cylinders:	4 petrol	4 turbo diesel
Output:	124 bhp/ 91 kW @ 5200 rpm	100 bhp/ 74 kW @ 4000 rpm
Torque:	145 lb ft/ 197 Nm @ 4000 rpm	163 lb ft/ 221 Nm @ 2200 rpm
Transmission:	five-speed manual	

The Ford Maverick.

Transfer box:	1.00:1/2.02:1
Four-wheel drive:	part-time – automatic freewheeling front hubs
Final drive:	4.63:1 – rear limited slip differential
Front suspension:	independent on torsion bars
Rear suspension:	live beam axle on coil springs
Brakes (front/rear):	disc/drum
Handbrake:	on rear drums
Wheels:	6J x 15
Base tyres:	215 R 15
Turning circle:	35.4 ft/10.8 m
	37.3 ft/11.4 m

Ford Raider – refer to Ford Explorer
Geo Tracker – refer to Suzuki Vitara
GMC Jimmy – refer to Chevrolet Blazer
GMC Suburban – refer to Chevrolet Suburban
GMC Yukon – refer to Chevrolet Tahoe
Holden Drover – refer to Suzuki SJ series
Holden Jackaroo – refer to Vauxhall Monterey
Honda Crossroads – refer to Land Rover Discovery
Honda Horizon – refer to Vauxhall Monterey
Honda Passport – refer to Vauxhall Frontera

ISUZU

Isuzu, Japan's longest-established vehicle manufacturer, must hold the record for the largest number of vehicles re-badged under other marques, though most of them have General Motors connections.

The long-wheelbase Isuzu Trooper.

Isuzu Amigo – refer to Vauxhall Frontera

Isuzu MU (Mysterious Utility) – As Vauxhall Frontera, but also available with 2.8-litre direct injection turbo diesel and automatic transmission.

Isuzu Rodeo – refer to Vauxhall Frontera

Isuzu Tönnermann – refer to Vauxhall Monterey

Isuzu Trooper – refer to Vauxhall Monterey

Jeep – refer to Chrysler

KIA SPORTAGE

A standard-design Korean-built 4x4 that is little bigger than a Vitara, but claims interior seating room in the Frontera/4Runner class. The engine is lively on-road, but the power comes in too high up the rpm range for off-road use, and four-wheel drive cannot be engaged on the move. Its main selling point is its low price.

Wheelbase:	104.4 in/2576 mm
Engine:	122 cu in/2.0 l
Cylinders:	4 petrol
Output:	139 bhp/102 kW @ 6000 rpm
Torque:	134 lb ft/82 Nm @ 4000 rpm
Transmission:	five-speed manual/four-speed automatic
Transfer box:	two ratio
Four-wheel drive:	part-time
Final drive:	4.78:1
Front suspension:	independent on coil springs
Rear suspension:	live beam axle on coil springs
Brakes (front/rear):	disc/drum

Handbrake:	on rear drums
Wheels:	6 x 15
Base tyres:	205/75 R 15
Turning circle:	34.8 ft/10.6 m

LADA NIVA/COSSACK

A Russian-built, sturdy, long-lasting workhorse, with full-time four-wheel drive, coil suspension and good approach, ramp breakover and departure angles, giving it good off-road performance at a very low price.

There are niggling little faults: the position of the coil gives problems when wading, the foot pedals are not for use when wearing boots, the rear view is poor due to a large spare wheel and a small window, and the engine has to be worked hard through the gearbox.

The Cossack looks more up to date, but the basic Niva is better value for money. Again, its main selling point is its low price.

Wheelbase:	88 in/2230 mm
Engine:	98 cu in/1.6 l
Cylinders:	4 petrol
Output:	78 bhp/61 kW @ 5400 rpm
Torque:	88 lb ft/119 Nm @ 3000 rpm
Transmission:	five-speed manual
Transfer box:	1.20:1/2.14:1
Four-wheel drive:	full-time
Final drive:	4.10:1
Front suspension:	independent on coil springs
Rear suspension:	live beam axle on coil springs
Brakes (front/rear):	disc/drum

The Lada Niva.

The Lada Cossack.

Handbrake:	on rear drums
Wheels:	5J x 16
Base tyres:	175 x 16 or 195 x 15
Turning circle:	36.3 ft/11.0 m

LAND ROVER

Land Rover Series III

Though no longer in production, its strength and reliability make the Series III the most sought-after expedition or overland vehicle. It does not have the full-time four-wheel drive or long-travel suspension of the modern versions, but it has a thicker chassis, thicker body panels, galvanized body capings, engines with camshafts driven by reliable chains and is far less prone to rust. Twenty-year-old models are a common sight around the world and, with few production changes, spare parts can usually be found or cannibalized.

The six-cylinder petrol engine had carburettor problems in dusty areas, and used oil. The diesel was never a good engine, but the four-cylinder and V8 petrol gave few problems. I have led convoys of these vehicles that were thrashed all over North and East Africa, Iran, Afghanistan, Pakistan, India and Nepal for 15 years without any serious problems.

Wheelbase:	88 in/2235 mm	
	109 in/2769 m	
Engine:	140 cu in/2.3 l	214 cu in/3.5 l
Cylinders:	4 petrol	V8 petrol
Output:	70 bhp/	135 bhp/
	52 kW	99 kW
	@ 4000 rpm	@ 3500 rpm

Torque:	120 lb ft/	205 lb ft/
	163 Nm	278 Nm
	@ 1500 rpm	@ 3000 rpm
Transmission:	four-speed manual	
Transfer box:	1.15:1/2.35:1	
	1.34:1/ 3.32:1	
Four-wheel drive:	part-time	full-time
Final drive:	4.70:1	3.54:1
Front suspension:	live beam axle on leaf springs	
Rear suspension:	live beam axle on leaf springs	
Brakes (front/rear):	drum/drum	
Handbrake:	transmission	
Wheels:	7.50 x 16	
Base tyres:	7.50 x 16	
Turning circle:	38 ft/11.6 m	
	47 ft/14.3 m	

Land Rover 1 Ton

This special long-wheelbase 109 in (2769 mm) model used the six-cylinder engine, heavier springs, the standard Salisbury rear axle but a stronger EMV front axle, 9.00 x 16 tyres and the Series IIA gearbox, which only had synchromesh on the top two gears. Four-wheel drive was part-time and the transfer box had a greater reduction, with ratios of 1.53:1 and 3.27:1.

Land Rover 101 in (2565 mm) 1 Tonne Forward Control

This vehicle was built for military use from 1975 to 1978 and was designed to be used with a Rubery Owen trailer, powered through a power take-off at the rear of the Land Rover. With a short wheelbase and the weight evenly distributed between all four wheels, this

A Land Rover 1 Ton in the North Teneré Desert.

vehicle has exceptional performance, making it a desirable expedition vehicle.

Wheelbase:	101 in/2565 mm
Engine:	214 cu in/3.5 l
Cylinders:	V8 petrol
Output:	135 bhp/99 kW @ 4700 rpm
Torque:	205 lb ft/278 Nm @ 3000 rpm
Transmission:	four-speed manual
Transfer box:	1.17:1/3.32:1
Four-wheel drive:	full-time
Final drive:	5.57:1
Front suspension:	live beam axle on leaf springs
Rear suspension:	live beam axle on leaf springs
Brakes (front/rear):	drum/drum
Handbrake:	transmission
Wheels:	9.00 x 16
Base tyres:	9.00 x 16

Land Rover Defender (90/110/130)

In 1983 Land Rover launched their 110, using a 110-inch (2794 mm) wheelbase Range Rover-type chassis, with massive axle articulation, long-travel coil spring suspension, excellent approach, departure and ramp break-over angles, and full-time four-wheel drive, with lockable centre differential. The short-wheelbase 90 (92.9 in/2360 mm) version followed just over a year later.

Initially the vehicle was available with a 2.5-litre four-cylinder diesel engine, a 2.25-litre (later 2.5 litre) four-cylinder petrol engine, and eventually the 3.5-litre V8 petrol engine.

These vehicles continue to evolve, especially in the engine and gearbox department, and were renamed Defender when the Discovery was launched. The Defender is without doubt the standard by which all other four-wheel drive vehicles are judged for off-road use. Despite not having cross-axle differential locks or limited slip differentials, in all true off-road situations they still beat all the opposition. On paper the

The Land Rover 110 County.

Mercedes Geländewagen and Toyota VX should do better than the Defender, but in practice they rarely do.

Well proven on the Camel Trophy, the Defender is an out-and-out off-road vehicle with few comforts. It has made immense progress in engineering and performance, but where other vehicles have made progress in rustproofing steel bodywork, on this vehicle Land Rover have gone backwards.

A combination of the fuel efficiency of the new direct injection diesel engines, buyer's preferences and new emission regulations means that currently the vehicle is only available with the 300 Tdi direct injection turbo diesel engine, though it is likely that the V8 petrol, as offered to the American market, will become available.

On the reliability side, the toothed camshaft drive belt is a major problem, though it must be said that several other manufacturers also fit these belts in the engines of their four-wheel drive vehicles.

As with their predecessors, Land Rover Special Products Division

A Land Rover Defender 110 showing good axle articulation.

The USA specification Land Rover V8 Defender 90.

manufacture all sorts of adaptations to Land Rovers, including 130 models on a 127-inch (3226 mm) wheelbase, with 6x6 or 6x4 drive.

90

Wheelbase:	92.9 in/2360 mm
Engine:	153 cu in/2.5 l
Cylinders:	4 turbo-diesel direct injection intercooled
Output:	111 bhp/83 kW @ 4000 rpm
Torque:	195 lb ft/265 Nm @ 1800 rpm
Transmission:	five-speed manual – synchromesh on reverse
Transfer box:	1.41:1/3.32:1
Four-wheel drive:	full-time
Final drive:	3.54:1
Front suspension:	live beam axle on long-travel coil springs
Rear suspension:	live beam axle on long travel coil springs
Brakes (front/rear):	disc/disc
Handbrake:	transmission
Wheels:	7.50 x 16
Base tyres:	250 R 16
Turning circle:	38.4 ft/11.7 m

The Land Rover 130.

110

Wheelbase:	109 in/2769 m
Base tyres:	265/75 R 16
Turning circle:	42 ft/12.8 m

Land Rover Discovery

Take the excellent suspension and full-time four-wheel drive of the Defender, add some of the luxury of the Range Rover and a modern body with designed-in crush zones, and you end up with an award-winning best-seller that keeps on going from strength to strength.

Now with uprated engines and better gearboxes, the Discovery is the best of the all-roaders in its class, with exceptional off-road performance when fitted with the V8 petrol or 300 Tdi diesel engine.

The Mpi (multipoint fuel injection) 2.0-litre petrol has now been added to the engine range. This engine is aimed at the normal 2-litre saloon or company car driver, and is really not the right engine for off-road or towing use. The ECU (Electronic Control Unit) can make some strange decisions, the belts driving the air conditioning, alternator, steering and water pumps look vulnerable to mud and grit, and the timing belt housing looks dodgy for deep wading.

Ignoring the Mpi engine, the vehicle is well proven on the Camel Trophy, and Honda thought it good enough to rebadge as the Honda Crossroads in Japan.

Land Rover are currently working on a new, small four-wheel drive vehicle.

V8i

Wheelbase:	100 in/2540 mm
Engine:	241 cu in/3.9 l
Cylinders:	V8 petrol injection
Output:	182 bhp/136 kW @ 4750 rpm
Torque:	231 lb ft/314 Nm @ 3100 rpm
Transmission:	five-speed manual – synchromesh on reverse – or four-speed automatic

The Land Rover Discovery.

Transfer box:	1.22:1/3.32:1
Four-wheel drive:	full-time
Final drive:	3.54:1
Front suspension:	live beam axle on long-travel coil springs
Rear suspension:	live beam axle on long-travel coil springs
Brakes (front/rear):	disc/disc with ABS
Handbrake:	transmission
Wheels:	7.50 x 16
Base tyres:	250 R 16
Turning circle:	39.4 ft/12.0 m

300 Tdi

Engine:	152 cu in/2.5 l
Cylinders:	4 turbo-diesel direct injection
Output:	111 bhp/83 kW @ 4000 rpm
Torque:	195 lb ft/265 Nm @ 1800 rpm

Mpi engine:

Engine:	122 cu in/2.0 l
Cylinders:	4 petrol multiport injection – intercooled
Output:	134 bhp/100 kW @ 6000 rpm
Torque:	140 lb ft/190 Nm @ 3600 rpm

Lotus Bighorn – refer to Vauxhall Monterey

MAHINDRA

A back-to-basics copy of the Jeep CJ3 (Bravo) and Jeep CJ5 (Marksman), built in India and fitted with Peugeot four-cylinder diesel engines. Used only for off-roading it has the performance of the vehicle it is based on, limited by lack of axle articulation and

The Mahindra.

with components in silly places, such as the clutch slave cylinder at the bottom of the bell housing and a junction box behind the rear wheel.

On-road it suffers from poor steering, gear change and brakes. Build quality on the early models was poor, but things have now improved.

Wheelbase:	80 in/2032 mm
Engine:	128 cu in/2.1 l
Cylinders:	4 diesel
Output:	62 bhp/46 kW @ 4500 rpm
Torque:	90 lb ft/122 Nm @ 2000 rpm
Transmission:	four-speed manual
Transfer box:	1.00:1/2.46:1
Four-wheel drive:	part-time
Final drive:	5.38:1
Front suspension:	live beam axle on leaf springs
Rear suspension:	live beam axle on leaf springs
Brakes (front/rear):	drum/drum
Handbrake:	transmission
Wheels:	7.00 x 15
Base tyres:	235/75 R 15
Turning circle:	38.4 ft/11.7 m 42 ft/12.8 m

Mazda Navajo – refer to Ford Explorer

MERCEDES BENZ G-SERIES (GELÄNDEWAGEN)

Developed in co-operation with cross-country vehicle specialists Steyr-Daimler-Puch, these luxury up-market vehicles are designed to be everything, both on and off-road. Manufactured by Steyr-Daimler-Puch at Graz in Austria to traditional Mercedes standards and quality, the vehicles are sold under the Steyr-Puch trademark in Austria, Switzerland, Greece, Yugoslavia and the COMECON countries. Military versions are also built under licence by Peugeot in France.

These vehicles, together with the Toyota VX, have the highest specifications of any non-military vehicles. Their only weakness is the engine power being a little high in the rpm range for the best off-road performance.

The G-Series now have full-time four-wheel drive, cross-axle differential locks front and rear, and ABS braking, but axle articulation is not quite up to that on Land Rover products. The differential locks can be engaged on the move and the engagement sequence is predetermined, so you cannot engage the front differential lock, therefore forfeiting stability, by mistake.

The ABS can be de-activated for off-road use and is automatically disengaged when one or more differential locks are activated; this is because it is not possible for ABS to exert control on each wheel individually when cross-axle locks are engaged. The braking system has an additional vacuum reservoir, so that servo-assisted braking is still possible in off-road operation when the engine is stalled.

The petrol engine can be switched to 'leaded regular fuel' by means of an adapter plug in the engine compartment, which is useful for Third World operation.

The diesel engine has automatic 'bleeding' of any air in the fuel system if the fuel in the tank has been allowed to become too low.

The doors are well sealed for wading, but this can lead to flotation, lowering traction.

Wheelbase:	94.4 in/2400 mm	
	112.2 in/2850 mm	
Engine:	181 cu in/3.0 l	183 cu in/3.0 l

The short-wheelbase Mercedes G Series.

Cylinders:	6 petrol	6 diesel
Output:	170 bhp/ 125 kW @ 5500 rpm	113 bhp/ 83 kW @ 4600 rpm
Torque:	173 lb ft/ 235 Nm @ 4500 rpm	141 lb ft/ 191 Nm @ 2800 rpm
Transmission:	five-speed manual/four-speed automatic	
Transfer box:	1.11:1/2.16:1	
Four-wheel drive:	full-time	
Final drive:	cross-axle differential locks front and rear	
Front suspension:	live beam axle on long-travel coil springs	
Rear suspension:	live beam axle on long-travel coil springs	
Brakes (front/rear):	disc/drum with ABS	
Handbrake:	on rear drums	
Wheels:	6J x 16	
Base tyres:	205 R 16	
Turning circle:	37.5 ft/11.4 m 42.0 ft/12.8 m	

MITSUBISHI

Mitsubishi Montero – refer to Mitsubishi Shogun
Mitsubishi Pajero – refer to Mitsubishi Shogun

Mitsubishi Shogun

Sold as the Pajero in most countries and the Montero in the USA, this vehicle has had considerable success in the Paris-Dakar rally, though the vehicles used are specialist rally cars, having little in common with production machines.

Subsequently remodelled, the

The long-wheelbase Mitsubishi Shogun.

current vehicles have proved very popular on-road, especially as a towing vehicle, though their performance is not so hot off-road and their over-complicated selection of four-wheel drive requires more knowledge of off-road driving skills than buyers are likely to have.

The suspension copes well most of the time, but is unhappy over rough bumps and corrugations, and you only notice any effect of the Variable Rate Suspension at extremes. Axle articulation is not up with that of Land Rover products or Toyota's VX.

The Super Select four-wheel drive system is either over the top, or sitting on the fence, depending on your point of view. There is full-time four-wheel drive with a viscous coupling unit centre differential, or you can have two-wheel drive by disconnecting the right-hand front propeller shaft. This is claimed to give improved fuel economy, less tyre wear and lower transmission noise, but as all the parts concerned are still rotating, less tyre wear and slightly improved steering will be the only true result.

Four-wheel drive can be engaged at speeds up to 62 mph

The short-wheelbase Mitsubishi Shogun.

(100 kph). Selecting low range automatically locks the centre differential and there is a cross-axle differential lock on the rear. Multi-mode ABS braking selects the optimum braking pattern for when two-wheel drive, four-wheel drive or the rear differential lock is in operation. Avoid the over-width tyres supplied as standard for Europe.

Multipoint petrol injection engines:

Wheelbase:	95.3 in/2420 mm	
	107.3/2725 mm	
Engine:	214 cu in/3.5 l	183 cu in/3.0 l
Cylinders:	V6	V6
Output:	205 bhp/	178 bhp/
	151 kW	131 kW
	@ 5000 rpm	@ 5500 rpm
Torque:	221 lb ft/	188 lb ft/
	300 Nm	255 Nm
	@ 3000 rpm	@ 4500 rpm
Transmission:	five-speed	
	manual/four-speed	
	automatic	
Transfer box:	1.00:1/1.90:1	
Four-wheel drive:	full-time/part-time	
	selection	
Final drive:	4.64:1 – cross-axle	
	differential lock on	
	rear	
Front suspension:	live beam axle on	
	torsion bars	
Rear suspension:	live beam axle on coil	
	springs – variable	
	rate suspension	
Brakes (front/rear):	disc/disc with ABS	
Handbrake:	on rear drums	
	integral with the	
	discs	
Wheels:	7JJ x 15	
Base tyres:	265/70 SR 15	
Turning circle:	34.8 ft/10.6 m	
	38.8 ft/11.8 m	

Turbo diesels, intercooled:

Engine:	171 cu in/2.8 l	153 cu in/2.5 l
Cylinders:	4	4
Output:	123 bhp/	98 bhp/
	91 kW	72 kW
	@ 4000 rpm	@ 4200 rpm
Torque:	215 lb ft/	177 lb ft/
	292 Nm	240 Nm
	@ 2000 rpm	@ 2000 rpm
Transmission:	five-speed	
	manual/four-speed	
	automatic	
Transfer box:	1.00:1/1.90:1	

Final drive:	4.90:1

Mitsubishi Lynx

Mitsubishi showed a Suzuki SJ rival, the 'Lynx' at the 1994 Tokyo motor show.

NISSAN

Nissan Terrano – refer to Nissan Pathfinder
Nissan Terrano II – refer to Ford Maverick

Nissan Pathfinder

Nissan Design International (NDI), in California, created the Pathfinder; derived from the 720 SEV6 series pick-ups, it was sold as the Terrano in Japan.

To the chagrin of many, it is not imported into the UK. Rather more expensive that its nearest competitors, Toyota's 4Runner and Vauxhall's Frontera, it is considered the sport utility for the person who likes driving, and with average ground clearance it is also pretty good off-road.

The four-wheel drive models come with any engine you like so long as it is the 3-litre V6 with multipoint fuel injection. The off-road options include disc brakes on the rear, a limited slip rear differential, driver-adjustable shock absorbers, 31 x 10.5 R 15 tyres and rear mounting for the spare.

The rear seats are individually adjustable, recline or fold down.

Wheelbase:	104.3 in/2650 mm
Engine:	183 cu in/3.0 l
Cylinders:	V6 petrol
Output:	153 bhp/113 kW @
	4800 rpm
Torque:	180 lb ft/244 Nm @
	4000 rpm
Transmission:	five-speed manual/
	four-speed automatic
Transfer box:	1.00:1/2.02:1
Four-wheel drive:	part-time
	automatic
	freewheeling front
	hubs

Final drive:	4.38:1/4.68:1
Front suspension:	independent on torsion bars
Rear suspension:	live beam axle on coil springs
Brakes (front/rear):	disc/drum with ABS on rear wheels; rear discs on off-road package
Handbrake:	on rear drums
Wheels:	6JJ x 15
Base tyres:	235/75 R 15
Turning circle:	42.0 ft/12.8 m

Nissan Patrol GR

Also sold as the Ford Maverick in Australia, the new coil-sprung Nissan Patrol is big (even bigger than the Toyota VX), butch, simple and reliable. Fitted with its largest engine it is very popular in Arabia, while in the West it is popular for towing. Current models have part-time four-wheel drive, but this vehicle really does require a full-time system.

The width of the vehicle takes some getting used to, and the long-wheelbase model lacks ramp breakover angle, despite the good axle articulation. The automatic freewheeling hubs can be locked in manually with the wheel wrench for genuine off-road work. The long-wheelbase models have cross-axle differential locks on the rear.

The automatic gearbox is not available on the naturally aspirated diesel engine, and the vertically split rear door and spare wheel lower rear vision.

However, you get a lot of four-wheel drive vehicle for the money, but avoid the over-width tyres supplied as standard for Europe.

The short-wheelbase Nissan Patrol.

Wheelbase:	94.5 in/2400 mm	
	117 in/2970 mm	
Engine:	256 cu in/4.2 l	256 cu in/4.2 l
Cylinders:	6 petrol	6 diesel
Output:	168 bhp/	122 bhp/
	124 kW	90 kW
	@ 4000 rpm	@ 4000 rpm
Torque:	235 lb ft/	201 lb ft/
	319 Nm	173 Nm
	@ 3200 rpm	@ 2000 rpm
Transmission:	five-speed manual/four-speed automatic; manual only on the diesel	
Transfer box:	1.00:1/2.02:1	
Four-wheel drive:	part-time – automatic or manual freewheeling front hubs	
Final drive:	4.11:1 – cross-axle differential lock on rear of long-wheelbase model	
Front suspension:	live beam axle on coil springs	
Rear suspension:	live beam axle on coil springs	
Brakes (front/rear):	disc/drum	
Handbrake:	transmission	
Wheels:	7 x 16	
Base tyres:	265/70 R 16	
Turning circle:	36 ft/11 m	
	43 ft/13 m	

OLDSMOBILE BRAVADA

An up-market version of the Chevrolet Blazer/GMC Jimmy, with less chrome than is usual on American vehicles. The vehicle has Smart-Trac full-time four-wheel drive, with the torque distribution of 35% front and 65% rear, a limited slip viscous clutch for the four-wheel drive and a limited slip rear differential.

There is no extra-low gearing and the ABS functions full time, rather than being disengaged when four-wheel drive is in operation. Aluminium wheels are standard.

Opel Monterey – refer to Vauxhall Monterey

RANGE ROVER

Twenty-five years old and still leading the field in off-road performance and luxury on-road cruising, though unashamedly aimed at the wealthy end of the market, the marque continues to evolve and remains at the forefront of engineering ingenuity. The Toyota VX gives it a close run with locks on everything, but the Range Rover's electronically controlled gismos just keep it ahead off-road, with no driver knowledge or input required or desired, and the electronic traction control system does not require strengthened components. Long term, all these electronic gismos will begin to malfunction. This will not worry buyers of new vehicles, but it will affect the pre-owned vehicle buyer market.

Over the years the petrol engines have got larger and the diesel engines more refined, the latest versions having a BMW diesel engine from Steyr-Daimler-Puch, and the on-road handling is improved.

As well as full-time four-wheel drive with a viscous coupled centre differential and ABS anti-lock braking, there is Electronic Traction Control (ETC), which senses when a wheel is likely to spin and puts a brake on it. There is also Electronic Air Suspension (EAS) – indeed, an electronic control unit to control almost everything! There is a display that tells you what is happening – how long will it be before there is a 'head-up display' on the windscreen?

The Range Rover HSE.

EAS, as well as keeping the ride level, automatically lowers for high-speed on-road use or easy entry and egress, has a standard position for normal conditions and a high-profile position for extra ground clearance, should you get high-centred, or for wading. The total height variance is 5 inches (130 mm).

The newer models have a stiffer chassis, stronger differentials, longer wheelbase for passenger comfort and a new electronic selector 'H'-gate automatic gearbox. The 'H'-gate gearbox has the high range on one side and the low range on the other, with neutral being the gate between them.

In the unlikely event that you take this vehicle seriously off-road, it is best to remove the front spoiler first.

The Range Rover Vogue will continue to be available as the Classic, as long as demand persists.

4.6 HSE:

Wheelbase:	108.1 in/2745 mm
Engine:	281 cu in/4.6 l
Cylinders:	V8 petrol
Output:	225 bhp/166 kW @ 4750 rpm
Torque:	280 lb ft/380 Nm @ 3000 rpm
Transmission:	four-speed automatic
Transfer box:	1.22:1/3.27:1
Four-wheel drive:	full-time – Electronic Traction Control
Final drive:	3.54:1
Front suspension:	live beam axle on air springs
Rear suspension:	live beam axle on air springs; variable ride height
Brakes (front/rear):	disc/disc with ABS
Handbrake:	transmission
Wheels:	8 x 16
Base tyres:	255/65 R 16
Turning circle:	39.4 ft/12 m

4.0 S and SE:

Engine:	244 cu in/4.0 l
Cylinders:	V8 petrol
Output:	190 bhp/140 kW @ 4750 rpm
Torque:	236 lb ft/320 Nm @ 3000 rpm
Transmission:	five-speed manual/four-speed automatic
Wheels:	7 x 16
Base tyres:	235/65 R 16

2.5 turbo diesel, intercooled:

Engine:	153 cu in/2.5 l
Cylinders:	6
Output:	136 bhp/100 kW @ 4400 rpm
Torque:	199 lb ft/270 Nm @ 2300 rpm
Transmission:	five-speed manual

SSANGYONG MUSSO

The SsangYong company, Korean for 'twin dragons', founded in 1939, acquired the Ha Dong Hwan Motor Company, a manufacturer of four-wheel drive vehicles since 1954, in 1988, and the Panther Car Company of the UK in the same year. Daimler-Benz has held a 5% stake in the company since 1992.

Combining their own and Mercedes expertise with the design of Ken Greenley, Head of Vehicle Design at the Royal College of Art, IM will bring the Musso to the UK in the spring of 1995. Shown at the 1994 Birmingham International Motor Show, the vehicle won the IBLAM (Institute of Vehicle Technology) British Steel Auto Design award in the £15,000 to £25,000 category.

Engine:	195 cu in/3.2 l	177 cu in/2.9 l
Cylinders:	6 petrol	5 diesel
Output:	225 bhp/ 166 kW @ 5000 rpm	190 bhp/ 140 kW @ 4000 rpm
Torque:	229 lb ft/ 310 Nm @ 4000 rpm	142 lb ft/ 193 Nm @ 2400 rpm
Transmission:	five-speed manual/four-speed automatic	
Four-wheel drive:	part-time – automatic freewheeling front hubs	

SUZUKI

Designed initially for the poorer Third World, where they failed miserably due to poor load-carrying capacity and unreliability, the tiny Suzuki Jimnys took off as cult vehicles in the opulent West. With typical Japanese foresight Suzuki developed the vehicle into a poser's dream, creating their own market where none had existed before.

Now with refined performance, larger engines and flash paintwork, you are as likely to find them outside a mews house in Chelsea, or with a mother taking the kids to school, as in competition or loaded with tourists as a hire car in sunny climates – but you will not see many in the Third World.

A light, fun vehicle with a gutsy engine, they are hard to get stuck, though you do get thrown around. The SJ/Samurai models were much too small for my height – my head was through the roof and my knees under my chin – but the Vitara series are much roomier.

Toyota have recently muscled in on the same market with their RAV4, though I have omitted it from this book as it is not a true off-roader, and Land Rover are known to have a small model under development.

Suzuki Samurai

One-time Holden Drover, Jimny, Rhino, Santana, SJ Series and Sierra, the Samurai is at the lowest end of the market. Old-fashioned, with rudimentary suspension, but with real off-road ability, it is

The Suzuki SJ Series hard top.

The Suzuki SJ Series soft top.

The Suzuki Vitara soft top.

being phased out in favour of the Vitara, as the buying public looks for more sophistication.

Wheelbase:	79.9 in/2029 mm
Engine:	79 cu in/1.3 l
Cylinders:	4 petrol
Output:	63 bhp/47 kW @ 6000 rpm
Torque:	74 lb ft/100 Nm @ 3500 rpm
Transmission:	five-speed manual
Transfer box:	two ratio
Four-wheel drive:	part-time – automatic or manual freewheeling front hubs
Final drive:	3.73:1
Front suspension:	live beam axle on leaf springs
Rear suspension:	live beam axle on leaf springs
Brakes (front/rear):	disc/drum
Handbrake:	on rear drums
Wheels:	15
Base tyres:	205/70 R 15
Turning circle:	33.5 ft/10.2 m

Suzuki Jimny – refer to Suzuki SJ Series

Suzuki Santana – refer to Suzuki SJ Series

Suzuki Sidekick – refer to Suzuki Vitara

Suzuki Sierra – refer to Suzuki SJ Series

Suzuki Vitara

Sold also as the Suzuki Sidekick and Geo Tracker (two-door hard-top model), the Vitara continues the Suzuki popularity, with independent front suspension, more power and more refinements all round.

It is noisy, and the engine has to be worked hard, but the long-wheelbase model handles well on-road, and wherever they have enough ground clearance both models perform well off-road. A rear limited slip differential is available on the X-EC, prices are good and little goes wrong.

The semi-rigid mud flaps are vulnerable, the side steps are flimsy and compromise ground clearance, and where the automatic gearbox is fitted it robs the engine of its performance. With the manual gearbox the vehicle is lively and fun.

Suzuki's own intention of adding a diesel engine option is currently delayed while they try to fit a small engine within the new emission regulations, and a 2.0-litre V6 is on the way. In the meantime Motor and Diesel can fit a 1.9-litre Peugeot diesel.

Wheelbase:	86.6 in/2200 mm 97.6 in/2480 mm
Engine:	97.6 cu in/1.6 l
Cylinders:	4 petrol
Output:	95 bhp/71 kW @ 5600 rpm
Torque:	97.6 lb ft/132 Nm @ 4000 rpm
Transmission:	five-speed manual/four-speed automatic
Transfer box:	two ratio
Four-wheel drive:	part-time – automatic or manual freewheeling front hubs
Front suspension:	independent on coil springs
Rear suspension:	live beam axle on coil springs
Brakes (front/rear):	disc/drum – ABS on rear in USA
Handbrake:	transmission
Wheels:	15
Base tyres:	195 R 15
Turning circle:	32 ft/9.8 m 35.4 ft/10.8 m

TOYOTA

Toyota is the world's largest manufacturer of four-wheel drive vehicles, with a standard of build quality and reliability by which all others are judged.

Until recently Toyota off-roaders were not particularly advanced in design, though dependable, with large engines and good slugging power, but with the Landcruiser VX and the new 4Runner they are right up there at the forefront, with the Landcruiser VX fighting it out with the new Range Rover HSE as the best on-road/off-road vehicle.

Some of the latest engines have the problems that I have criticised on other manufacturers' modern engines. I have already had one fail on me in the Yemeni Rub al Khali Desert, the first time a Landcruiser has ever let me down. So it remains to be seen if they can keep up their reliability record.

The power steering is too light, the VX is too heavy, the long-wheelbase models have poor approach, ramp break-over and departure angles, some models have the spare wheel slung underneath the vehicle, and the tyres supplied as standard are too wide for use in Europe.

The vehicles are made in many versions worldwide, with only the top models and top specifications available in the UK. In countries where off-road tracks are more common than paved roads, Toyota four-wheel drives outsell all others.

Toyota Landcruiser VX

Toyota's flagship, the VX is big and sophisticated, with permanent four-wheel drive, viscous coupling centre differential in high range, live beam axles on long-travel coil springs, cross-axle differential locks

The Toyota Landcruiser VX.

front and rear and ABS brakes that are automatically disengaged when low range is engaged. The viscous coupling is automatically locked when low range is engaged. The vehicle only stops when its weight causes it to sink into soft sand or mud.

On the other hand, with the over-large tyres that come as standard it is easy to spin the wheels on wet roads, wet grass, or loose-topped tracks. The spare wheel is underneath, it does not have a transmission handbrake, the axle articulation is not quite as good as that on Land Rover products, and it requires more driver input than a Range Rover. When it is at a standstill without the brakes applied some testers have experienced the vehicle creeping forward when the automatic air conditioning cuts in, thus increasing engine speed.

If you can afford it, only the Range Rover can beat it, but it is a close-run contest.

Wheelbase:	112.2 in/2850 mm
Engine:	256 cu in/4.2 l
Cylinders:	6 turbo diesel direct injection
Output:	158 bhp/116 kW @ 3600 rpm
Torque:	266 lb ft/361 Nm @ 1800 rpm
Transmission:	five-speed manual/four-speed automatic
Transfer box:	1.00:1/2.49:1
Four-wheel drive:	full-time
Final drive:	4.10:1 – cross-axle differential locks front and rear
Front suspension:	live beam axle on long-travel coil springs
Rear suspension:	live beam axle on long-travel coil springs
Brakes (front/rear):	disc/disc with ABS
Handbrake:	on integral rear drums
Wheels:	8JJ x 16
Base tyres:	275/70 HR 16
Turning circle:	39.4 ft/12 m

Toyota Landcruiser II

Available only in short-wheelbase form in the UK, but elsewhere also as long-wheelbase and, in some cases, with leaf springs, the Landcruiser II is now the basic vehicle of the Toyota four-wheel drive range. Derived from the old 70-Series range, this is Toyota's answer to the Defender 90 – built like a tank and now with a better engine, part-time four-wheel drive, a limited slip rear differential and manual freewheeling front hubs. It is a rugged, reliable working vehicle; only its axle articulation is not up to that of Land Rover products.

The seats let it down and the heater controls should be set to 'recirculate' before wading, or you get wet feet. Exhaust pipes are vulnerable off-road, as is the gearbox protection plate when in reverse.

Wheelbase:	91 in/2310 mm
Engine:	183 cu in/3.0 l
Cylinders:	4 turbo diesel direct injection
Output:	123 bhp/91 kW @ 3600 rpm
Torque:	218 lb ft/296 Nm @ 2000 rpm
Transmission:	five-speed manual
Transfer box:	two ratio

The long-wheelbase Toyota Landcruiser II.

The short-wheelbase Toyota Landcruiser II.

Four-wheel drive:	part-time – manual freewheeling front hubs
Final drive:	limited slip rear differential
Front suspension:	live beam axle on coil springs
Rear suspension:	live beam axle on coil springs
Brakes (front/rear):	disc/drum
Handbrake:	on rear drums
Wheels:	15
Base tyres:	265/75 R 15
Turning circle:	34.8 ft/10.6 m

Toyota 4Runner

The 4Runner is based on the SR5 Prerunner pick-up, in the same way as the Vauxhall Frontera and Nissan Pathfinder are based on similar pick-ups. It is new to the UK, but has been on sale in other countries for some time.

The engines are superb, there is part-time four-wheel drive, a limited slip rear differential, an automatically disconnecting front differential when you engage two-wheel drive, and independent front suspension. The claims for the disengaged front differential are as dubious as those on the Jeep Cherokee and Mitsubishi Pajero,

The Toyota 4Runner.

but it will decrease tyre wear and allow more sporty driving.

The suspension is rather soft, the floor is high, the seats low and, together with the running boards, these make entry and egress difficult. There is not a lot of foot room when wearing boots. The spare wheel is stowed under the vehicle, the handbrake is of the horrible twist and pull or push, dash-mounted type, and the awkward rear tailgate access system is not to everyone's liking. The standard tyres supplied are too wide and off-road departure angle is poor. However, this vehicle has sold well around the world, and only time will tell how it gets on in the UK.

Wheelbase:	103.3 in/2625 mm	
Engine:	183 cu in/3.0 l	183 cu in/3.0 l
Cylinders:	V6 petrol	4 turbo diesel direct injection
Output:	141 bhp/ 104 kW @ 4600 rpm	123 bhp/ 91 kW @ 3600 rpm
Torque:	177 lb ft/ 240 Nm @ 3400 rpm	218 lb ft/ 300 Nm @ 2000 rpm
Transmission:	four-speed manual	
Transfer box:	1.00:1/2.57:1	
Four-wheel drive:	part-time	
Final drive:	4.3:1 – limited slip rear differential	
Front suspension:	independent on torsion bars	
Rear suspension:	live beam axle on coil springs	
Brakes (front/rear):	disc/drum	
Handbrake:	on rear drums	
Wheels:	7 x 15	
Base tyres:	265/70 SR 15	
Turning circle:	37.1 ft/11.4 m	

Toyota Tracker

The long-wheelbase version of the Landcruiser II, available in the Far East.

Vauxhall Frontera

Based originally on the Isuzu Rodeo pick-up and now also sold variously as the Isuzu Rodeo, MU (Mysterious Utility), Amigo and the Honda Passport, this vehicle is now put together in the UK, USA and Japan, with different names for different wheelbase, soft- or hard-top versions, different sizes of engine and final drive ratios in different countries. 2.6-litre and 3.2-litre petrol engines and a four-speed automatic transmission are available in some countries, together with disc brakes all round and ABS on the rear wheels.

Although now rather dated in design, the vehicle is a good compromise between on and off-road use and good value for money, with good build quality. Vauxhall have already made several changes since its launch in the UK and it is selling so well that Vauxhall's main problem could be selling it to drivers with no off-road knowledge. In the UK a free one-day off-road training course is offered to buyers.

Despite being put together in the UK, in terms of reaching controls, particularly those of the gears, the conversion from left-hand drive to right-hand drive has not been very thorough.

Off-road the transfer box reduction is not low enough, low-range first gear has to be used for most situations, axle articulation is limited and underneath the low points are not in line. A limited slip rear differential is optional, but the toothed camshaft drive belt on the engine precludes serious use away from civilisation.

The Vauxhall Frontera now has coil springs on the rear axle and two new engines. The 2.4 litre diesel is replaced by a 2.8 litre unit and the 2.4 litre petrol engine is replaced by a 2.2 litre, 16 valve unit.

Wheelbase:	91.8 in/2330 mm	
	108.7 in/2760 mm	
Engine:	122 cu in/2.0 l	134 cu in/2.2 l
Cylinders:	4 Petrol	4 Petrol
Output:	115 bhp/ 85 kW @ 5200 rpm	136 bhp/ 100 kW @ 5200 rpm

The Vauxhall Frontera.

Torque:	125 lb ft/ 170 Nm @ 2600 rpm	149 lb ft/ 202 Nm @ 2600 rpm
Transmission:	5 speed manual	
Transfer box:	1.00:1/1.87:1	
Four-wheel drive:	part-time automatic freewheeling front hubs	
Final drive:	4.9:1 – optional limited slip rear differential	
Front suspension:	independent on torsion bars	
Rear suspension:	live beam axle on coil springs	
Brakes (front/rear):	disc/drum – ABS optional	
Handbrake:	on rear drums	
Wheels:	6J x 15	
Base tyres:	225/75 R 15	
Turning circle:	32.4 ft/9.87 m	
	37.7 ft/11.5 m	

Turbo Diesel intercooled engine:

Engine:	171 cu in/2.8 l
No. of cylinders:	4
Output:	113 bhp/83 kW @ 3600 rpm
Torque:	179 lb ft/243 Nm @ 2100 rpm

Vauxhall Monterey

Isuzu's Trooper also comes variously as the Holden Jackaroo, the Honda Horizon, Lotus Bighorn, Isuzu Tönnermann, Opel Monterey, and now Vauxhall Monterey. In the UK the Trooper was successfully imported by IM (International Motors), but this is now being wound down as Vauxhall, whose parent company General Motors owns a large percentage of Isuzu, takes over the marque.

The Vauxhall Monterey.

Currently Vauxhall are only offering the highest specification models, so as not to present a challenge to their highly successful Frontera sales; but this is likely to change as the IM-imported models clear from the market place.

The vehicle comes in various levels of hard or soft suspension and engine, according to the importer, various levels of trim and accessories and automatic or manual freewheeling hubs.

The rear door still has a 70%/30% vertical split, which both hinders rear vision (not a vehicle to reverse downhill on a failed ascent!) and opens on the wrong side for loading from the kerb on right-hand drive vehicles. This continues to surprise me, as Japan uses right-hand drive.

The vehicle has evolved considerably over the years. All the latest versions are longer, sophisticated, have high build quality and a fully galvanized body, though the interiors are considered dull. The manual gearbox can be notchy and the on-road ride is a bit soft, with a tendency to wallow about when fully laden.

Off-road the departure angle is poor, the underbody protection plates lower the ground clearance and the limited slip differential does not always want to play, unless tweaked with the handbrake.

The new engines are over-sophisticated for outback use, the toothed camshaft drive belt is particularly worrying, but this vehicle is now firmly aimed at a more sophisticated market, where is does well what is asked of it.

The Dunlop Grand Trek tyres fitted as standard have been criticised for premature wear.

Engine:	195 cu in/3.2 l	189 cu in/3.1 l
Cylinders:	V6 petrol	4 turbo diesel intercooled
Output:	177 bhp/ 130 kW @ 5200 rpm	114 bhp/ 84 kW @ 3600 rpm
Torque:	192 lb ft/ 260 Nm @ 3750 rpm	192 lb ft/ 260 Nm @ 2000 rpm
Transmission:		five-speed manual with synchromesh on reverse/four-speed automatic
Transfer box:		1.00:1/2.28:1
Four-wheel drive:		part-time – automatic or manual freewheeling front hubs
Final drive:	4.3:1	4.56:1 limited slip rear differential
Front suspension:		independent on torsion bars
Rear suspension:		live beam axle on coil springs
Brakes (front/rear):		disc/disc with ABS
Handbrake:		on integral rear drums
Wheels:		7JJ x 16
Base tyres:		245/70 R 16
Turning circle:		32.8 ft/10 m 38 ft/11.6 m
Wheelbase:		91.7 in/2330 mm 108.7 in/2760 mm

Sources of supply

VEHICLES

**AMPHI-RANGER –
FAHRZEUGBAU GmbH**
Ostrasse 17
D-77694
Kehl
Rhein
Germany
Tel 0049 7851 86839
Fax 0049 7851 86813

ASIA MOTORS (UK) LTD
77 Mount Ephraim
Tunbridge Wells
Kent TN4 8BS
Tel 01892 513454

AUVERLAND
Stanford Road Garage
Stanford Road
Lydney
Glos GL15 5HT
Tel/fax 01594 842116

DAIHATSU (UK) LTD
Poulton Close
Dover
Kent CT17 0HP
Tel 01304 213030
Fax 01304 213525

**FORD MOTOR COMPANY
LTD**
Brentwood
Essex CM13 3BW
Tel 01277 253000
Fax 01277 253067

**FORD NORTH AMERICAN
AUTOMOTIVE
OPERATIONS**
Export Sales
PO Box 600
Wixom
Michigan 48393-0600
USA

**GENERAL MOTORS
CORPORATION**
General Motors Building
3044 West Grand Boulevard
Detroit
Michigan 48202
USA

ISUZU CARS
IMI Group
Ryder Street
West Bromwich
West Midlands B70 0EJ

JEEP
Chrysler Jeep Imports UK
Poulton Close
Dover
Kent CT17 0HP
Tel 01304 228877
Fax 01304 208001

LADA CARS
3120 Park Square
Birmingham Business Park
Birmingham B37 7YN
Tel 0121 717 9000
Fax 0121 717 9004

LAND ROVER
Lode Lane
Solihull
B92 8NW
Tel 0121 722 2424
Fax 0121 742 1927

MAHINDRA
UK 4x4 LTD
Ipsden
Oxfordshire
OX10 6AF
Tel 01491 836666
Fax 01491 832290

MERCEDES-BENZ
Tongwell
Milton Keynes
Bucks MK15 8BA
Tel 01908 245946
Fax 01908 245096

MITSUBISHI
The Colt Car Company Ltd
Watermoor
Cirencester
Glos GL7 1LF
Tel 01285 655777
Fax 01285 657351

NISSAN MOTORS (GB) LTD
London SW1A 1RD
Tel 0171 493 3088

NISSAN USA
Nissan Motor Corporation
Gardena
Suburb of Los Angeles
California
USA

OKA UK Ltd
Unit 2
Dillybrook Business Park
Wingfield
Wiltshire
BA14 9NB
Tel 01225 428001
Fax 01225 428980

Personal imports of vehicles that are not normally available on the UK market, including the Nissan Patrol, the Australian OKA and various double-cab pick-ups.

SSANGYONG MOTOR
    DISTRIBUTORS LTD
Ryder Street
West Bromwich
West Midlands B70 0EJ
Tel 0121 522 2000
Fax 0121 520 5025

SUZUKI GB PLC
46-62 Gatwick Road
Crawley
West Sussex RH10 2XF
Tel 01293 518000

TOYOTA (GB) LTD
Head Office and Tax Free Sales
The Quadrangle
Redhill
Surrey RH1 1PX
Tel 01737 768585
Fax 01737 771728

VAUXHALL MOTORS LTD
Griffin House
Osborne Road
Luton
Beds LU1 3YT
Tel 01582 21122
Fax 01582 427400

TYRES

AVON:

AVON TYRES LTD
Melksham
Wilts SN12 8AA
Tel 01225 703101
Fax 01225 707880

BRIDGESTONE/FIRESTONE:

BRIDGESTONE/FIRESTONE
    UK LTD
Bridgestone House
Birchley Trading Estate
Oldbury
Warley
West Midlands B69 1DT
Tel 0121 552 3331
Fax 0121 552 5559

DICK CEPEK:

Transatlantic 4x4
Atlantic House
Unit 4, Oaktree Business Park
Mansfield
Notts NG18 3HQ
Tel 01623 422280
Fax 01623 422553

COOPER:

Sinton Tyres Ltd
Broughton Manor Farm
Broughton
Milton Keynes
MK10 9AA
Tel 01908 665591
Fax 01908 604667 also

Tyre Tech Auto Centre
Unit 4, Windsor Industrial Estate
424 Ware Road
Hertford
Herts
Tel 01992 504199

DUNLOP:

SP Tyres UK Ltd
Fort Dunlop
Erdington
Birmingham B24 9QT
Tel 0121 384 4444
Fax 0121 306 2359

FULDA:

Transatlantic 4x4
Atlantic House
Unit 4, Oaktree Business Park
Mansfield
Notts NG18 3HQ
Tel 01623 422280
Fax 01623 422553

GENERAL TIRE:

Bond International
Tel 01759 303942

Sinton Tyres Ltd
Broughton Manor Farm
Broughton
Milton Keynes
MK10 9AA
Tel 01908 665591
Fax 01908 604667

Transatlantic 4x4
Atlantic House
Unit 4, Oaktree Business Park
Mansfield
Notts NG18 3HQ
Tel 01623 422280
Fax 01623 422553

Tyre Tech Auto Centre
Unit 4, Windsor Industrial Estate
424 Ware Road
Hertford
Herts
Tel 01992 504199

BF GOODRICH:

John Craddock Ltd
70–76 North Street
Bridgtown
Cannock
Staffs WS11 3AZ
Tel 01543 577207
Tel 01543 504818

BJ Fielden
Starhouse Farm
Onehouse
Stowmarket
Suffolk IP14 3EL
Tel 01449 675071
Fax 01449 678282

Southam Tyres Ltd
Westfield Road Industrial Estate
Southam
Warks
Tel 01926 813888

Transatlantic 4x4
Atlantic House
Unit 4, Oaktree Business Park
Mansfield
Notts NG18 3HQ
Tel 01623 422280
Fax 01623 422553

GOODYEAR:

GOODYEAR GREAT BRITAIN
 LTD
Stafford Road
Wolverhampton WV10 6DH
Tel 01902 22321

KELLY:

BJ Fielden
Starhouse Farm
Onehouse
Stowmarket
Suffolk IP14 3EL
Tel 01449 675071
Fax 01449 678282

Transatlantic 4x4
Atlantic House
Unit 4, Oaktree Business Park
Mansfield
Notts NG18 3HQ
Tel 01623 422280
Fax 01623 422553

MAXI CROSS:

Simmonites 4x4
755 Thornton Road
Thornton
Bradford
West Yorks
Tel 01274 833351
Fax 01274 835117

MICHELIN:

MICHELIN TYRE PLC
The Edward Hyde Building
38 Clarendon Road
Watford
Herts WD1 1SX
Tel 01923 415000
Fax 01923 415250

PIRELLI:

PIRELLI LTD
Derby Road
Burton-on-Trent
Staffs DE13 0BH
Tel 01283 66301

MICKEY THOMPSON:

MICKEY THOMPSON
 PERFORMANCE TYRES
Unit B, Chelford Court
37 Robjohns Road
Chelmsford
Essex CM1 3AG
Tel 01245 344170
Fax 01245 344172

TOYO TYRE:

TOYO TYRE (UK)
Toyo House
Shipton Way
Northampton Road
Rushden
Northants NN10 9GL
Tel 01933 411144
Fax 01933 410945

YOKOHAMA:

YOKOHAMA HPT LTD
4A Hicks Road
Markyate
St Albans
Herts AL3 8LJ
Tel 01582 842233

All Land Rover dealers plus

ADI ENGINEERING
Unit 6, Brickfield Lane
Chandlers Ford
Eastleigh
Hants SO53 4DP
Tel 01703 270600
Fax 01703 266661

ALLMAKES LTD
176 Milton Park
Abington
Oxon
Tel 01235 821122
Fax 01135 821133

ARROW SERVICES
 (DONCASTER) LTD
Unit 4, Churchill Buildings
Churchill Road
Doncaster
DN1 2TF
Tel 01302 341154
Fax 01302 341736

AUTOPOST LTD
Unit 21, Zennor Road Trading
 Estate
Balham
London SW12 0PS
Tel 0181 675 4022
Fax 0181 673 4287

AYLMER MOTOR WORKS
 LTD
The Old Coach Station
Great North Road
Bellbar
Nr Brookmans Park
Herts AL9 6NA
Tel 01707 665588
Fax 01707 665206

P. A. BLANCHARD
Clay Lane
Shiptonthorpe
York YO4 3RU
Tel 01430 872765
Fax 01430 872777

JOHN CRADDOCK LTD
70–76 North Street
Bridgtown
Cannock
Staffs WS11 3AZ
Tel 01543 577207
Fax 01543 504818

Everything you might require

DINGO CROFT
High Street
Downley
High Wycombe
Herts HP13 5XJ
Tel 01494 448367
Fax 01494 459964

DLS
Water Lane
Wirksworth
Matlock
Derbyshire DE4 4AA
Tel 01629 822185
Fax 01629 825683

KEITH GOTT
Greenwood Farm
Old Odiham Road
Alton
Hants GU34 4RW
Tel 01420 543210
Fax 01420 544331

GUMTREE ENTERPRISES
Plumpton
East Sussex
Tel 01273 890259
Fax 01273 891010

MARSHLAND CHASSIS
Salt Pie Works
Whitehough
Chinley
Nr Stockport
Ches SK12 6BX
Tel 01663 750484
Fax 01663 751015

Series I, II and III Chassis

AEW PADDOCK MOTORS LTD
The Showground
The Cliff
Matlock
Derbyshire DE4 5EW
Tel 01629 584499
Fax 01629 584498

PRB SERVICES
Wortley Moor Garage
Tong Road
Leeds LS12 4NW
Tel 01132 796039
Fax 01132 310708

R. H. ENGINEERING
    SERVICES
The Meads
Llechwedd
Conwy
Gwynedd LL32 8DX
Tel/fax 01492 573320

*Suspension bushes, bush, drop arm,
crankshaft and steering wheel
pullers*

SIMMONITES 4x4
755 Thornton Road
Thornton
Bradford
West Yorks
Tel 01274 833351
Fax 01274 835117

WARWICK 4x4 LTD
Princes Drive
Coventry Road
Kenilworth
Warwickshire CV8 2F
Tel 01926 864421
Fax 01926 864427

OVERLAND PREPARATION AND OUTFITTING

BROWNCHURCH LTD
Hare Row
London E2 9BY
Tel 0171 729 3606
Fax 0171 729 9437

DÄRR EXPEDITIONSSERVICE
Theresienstr 66
D-80333 Munich
Germany
Tel 0049 89 282032
Fax 0049 89 292525

*Send a £1 coin for comprehensive
catalogue. All off-road expedition
supplies and outfitting from
perforated aluminium plate to good
maps of North Africa.*

BERND WOICK GmbH
Woick Travel Center
Plieningerstr 21 (B312)
70794 Filderstadt – Bernhausesn
Germany
Tel 0049 711 7096700
Fax 0049 711 7096770

*All off-road expedition supplies and
outfitting from perforated plate to
good maps of North Africa.*

KEITH GOTT
Greenwood Farm
Old Odiham Road
Alton
Hants GU34 4RW
Tel 01420 544330
Fax 01420 544331

QUEST LIMITED
Cow Pasture Farm
Louth Road
Hainton
Lincs LN3 6LX
Tel 01507 313401
Fax 01507 313609

SURREY OFF-ROAD
    SPECIALISTS LTD
Alfold Road
Dunsfold
Surrey GU8 4NP
Tel 01483 200046
Fax 01483 200047

BOOTS, CLOTHING AND CAMPING EQUIPMENT

COTSWOLD
Broadway Lane
South Cerney
Cirencester
Glos GL7 5UQ
Tel 01285 860612
Fax 01285 860483

Branches around the UK.

DÄRR EXPEDITIONSSERVICE
Theresienstr 66
D-80333 Munich
Germany
Tel 0049 89 282032
Fax 0049 89 292525

*Send £1 coin for a comprehensive
catalogue. All off-road expedition
supplies and outfitting from
perforated aluminium plate to
good maps of North Africa.*

FIELD AND TREK PLC
3 Wates Way
Brentwood
Essex CM15 9TB
Tel 01277 224647
Fax 01277 260789

Branches around the UK.

WOICK – TRAVEL CENTER
Bernd Woick GmbH
Plieningerstr 21 (B312)
70794 Filderstadt – Bernhausen
Germany
Tel 0049 711 7096700
Fax 0049 711 7096770

All off-road expedition supplies and outfitting from perforated plate to good maps of North Africa.

Hard tops, soft tops, wheel covers:

F. CUTLER
Twites Corner
Great Saxham
Bury St Edmunds
Suffolk IP29 5JR
Tel 01284 810167

Wheel covers.

FORCE TEN HARD TOPS
Albatross G/F Products Ltd
Rotherwas Industrial Estate
Hereford HR2 6JX
Tel 01432 275058
Fax 01432 278236

GRP hard tops.

KIM JOHNSON CAR
    TRIMMERS
Unit F, Swain Court
Avenue 2
Station Lane
Witney
Oxon
Tel 01993 776800
Fax 01993 705352

Wheel covers and soft tops.

MASTER COVERS
Unit 6, The Slipway
Port Solent
Portsmouth
Hants PO6 4TJ
Tel 01705 374739

Replacement soft tops.

TOPPER HARDTOPS
Inkberrow
Worcs WR7 4HD
Tel 01527 597870
Fax 01386 792156

Hard tops and soft tops.

Anti-theft:

CARWOOD MOTOR UNITS
    LTD
Herald Way
Binley
Coventry CV3 2RQ
Tel 01203 449553
Fax 01203 452074

MED electronic anti-theft fuel immobilisers.

TOAD INNOVATIONS
The Quorum
Barnwell Road
Cambridge CB5 8RE
Tel 01223 214555
Fax 01223 214844

Off-road vehicle steering wheel locks.

Racks:

MP PRODUCTS
Tel 01952 550056

ON THE BALL BIKE RACKS
    LTD
On the Ball Ltd
Stanchils
Hengrave
Bury St Edmunds
Suffolk IP28 6NB
Tel 01284 704730
Fax 01284 724170

RAY WAITE ENGINEERING
Tel 0161 367 884

Rear-mounting luggage racks.

Strengthened and locking differentials:

KAM DIFFERENTIALS LTD
Clockbarn House
Hambledon Road
Godalming
Surrey GU8 4AY
Tel 01483 419779
Fax 01483 417558

LOCK RIGHT
AUTOMOTIVE POSITIVE
    LOCKING DIFFERENTIALS
UK 4x4
Ipsden
Oxon OX10 6AF
Tel 01491 836666
Fax 01491 832290

JACK McNAMARA
DIFFERENTIAL SPECIALIST
    PTY LTD
25 Levanswell Road
Moorabbin 3189
Victoria
Australia
Tel 0061 3 555 2213
Fax 0061 3 555 0251

SURREY OFF-ROAD
    SPECIALISTS LTD
Alfold Road
Dunsfold
Surrey GU8 4NP
Tel 01483 200046
Fax 01483 200047

Sound-proofing:

ACOUSTIKIT
Lees Brook Mill
Lees Road
Oldham
Lancs OL4 5JL
Tel 0161 652 2773

AUTO INTERIORS
56 Norfolk Street
Liverpool L1 0BE
Tel 0151 708 8881
Fax 0151 708 6002

BJ ACOUSTICS LTD
Unit 6, Neville Street
Middleton Road Industrial Estate
Chadderton
Oldham
Lancs OL9 6LD
Tel 0161 627 0873

Engine and vehicle heating and pre-heating systems:

EBERSPÄCHER (UK) LTD
Headlands Business Park
Salisbury Road
Ringwood
Hants BH24 3PB
Tel 01425 480151
Fax 01425 480152

Burns fuel independently of the engine.

KENLOWE LTD
Maidenhead
Berks SL6 6QU
Tel 01628 823303
Fax 01628 823451

Electric engine fans and electrical engine pre-heating systems.

WEBASTO THERMOSYSTEMS
(UK) LTD
Webasto House
White Rose Way
Doncaster Carr
South Yorks DN4 5JH
Tel 01302 322232
Fax 01302 322231

Burns fuel independently of the engine; also Thermotronic portable refrigerators.

WINCHES AND WINCH ACCESSORIES:

DAVID BOWYER'S OFF ROAD
CENTRE
East Foldhay
Zeal Monachorum
Crediton
Devon EX17 6DH
Tel 01363 82666
Fax 01363 82782

Telephone between 9 and 5 Monday-Friday. Weekend visitors by appointment.

SOUTHERN WINCH CENTRE
LTD
Unit 13, Monks Brook Industrial
Park
School Close
Chandlers Ford
Eastleigh
Hants SO5 3RA
Tel 01703 270600
Fax 01703 271242

SUPERWINCH
Abbey Rise
Whitchurch Road
Tavistock
Devon PL19 9DR
Tel 01822 614101
Fax 01822 615204

TRUCKERS
Providence Street
Lye
Stourbridge
West Midlands DY9 8HS
Tel 01384 895700
Fax 01384 891994

UK WIRE & ROPE
15 Ronald Court
Wadloes Road
Cambridge CB5 8PX
Tel 01223 414361
Fax 01223 416657

WARN WINCH DIVISION
RYDERS INTERNATIONAL
Knowsley Road
Bootle
Liverpool L20 4NW
Tel 0151 933 4338
Fax 0151 944 1424

Hand winches and pullers:

BRANO:
DAVID BOWYER'S OFF ROAD
CENTRE
East Foldhay
Zeal Monachorum
Crediton
Devon
EX17 6DH
Tel 01363 82666
Fax 01363 82782

Telephone between 9 and 5 Monday-Friday. Weekend visitors by appointment.

SOUTHERN WINCH CENTRE
LTD
Unit 13, Monks Brook Industrial
Park
School Close
Chandlers Ford
Eastleigh
Hants SO5 3RA
Tel 01703 270600
Fax 01703 271242

TIRFOR LTD
Old Lane
Halfway
Sheffield S19 5GZ
Tel 01742 482266
Fax 01742 475649

MAASDAM PULLERS:
ASHWOOD UK
PO Box 1221
Chester CH3 6ZD
Tel/fax 01224 321407

Ground anchors:

DAVID BOWYER'S OFF ROAD
CENTRE
East Foldhay
Zeal Monachorum
Crediton
Devon EX17 6DH
Tel 01363 82666
Fax 01363 82782

Telephone between 9 and 5 Monday-Friday. Weekend visitors by appointment.

Pull-Pal ground anchor:

PO Box 639
Carbondale
Colorado 81623
USA
Tel/fax 00 1 303 963 1817

JB SERVICES
8 Falcon Park
Pipps Hill Industrial Estate
Basildon
Essex
Tel 01268 282122
Fax 01268 288775

Snow chains:

(Check fittings with your vehicle manufacturer.)

GREFSTEG:
RUD CHAINS LTD
John Wilson Business Park
Units 10-12
Thanet Way
Whitstable
Kent CT5 3QT
Tel 01227 276611
Fax 01227 276586

PEWAG:
BRINDLY CHAINS LTD
1 Tatton Court
Kingsland Grange
Warrington
Cheshire WA1 4RR
Tel 01925 825555
Fax 01925 825338

WEISSENFELS:
SNOWCHAINS LTD
The Bourne Enterprise Centre
Wrotham Road
Borough Green
Kent TN15 8DG
Tel 01732 884408
Fax 01732 884564

Styling:

Individual vehicle manufacturers' own accessories plus:

AP TRANSPORT
    ACCESSORIES
Unit 2, Elliot Centre
20 Elliot Road
Cirencester
Glos GL7 1YS
Tel 01285 642727
Fax 01285 642526

AUTOMOTIVE STYLING LTD
12, Poplar View
GEC Estate
East Lane
Wembley
Middlesex
HA9 7PX
Tel 0181 9040043
Fax 0181 9040415

BETTAWELD
Oldfield Lane
Stainforth
Doncaster DN7 5AA
Tel 01302 351264

Roll cages, racks and roof racks.

DAVID BOWYER'S OFF ROAD
    CENTRE
East Foldhay
Zeal Monachorum
Crediton
Devon EX17 6DH
Tel 01363 82666
Fax 01363 82782

Telephone between 9 and 5 Monday-Friday. Weekend visitors by appointment.

CYCLONE WHEELS
Unit 1, Dave Close
Greenstead Road
Colchester
Essex CO1 2XL
Tel 01206 794610
Fax 01206 794611

Wheels and tyres.

EXPLORER PRO COMP
Warrington Road
High Legh
Nr Knutsford
Cheshire WA16 0RT
Tel 01925 757575
Fax 01925 755146

FAMOUS FOUR PRODUCTS
Tattershall Way
Fairfield Industrial Estate
Louth
Lincs LN11 0Y7
Tel 01507 609444
Fax 01507 609555

HIGHLANDER 4X4
Tel 01249 783077

MOBILITY ACCESSORIES
20-22 Dunster Street
Northampton NN1 3JY
Tel 01604 28223

MOTOR CITY
Telford Way
Kettering
Northants NN16 8UW
Tel 01536 414121
Fax 01536 414122

NORTH STAFFS 4x4 CENTRE
Lingwood Road
Longton
Stoke-on-Trent
Staffs ST3 4JJ
Tel 01782 593091
Fax 01782 593215

PERFORMANCE INDUSTRIES
    (UK) LTD
1 Hatton Garden Industrial Estate
Kington
Herefordshire HR5 3RB
Tel 01544 231214
Fax 01544 230904

PWS NUDGE BARS
DAVID SPREADBURY
Unit 5, Chalwyn Industrial Estate
St Clements Road
Parkstone
Poole
Dorset BH15 3PE
Tel 01202 746851
Fax 01202 738135

R. K. AUTOMOTIVE
Unit 2B, Mariner
Lichfield Road Industrial Estate
Tamworth
Staffs B79 7UL
Tel 01827 63866
Fax 01827 63865

SURREY OFF ROAD
    SPECIALISTS
Alford Road
Dunsfold
Surrey GU8 4NP
Tel 01483 200046
Fax 01483 200047

TRANSATLANTIC 4x4 UK
Atlantic House
Unit 4, Oak Tree Business Park
Mansfield
Notts NG18 3HQ
Tel 01623 422280
Fax 01623 422553

UP COUNTRY PRODUCTS
(UK) LTD
Norwich Road
Halesworth
Suffolk IP19 8QH
Tel 01986 875171
Fax 01986 875260

WEST COAST OFF-ROAD
CENTRE
71 Gorsey Lane
Banks
Southport
Lancs
Tel 01704 29014
Fax 01704 232911

Tow bars/hitches:

DIXON – BATE
First Ave
Deeside Industrial Park
Deeside
Ches CH5 2LG
Tel 01244 288925
Fax 01244 288462

WITTER TOWBARS
Chester
CH1 3LL
Tel 01244 341166

MISCELLANEOUS

DAMPERTECH
12 Armley Close
Long Buckly
Northants NN8 7YG
Tel/fax 01327 843112

*'Polyair' pneumatic assister springs
for coil springs.*

'EASYLIFT' AIR JACK
NEW CONCEPT
PO Box 61
Winchester
Hants SO23 8XR
Tel 01962 840769

RICHBROOK
INTERNATIONAL LTD
2 Munro Terrace
112 Cheyne Walk
London SW10 0DL
Tel 0171 351 9333
Fax 0171 351 7732

Fused battery isolators.

SOUTHDOWN 4x4
PRODUCTS
South Down
Zeal Monachorum
Crediton
Devon EX17 6DR
Tel 01363 83819
Fax 01363 83472

Under-chassis protection plates.

TECHNO WELD
Aston Works
Back Lane
Aston
Oxon
Tel 01993 851028
Fax 01993 851036

*Low-temperature aluminium
welding kits.*

ZEUS
8 Devon Units
Budlake Road
Marsh Barton
Exeter EX2 8PY
Tel 01392 438833
Fax 01392 422099

*Gear drive replacement for
camshaft driving belts.*

NAVIGATION

Global Positioning Systems:

MAGELLAN TRAILBLAZER
Trailblazer UK
PO Box 164
Edinburgh EH7 4EH
Tel 01705 791188
Fax 01705 792188

ENSIGN GPS
Trimble Navigation Europe Ltd
Tel 01256 760150

SONY PYXIS GPS
Sony Consumer Products
Tel 01784 467284

PANASONIC GPS
Panasonic Business Systems
Tel 01344 853176

Combined GPS and compass:

SILVA GPS COMPASS
Silva (UK) Ltd
Tel 01784 471721

Compass:

S. I. R. S. NAVIGATION LTD
186A Milton Road
Swanscombe
Kent DA10 OLX
Tel 01322 383672

*'Navigation' aircraft standard
auto compass.*

Index